Britische und Irische Studien
zur deutschen Sprache und Literatur

British and Irish Studies
in German Language and Literature

Etudes britanniques et irlandaises
sur la langue et la littérature allemandes

Edited by H.S. Reiss and W.E. Yates

Band 50

PETER LANG
Oxford · Bern · Berlin · Bruxelles · Frankfurt/M. · New York · Wien

Rereading Monika Maron

Text, Counter-Text and Context

Deirdre Byrnes

PETER LANG
Oxford · Bern · Berlin · Bruxelles · Frankfurt/M. · New York · Wien

Bibliographic information published by Die Deutsche Nationalbibliothek.
Die Deutsche Nationalbibliothek lists this publication in the Deutsche
Nationalbibliografie; detailed bibliographic data is available on the
Internet at http://dnb.d-nb.de.

A catalogue record for this book is available from the British Library.

Library of Congress Cataloging-in-Publication Data:

Byrnes, Deirdre, 1972-
  Rereading Monika Maron : text, counter-text and context / Deirdre
Byrnes.
       p. cm. -- (British and Irish studies in German language and
literature ; v. 50)
  Includes bibliographical references and index.
  ISBN 978-3-03911-422-1 (alk. paper)
  1. Maron, Monika--Criticism and interpretation. 2. Maron,
Monika--Political and social views. 3. Germany (East)--In literature.
4. Socialism in literature. I. Title.
  PT2673.A4686Z65 2010
  833'.914--dc22
                               2010036976

This publication was grant-aided by the Publications Fund of the National
University of Ireland, Galway.

ISSN 0171-6662
ISBN 978-3-03911-422-1

© Peter Lang AG, International Academic Publishers, Bern 2011
Hochfeldstrasse 32, CH-3012 Bern, Switzerland
info@peterlang.com, www.peterlang.com, www.peterlang.net

All rights reserved.
All parts of this publication are protected by copyright.
Any utilisation outside the strict limits of the copyright law, without
the permission of the publisher, is forbidden and liable to prosecution.
This applies in particular to reproductions, translations, microfilming,
and storage and processing in electronic retrieval systems.

Printed in Germany

For my parents and my uncle Jimmy

Contents

Acknowledgements ix
Introduction 1

CHAPTER ONE
Writing Herself out of the System: The Early Texts 17

CHAPTER TWO
Transgressing in Style: *Das Mißverständnis* and *Die Überläuferin* as Counter-Texts 43

CHAPTER THREE
Writing and Rewriting: The Problem of History in *Stille Zeile Sechs* 63

CHAPTER FOUR
Love and Loss after the Wall: *Animal triste* 97

CHAPTER FIVE
Exposing the Gaps in Memory: Forgetting and Remembering in *Pawels Briefe* 117

CHAPTER SIX
Lebensentwürfe, Zeitenbrüche: Biographers and Biographies in *Endmoränen* and *Ach Glück* 149

Conclusion 175
Bibliography 181
Index 191

Acknowledgements

There are so many people who encouraged and supported me in the writing of this book. I am forever grateful to Professor Hugh Ridley for his supervision of my doctoral thesis, from which this book emerged. His generosity and support continue to be a source of inspiration. I also wish to thank Professor Dennis Tate and Dr Hannes Krauss, who acted as external assessors for the dissertation and who encouraged me to embark upon this project. I would like to remember the late Dr Beate Dreike, who first introduced me to the texts of Monika Maron when I was an undergraduate student at University College Cork.

I wish to express my gratitude to Monika Maron for being so generous with her time when I interviewed her during my doctoral studies. I am most thankful for the funding that I received from the National University of Ireland, Galway. The Millennium Research Fund facilitated productive research trips to Berlin in 2005; the Triennial Travel Grant Scheme financed a further research trip to the German capital in 2008. I would like to acknowledge the support of the Publications Fund of NUI Galway, which helped to finance the publication of this book.

I am very grateful to Professor Edgar Yates for his helpful comments and careful reading of the manuscript. My colleagues in German in the School of Languages, Literatures and Cultures at NUI Galway were constant in their support. I am indebted to a cherished circle of friends, in particular to Catriona, Elaine, Helen, Karen, Lindsay, Lorraine, Máire Áine, Micheál and Therese, whose encouragement and help mean so much. I am especially grateful to Richard for his kindness and untiring support, particularly during the final months of this project.

Most especially I want to thank my mother Maura and my sister Ciara for always believing in me. I would like to remember my late uncle Jimmy Clune, whose deep appreciation of language was a privilege to experience. I am forever grateful to my parents – to my mother Maura and to my late father Thady Byrnes – who have been such inspirational figures in my life. This book is dedicated to them, with love and gratitude.

Galway, July 2010

Introduction

Monika Maron is one of the most significant authors of her generation. She is an accomplished essayist, a critically acclaimed novelist, and a trenchant social and political commentator. She is the recipient of many literary awards, including the Kleist Prize and the Carl Zuckmayer Medal. Together with Erich Loest and Uwe Tellkamp, she was awarded the *Deutscher Nationalpreis* in June 2009. The interest in her writing is reflected not only in such accolades from her peers, but also in the extent and frequency with which her texts are being translated. Her oeuvre is thus reaching a growing international readership.

Monika Maron began her writing career as a journalist. In the mid-1970s she was a regular contributor to the East German weekly newspaper *Die Wochenpost*. Even as she embarked upon her journalistic career, she clearly felt confined by the GDR state and was already testing out the boundaries of the official discourse system, particularly in her articles on Bitterfeld, the East German town that was to become synonymous with environmental pollution. Her debut novel *Flugasche*, published in West Germany in 1981, chronicled the problems of a journalist confined by official narratives. Scathing in its depiction of environmental conditions and of journalistic practice in the socialist state, the novel was denied publication in the GDR. This began a pattern that was to be repeated until 1989; it was only after the collapse of the socialist state that her novels finally secured an East German readership.

'Lebensentwürfe, Zeitenbrüche': Monika Maron's Biography

In this study I will explore the work of a provocative and dissenting literary voice that has been constant in its critique of socialist practice in the GDR. Maron's biography charts a complex relationship with the GDR state, from initial identification to rebellion, from a collaboration of sorts to radical rejection.

During her address 'Lebensentwürfe, Zeitenbrüche', delivered at the 2002 *Historikertag*, the biennial German Historians' Conference, Monika Maron reflected on the fashioning of individual biographies and on our limited autonomy in this respect: 'Obwohl wir ahnen, sogar wissen, wie klein unser Spielraum zwischen Schicksal und Zufall ist, kämpfen wir verzweifelt um [...] unsere selbst gestaltete Biografie.'[1] She spoke of our deep-seated desire to bestow meaning, albeit retrospectively, on our biography. It was precisely this need to bestow meaning on her family's past and thus to arrive at a better understanding of her own identity that had led to the composition of the autobiographical text *Pawels Briefe*, published in 1999.

Monika Maron was born in Neukölln, a working-class area of Berlin, in June 1941. Her maternal grandparents, the Jewish-born Pawel Iglarz and his Catholic wife Josefa, had converted to the Baptist faith and were subsequently disowned by their respective families. They left their native Poland and arrived in Berlin in 1905. Pawel established a successful tailoring business in Neukölln, where the family lived until his expulsion from Germany in 1939. He and Josefa returned to Poland; their four children remained in Berlin. Pawel was executed in 1942. *Pawels Briefe: Eine Familiengeschichte* spans three generations and situates Maron's turbulent family biography within the interstices of twentieth-century German history. 'Das Schicksal unserer Familie ist wie ein Muster in das Schicksal dieses Landes eingezeichnet,'[2] Maron explained in an interview, thereby emphasising the exemplary and typical aspects of her family story.

In *Pawels Briefe* Maron seeks to reconstruct a family biography that historical forces had brutally ruptured. In so doing, she explores her own identity and those figures that shaped it, in particular her grandfather Pawel and mother Hella. Her Jewish ancestry meant that Hella was prevented from marrying Walter, the man who had fathered her child. Monika thus grew up without paternal influence, surrounded, instead, by a group of strong female

---

1   Monika Maron's lecture at the *Historikertag* in Halle was published the following day in the *Süddeutsche Zeitung* as 'Lebensentwürfe, Zeitenbrüche. Vom Nutzen und Nachteil dunkler Brillen: Wer es sich zu einfach macht beim Rückblick auf seine Geschichte, beraubt sich seiner Biografie', 13 September 2002, p. 18.
2   Michael Hametner, 'Von Opfern, die Täter wurden', *Börsenblatt für den Deutschen Buchhandel*, 26 June 1992, pp. 40–44 (p. 42).

Introduction

figures, including Hella and Hella's sister Marta. A dedicated communist, Hella ensured that her only child received the appropriate socialist education: Monika was a member of the Young Pioneers, the communist youth organisation. 'Ich war das Kind von Kommunisten', Maron announced in the very opening sequence of her autobiographical essay 'Ich war ein antifaschistisches Kind', written in 1989: 'Ich habe gelernt, daß die Welt sich nicht in Nationen teilt, sondern in Klassen'.[3] Mother and daughter moved from West to East Berlin in 1951. Maron welcomed the move to a community of political and ideological equals: 'Nun war ich gleich mit allen, glaubte ich. Ich wohnte auf der Seite der Wahrheit und der historischen Sieger. Ich war zehn Jahre alt und das Wort Kommunist war für mich ein Synonym für guter Mensch. Alle Menschen, die mir nahestanden und die ich liebte, waren Kommunisten' (*Begreifungskraft*, p. 17). This identification with the state was to define her childhood and early youth.

Hella's marriage in 1955 to Karl Maron, Chief of the People's Police and GDR Interior Minister from 1955 until his retirement in 1963, sealed the relationship between personal story and official GDR history. In her essay 'Ein Schicksalsbuch', written in 1997, Maron described her childhood and earlier youth in terms of this symbiotic relationship between individual and state: 'aufgewachsen in einer Familie, die sich mit der DDR nicht nur identifizierte, sondern sie auch repräsentierte.'[4] Hella's marriage to Karl Maron marked a caesura in her daughter's life. The relationship between stepdaughter and the man whom Maron was to describe ominously as her 'biographisches Schicksal'[5] in *Pawels Briefe* was fraught from the outset. The strained father–daughter

---

[3] Monika Maron, 'Ich war ein antifaschistisches Kind', in *Nach Maßgabe meiner Begreifungskraft: Artikel und Essays* (Frankfurt am Main: Fischer Taschenbuch Verlag, 1995), pp. 9–28 (p. 9). The essay collection was originally published by S. Fischer in 1993. I will be referring to the paperback edition. Quotations from this volume of essays will be followed in parentheses by the word *Begreifungskraft* and the relevant page number.

[4] Monika Maron, 'Ein Schicksalsbuch', in *Quer über die Gleise: Artikel, Essays, Zwischenrufe* (Frankfurt am Main: S. Fischer, 2000), pp. 7–23 (p. 13). Quotations from this volume of essays will be followed in parentheses by the words *Quer über die Gleise* and the relevant page number.

[5] Monika Maron, *Pawels Briefe: Eine Familiengeschichte* (Frankfurt am Main: S. Fischer, 1999), p. 83. Quotations from the text will be followed in parentheses by the abbreviation PB and the relevant page number.

relationship is a topos throughout Maron's writing. In *Stille Zeile Sechs* the protagonist's confrontation with an ageing communist functionary is simultaneously a revisiting of her own childhood, which was overshadowed by her father's allegiance to communism at the expense of paternal affection. 'Das Schlimmste ist, wenn draußen die gleiche Macht herrscht und das gleiche Gesetz wie im eigenen Haus',[6] Rosalind comments, thus allowing Maron to foreground the politicisation of the private sphere in the GDR.

Hella and Monika suddenly belonged to the GDR nomenklatura, living in the fashionable district of Pankow, which was inhabited by prominent communist officials. As befitted the stepdaughter of the Interior Minister, Maron attended the Wilhelm-Pieck school. Despite such preparation for a model communist life, the young and wilful Monika had other ideas; as Marcel Reich-Ranicki observes: 'Der schönen und vermutlich steil aufwärts führenden Karriere in der DDR stand nichts im Wege – nur sie selbst.'[7] After an excellent performance in the *Abitur*, Maron promptly left home and spent a year working in an aeroplane factory in Dresden. Upon her return to Berlin, she worked as an assistant producer with GDR television. From 1962 to 1966 she studied theatre and art history at the Humboldt University. She was also a research assistant at the *Schauspielschule*, the renowned drama academy in Berlin. Her only child – a son Jonas – was born in 1969.

In the early 1970s Maron embarked upon a career as a journalist. She wrote for the women's magazine *Für Dich* before moving to the *Wochenpost*. From 1974 to 1976 she contributed articles to this weekly newspaper, one of the most influential in the GDR. While recognising the relatively progressive intellectual climate of the *Wochenpost* newspaper offices, she was also frustrated by the confines of the official discourse system: 'Als ich Journalistin war, blieb bei allem, was ich schrieb, sehr viel übrig', she revealed in an interview. 'Was meine Aufregung ausgemacht hat, war nur indirekt benennbar – sehr

---

6   Monika Maron, *Stille Zeile Sechs: Roman* (Frankfurt am Main: Fischer Taschenbuch Verlag, 1996), p. 135. The novel was first published by S. Fischer in 1991. I will be referring to the paperback edition. Quotations from the text will be followed in parentheses by the abbreviation SZS and the relevant page number.

7   Marcel Reich-Ranicki, 'Keine Frucht ohne Schale: Rede bei der Verleihung des Kleist-Preises 1992 an Monika Maron', in *Kleist Jahrbuch 1993*, ed. by Hans Joachim Kreutzer (Stuttgart: Metzler, 1993), pp. 8–20 (p. 12).

gedämpft. Das alles sammelte sich über Jahre hinweg an.'[8] The inheritance bequeathed to Maron upon the death of her stepfather meant that she was able to resign from the *Wochenpost* and pursue her career as a freelance writer. In *Pawels Briefe* she recalls her sense of liberation following the death of Karl Maron: 'An die ersten Jahre nach Karls Tod erinnere ich mich wie an einen Rausch. Alles schien möglich' (PB, pp. 193–94). It was during this period that she wrote her debut novel *Flugasche*, which was published in West Germany by the Fischer publishing house in 1981. It was also in the late 1970s that she withdrew from the SED, having been a member of the party for twelve years. In retrospect she described her SED membership, propelled by what she called youthful activism, in unequivocal terms as 'de[n] größte[n] Fehler meines Lebens.'[9]

Das Mißverständnis, a collection of four short stories and a play, was published in 1982. A second novel, *Die Überläuferin*, followed in 1986. Between July 1987 and March 1988 the *Zeit Magazin* provided the forum for regular correspondence between Maron and the West German journalist Joseph von Westphalen. The letters were subsequently published by Fischer as *Trotzdem herzliche Grüße: Ein deutsch-deutscher Briefwechsel*. Their correspondence addressed such issues as the divergent political and economic systems in East and West Germany and the role of the writer.

In June 1988 Maron obtained a visa and moved, together with her husband and son, from East Berlin to Hamburg, remaining there until 1992. The author identified the apathy of life in the GDR as catalyst for the move: 'Man kam sich uralt vor', she explained in an interview, 'das war ja ein allgemeines Lebensgefühl, die permanente Abwesenheit von Lebensgenuß, wie ein langsames Einschlafen.'[10] It was in Hamburg that her third novel was composed; set in Pankow in the mid-1980s and portraying just such an environment of stagnation and decay, *Stille Zeile Sechs* was published in 1991 to widespread critical acclaim.

---

8   Wilfried F. Schoeller, 'Literatur, das nicht gelebte Leben: Gespräch mit der Ostberliner Schriftstellerin Monika Maron', *Süddeutsche Zeitung*, 6 March 1987, p. 47.
9   Hametner, 'Von Opfern, die Täter wurden', p. 43.
10 Gerhard Richter, 'Verschüttete Kultur – Ein Gespräch mit Monika Maron', *GDR Bulletin*, 18 (1992), 2–7 (p. 6).

Maron's status as social and political commentator was firmly established with the publication in 1993 of the essay collection *Nach Maßgabe meiner Begreifungskraft*. As a result of their controversial content and critical tone, her novels were denied publication in the East; as an essayist, too, Maron was unrelenting in her criticism of the GDR. In 'Ich war ein antifaschistisches Kind', for example, she reflects upon the devastating effect of political ideology:

> Es bleibt die Frage, wie eine Idee, die zum Glück aller erdacht war, sich in das Unglück aller, selbst ihrer treuesten Anhänger verkehren konnte.
> Es bleibt die Frage, warum Menschen, die in ihrer Jugend gegen Ungerechtigkeit und Unterdrückung gekämpft und ihr Leben dafür eingesetzt haben, in Jahrzehnten unangefochtener Macht ihr eigenes Volk mit den Mitteln von Gangstern betrogen und beherrschten. Und andere es duldeten. (*Begreifungskraft*, p. 28)

Unsurprisingly, Maron was an advocate of unification. However, in the final essay of the volume, the explosive 'Zonophobie', she castigates her fellow-East Germans for their passivity, their servile nature, and especially for their incessant feeling of victimisation as they constantly attribute blame to the West: 'ein neues Wir ist geboren', she comments sarcastically, '"wir aus dem Osten"; endlich dürfen alle Opfer sein, Opfer des Westens' (*Begreifungskraft*, p. 118).

An explosive *Spiegel* article 'Stasi-Deckname "Mitsu"', published in August 1995, sensationally revealed that Maron had worked as a contact for the *Hauptverwaltung Aufklärung*, the foreign intelligence branch of the Stasi between 1976 and 1978.[11] She was recruited in October 1976 and agreed to provide information on West German citizens, but with the stipulation that she would not be required to inform upon her friends and colleagues in the East. In return, she was granted travel visas to West Berlin where she could fulfil her wish to revisit 'Stätten ihrer Kindheit' and conduct 'Milieu-Studien für einen autobiographischen Roman'.[12] In *Pawels Briefe* she cites curiosity, an adventurous spirit and a desire for action as reasons for her Stasi-involvement (PB, p. 196), insisting that it was nothing more than 'eine kuriose und komische

---

11 'Stasi-Deckname "Mitsu"', *Der Spiegel*, 7 August 1995, pp. 146–49 (author unknown). In his article 'Escaping the Autobiographical Trap?: Monika Maron, the Stasi and *Pawels Briefe*', Andrew Plowman provides a detailed account of Maron's Stasi-involvement. *German Writers and the Politics of Culture: Dealing with the Stasi*, ed. by Paul Cooke and Andrew Plowman (Hampshire and New York: Palgrave Macmillan, 2003), pp. 227–42.
12 'Stasi-Deckname "Mitsu"', p. 147.

Episode [...] auf die ich nicht sonderlich stolz war, für die ich mich aber auch nicht schämte, weil sie eben keine Spitzelaffäre war' (PB, p. 199). Her two reports for the Stasi are included in the collection of essays *Quer über die Gleise*, published in 2000. In the first report, written following her trip to West Berlin, Maron furnishes a glowing description of life in the West, contrasting this with the lack of freedom in the GDR and daring even to condemn the constant presence of the Stasi: 'Die Leute haben einen Stasikoller, fühlen sich beobachtet, abgehört und denunziert' (*Quer über die Gleise*, p. 31). West Berlin is described as a pulsating city – 'unvorstellbaren Ausbund an Vielfalt und Vitalität' – which merely serves to reinforce the lethargy of its East German counterpart: 'die Starre und Unbewohnbarkeit unserer Stadt' (*Quer über die Gleise*, p. 26). A second, shorter report concerns a reception at the West German diplomatic office in East Berlin in December 1976. Although she does provide the names of West German journalists present, Maron devotes much of this report to explaining why she is unwilling to inform upon her fellow GDR citizens. Having requested release from Stasi-activity in May 1978, she subsequently became an object of long-term surveillance over a ten-year period; eight volumes of files, code name 'Wildsau', was the result.

In a newspaper article 'Heuchelei und Niedertracht', published two months after the *Spiegel* revelations, Maron expressed her fury at a post-*Wende* society that had forced a very public confrontation with her past.[13] On the final pages of *Pawels Briefe* she continues in similar fashion: 'das öffentliche Gedächtnis [...] stellte meine Biographie ab 1976 auf den Kopf, damit sie in eine allgemeine Biographie paßte. Die Bedeutung des Vorfalls wurde nicht aus ihm selbst geleitet, sondern aus dem Bedürfnis nach Umdeutung' (PB, p. 199).

Despite such upheaval, Maron's literary production continued unabated throughout the 1990s. The novel *Animal triste* was published in 1996, followed by the autobiographical *Pawels Briefe* in 1999. Her essay-writing continued apace with the publication in 2000 of the thematically diverse volume *Quer über die Gleise: Artikel, Essays, Zwischenrufe*. The essay collection *Geburtsort Berlin*, Maron's homage to the city in which she has spent almost all of her life, followed in 2003.

---

13 Monika Maron, 'Heuchelei und Niedertracht', *Frankfurter Allgemeine Zeitung*, 14 October 1995, *Bilder und Zeiten*, p. B1. The article was later published in the anthology *Quer über die Gleise* (pp. 34–43).

Whether in newspaper reports, incisive essays, or in the guise of fiction, Maron's oeuvre offers a damning commentary on the GDR. It is all the more significant, then, that her novel *Endmoränen*, published in 2002, offers a melancholic meditation on the sobering reality of life after socialism. In 2005 she was a guest lecturer at the Goethe University, Frankfurt am Main; the series of lectures in which she described her difficulties in writing a new novel were subsequently published as *Wie ich ein Buch nicht schreiben kann und es trotzdem versuche*. *Ach Glück*, the sequel to *Endmoränen*, appeared in 2007. In *Bitterfelder Bogen*, published in 2009, Maron revisits the East German town that played such a significant role in her contributions to the *Wochenpost* more than three decades previously.

Maron's biography is inextricably bound to the state. Her childhood and early youth followed a model communist trajectory. However, she soon began to challenge the unwavering identification with the GDR that was exhibited by her mother and, more obviously still, by her stepfather. Although she remained a member of the SED until the late-1970s as she still harboured hopes of changing the system from within, Maron became increasingly disillusioned with socialist practice in the GDR. Her move to Hamburg in 1988 marked an irrevocable break and she returned only after unification. The revelation about her Stasi-involvement was all the more surprising in light of the unrelenting criticism of the GDR present throughout her writing.

Beyond Unification: The Challenge to Reread

The collapse of an entire political and literary system in late 1989 necessitated a review of critical practice. The literary historian Wolfgang Emmerich called for a rereading of traditional approaches to those texts emerging from a suddenly defunct state. The third edition of his seminal text *Kleine Literaturgeschichte der DDR*, published in 1996, opens with a chapter provocatively entitled 'Was heißt und zu welchem Ende studiert man die Geschichte der DDR-Literatur?' The rereading that he advances has paradigmatic significance for the present study, which situates its reflections on Monika Maron's writing against the backdrop of a changing critical landscape.

In order to understand the difficulties facing writers and critics alike following the tumultuous and far-reaching events of late 1989, we should first recall the very specific function ascribed to literature in the GDR and the clearly defined position of the writer within the socialist state. From its very inception, the GDR as an antifascist state had a pronounced sense of its own cultural and literary identity. As early as 1956 the Minister for Culture Johannes R. Becher delivered an impassioned speech 'Von der Größe unserer Literatur' at the Fourth Writers' Conference, a landmark event in GDR literary history. Becher advocated the formation of a *Literaturgesellschaft*, a literary community of writers and their readers, an egalitarian society in which literature would be accessible to all.

Cultural politics was dominated by socialist realism during the initial decades of the GDR's existence. Developed in the Soviet Union in the 1930s, this doctrine saw the writer's role as a pedagogical one. Andrei Zhdanov's much-quoted definition illuminates this didactic element. The socialist realist writer was to furnish a 'wahrheitsgetreue, historisch konkrete Darstellung der Wirklichkeit in ihrer revolutionären Entwicklung.' Zhdanov continues: 'Wahrheitstreue und historische Konkretheit der künstlerischen Darstellung müssen mit den Aufgaben der ideologischen Umgestaltung und Erziehung der Werktätigen im Geiste des Sozialismus verbunden werden.'[14] Socialist realist texts were characterised by their consistently positive reflection of socialist reality, by an unwavering belief in a historical teleology, culminating in the triumph of the antifascist state, and by the presence of a positive hero who espoused the virtues of socialism.

Despite official cultural policy dictates that continued to champion the socialist realist doctrine, increasingly modernist tendencies began to emerge throughout the 1960s and 1970s. During his speech at the Fourth Plenum of the SED Central Committee in December 1971, the party's General Secretary Erich Honecker famously advocated the lifting of all taboos in literature and art. Despite the much-trumpeted heralding of an emancipatory period in GDR cultural politics, this apparently liberal climate came to an abrupt end with the expatriation of the singer and songwriter Wolf Biermann in 1976, one of the canonical moments of GDR literary and, indeed, political history. The

---

14   Quoted in Manfred Jäger, *Kultur und Politik in der DDR: Ein historischer Abriß*, Edition Deutschland Archiv (Cologne: Verlag Wissenschaft und Politik, 1982), p. 37.

highly controversial decision provoked an immediate reaction in the form of a petition signed by many eminent GDR writers. The Biermann affair, seen by a generation of critics as marking a caesura in the development of cultural policy, ushered in a whole array of restrictive measures, such as house arrest, censorship and expulsion from the Party. Maron reads this rupture back into the writing of her first novel *Flugasche*: 'Der Bruch im Buch, als ein formaler durchaus zu bemerken, ging auf die Ausweisung Biermanns zurück. In dieser Zeit habe ich es geschrieben. Ich dachte, so naiv und blöd kann die Heldin nicht bleiben, wie sie bis zur Mitte des Buches gediehen ist. Mit soviel Illusionen und Gutwilligkeit bin ich nicht mehr ausgestattet.'[15] A veritable exodus of writers followed Biermann's expatriation. Paradoxically, those who remained often contributed to the diversification of GDR literature. Plurality became the order of the day. In retrospect, this heterogeneity appeared to be a sign of the state's inability to exercise its desired stringent control. The final decade of the socialist state was characterised by an increasing experimentation with form, making more difficult the kind of separation of East and West German literature that the heroic age of socialist realism had seemed to legitimate. This stylistic experimentation also characterised Maron's writing from the period. Literary critics frequently pointed to the dichotomy between the stagnant political state and its diverse literary landscape, illustrated particularly in the counterculture of Prenzlauer Berg. However, the post-*Wende*[16] revelation that influential Prenzlauer Berg figures such as Rainer Schedlinski and Sascha Anderson had worked for the Stasi destroyed the comforting illusion of autonomy in this alternative literary milieu.

Although socialist realism remained the official doctrine throughout the existence of the GDR, literature increasingly fulfilled a compensatory role, acting, to quote Wolfgang Emmerich, as an 'Ersatzöffentlichkeit anstelle einer nicht zugelassenen Presse- und Medienöffentlichkeit'.[17] Literature's function

---

15 Schoeller, p. 47.
16 The term *Wende*, which literally means turning point, is used to describe the period of momentous change, encompassing the fall of the Berlin Wall, the months following the collapse of the German Democratic Republic, and the reunification of Germany in 1990. Subsequent use of this term will be in normal script.
17 Wolfgang Emmerich, *Kleine Literaturgeschichte der DDR*, 3rd edn (Leipzig: Kiepenheuer, 1996), p. 13. Quotations from the text will be followed in parentheses by the word *Literaturgeschichte* and the relevant page number.

Introduction

was to articulate public opinion and, more importantly, the discontent that could not find expression in the official press and media. It was precisely the writer's oppositional role in the creation of a substitute public arena that Maron recalled in her 1990 essay 'Das neue Elend der Intellektuellen':

> Und wie fast jede lebenserhaltende Symbiose in diesem Land durch den Mangel gestiftet war, so auch die zwischen Lesern und Schreibern. In einem Staat, der den Mangel an bürgerlichen Freiheiten zur Doktrin erhebt, sammelt sich die verbotene Öffentlichkeit in den verbleibenden Rinnsalen der Kommunikation: in privaten Zirkeln, in den Kirchen, in der Kunst. Der konspirative Diskurs wird zu einer Form des Widerstands. (*Begreifungskraft*, p. 85)

Maron described the privileged status of writers in the GDR: 'Diese leidvollen Bedingungen bescherten den Schriftstellern und Künstlern der DDR ihre exklusive Bedeutung. Wie selbstverständlich wuchs ihnen das Recht, sogar die Pflicht zu, im Namen der zum Schweigen gezwungenen Mehrheit zu sprechen' (*Begreifungskraft*, p. 85). In an interview published in February 1990, Maron once again foregrounded the very specific function accorded to writers in the GDR. In what she termed the symbiotic relationship between writers and their readers, the former quickly emerged as figureheads:

> Sie waren mehr als nur Autoren, sie waren selbst für Leute, die mit Literatur noch nie viel anfangen konnten, Galionsfiguren. Das hatte etwas Rührendes. Es konnte vorkommen, dass die Briefträgerin oder der Wäschemann einem gratulierte – wozu eigentlich? Zum Mut, den es brauchte, Sätze zu sagen, die auch seine waren und die sonst nirgends zu hören waren.[18]

For many writers in the GDR, the political turmoil of late 1989 resulted in an abrupt and definitive loss of purpose. Authors were suddenly bereft of their privileged role. The disorientation experienced by these writers in the aftermath of political collapse was mirrored in the uncertainty of literary critics, confronted with the problematic task of analysing texts that emerged from a suddenly defunct state. Wolfgang Emmerich has charted the uncomfortable shifts in critical discourse since the Wende. In his 1992 essay 'Für eine andere

---

18   Sabine Sütterlin, '"Soll ich Not beschwören, damit Leute nett sind?": Die im Westen lebende DDR-Autorin Monika Maron über deutsche Einheit und Irrtümer ihrer Schriftsteller-Kollegen', *Die Weltwoche*, 8 February 1990, p. 59.

Wahrnehmung der DDR-Literatur: Neue Kontexte, neue Paradigmen, ein neuer Kanon', he put forward an alternative literary historiography of the GDR, an analysis that would focus on the imaginative and aesthetic elements of the writing. He explained his understanding of literature's potential as follows:

> Die bessere DDR-Literatur löst sich vom Offizialdiskurs und entwirft Literatur als 'Gegentext', als Subversion des Leitdiskurses. Damit meine ich gerade nicht das Aussprechen von tabuisierten Sachverhalten im Sinne einer Ersatzöffentlichkeit, sondern ich meine die Mobilisierung von Phantasie, verrückte Erzählhaltungen, fragmentierte, dezentrierte dramatische Fabeln, Intertextualität und Redevielfalt in der Lyrik.[19]

The rereading of Maron's texts that I will advance in the ensuing chapters explores at various points the imaginative dimensions of her writing. It identifies the protagonists' desire to transcend the stultifying conditions of life in the GDR and move into the imaginative realm; this desire is frequently expressed in the creation of potent counter-texts. However, her protagonists remain rooted in the reality of their GDR experience, even as they attempt to transcend it.

In the 1996 edition of his literary history, Emmerich continued to argue for a new perception of the literature emerging from the GDR. His proposal can hardly be ignored by subsequent critics: 'Was zu tun war und noch ist, das ist ein skeptisches, kritisches *rereading* dieser Entwürfe und Konstrukte [der Geschichtsschreibung zur DDR-Literatur]. Im folgenden wird ein solcher (in vieler Hinsicht notwendig selbstbezüglicher) Versuch unternommen' (*Literaturgeschichte*, p. 17). Emmerich emphasised that the sociopolitical approach which had dominated literary criticism up to 1989 – whereby texts were viewed as mere reflection of or, more interestingly, as protest against societal conditions – had been at the expense of stylistic analysis. The third edition of his literary history sought the middle ground: analysis of the texts as aesthetic constructs was tempered by the realisation that it was impossible to extract them completely from their political context. In Emmerich we thus

---

19   Wolfgang Emmerich, 'Für eine andere Wahrnehmung der DDR-Literatur: Neue Kontexte, neue Paradigmen, ein neuer Kanon', in *Geist und Macht: Writers and the State in the GDR*, ed. by Axel Goodbody and Dennis Tate, German Monitor, 29 (Amsterdam and Atlanta, GA: Rodopi, 1992), pp. 7–22 (p. 17). Quotations from this essay will be followed in parentheses by the words 'Für eine andere Wahrnehmung' and the relevant page number.

recognise both a model and a dilemma. This is the fundamental paradox of GDR literary analysis post-1989, a dilemma that I hope to acknowledge and explore in the ensuing reading of Maron's oeuvre: the problem of history in an age that, if not directly post-historical, is at least unsure of its historical foundations. The experience of socialism continues to exert an influence, even in those texts written after 1989.

The Writing of Monika Maron

In this study I will trace the development of Maron's writing from her journalistic beginnings to the publication of her most recent novel *Ach Glück*. Chapter One, 'Writing Herself out of the System: The Early Texts', illustrates the significance of a previously neglected aspect of Maron's oeuvre: her contributions to the *Wochenpost* in the mid-1970s. Through analysis of her articles, a combination of incisive reports on environmental and working conditions and of light-hearted observations on daily life in the socialist state, the chapter explores how she negotiated the compromise manoeuvres of reportage in the GDR. The first chapter also analyses her debut novel *Flugasche*, a text that chronicles the disillusioning experience of writing in a restrictive society. Its protagonist is a journalist in East Berlin who literally writes herself out of the official discourse system and withdraws into a turbulent inner landscape. The imaginative realm thus acts as a counter-text to the scripted existence of life in the socialist state.

Critics have posited a direct link between the privileging of fantasy in Maron's writing from the early- to mid-1980s and her increasing sense of confinement within the GDR. In his entry for the *Kritisches Lexikon zur deutschsprachigen Gegenwartsliteratur*, Eckhard Franke notes that 'das (literarische) Traumspiel, das Hinübergleiten in Freiräume, die sich nur (noch) der Fantasie eröffnen, die expressiven Visionsbilder' are characteristic of Maron's pre-Wende writing.[20] Chapter Two, 'Transgressing in Style: *Das*

---

20   Eckhard Franke and Roman Luckscheiter, 'Monika Maron', in *Kritisches Lexikon zur deutschsprachigen Gegenwartsliteratur*, March 2005.

Mißverständnis and *Die Überläuferin* as Counter-Texts', explores the radical stylistic experimentation of these texts, published in 1982 and 1986 respectively. *Das Mißverständnis*, a collection of four short stories and a play, abounds in surreal sequences and is strewn with enigmatic images. In the Kafkaesque opening sequence of *Die Überläuferin*, the protagonist awakes one morning to find her body paralysed. Rosalind Polkowski is a GDR state historian who withdraws from society and retreats into the imaginative realm. Depicting the intellectual and emotional stultification of life in the socialist state and overtly flouting stylistic conventions, *Die Überläuferin* followed the fate of its predecessors and was published only in West Germany.

In the context of Maron's literary development, her third novel *Stille Zeile Sechs*, published in 1991, occupies an important position because it established a concern with the writing of history as a central theme in her oeuvre. Its protagonist Rosalind Polkowski, heroine of her previous novel *Die Überläuferin*, is a former GDR state historian who agrees to transcribe the memoirs of an ageing communist. More overtly than in any of Maron's previous texts, *Stille Zeile Sechs* charts the inexorable decline of a stagnant political order, which is embodied in the figure of the ailing, once powerful communist Herbert Beerenbaum. Chapter Three, 'Writing and Rewriting: The Problem of History in *Stille Zeile Sechs*', explores the bitter struggle to write and rewrite GDR history that is played out in the text. Through the juxtaposition of conflicting memories of life in the GDR, *Stille Zeile Sechs* considers the problems of historical representation.

Maron's literary output continued throughout the 1990s but with a significant shift in thematic focus. Post-Wende sexual politics are explored in the 1996 novel *Animal triste*, which forms the focus of Chapter Four, 'Love and Loss after the Wall: *Animal triste*'. The novel is an exploration of all-consuming passion and loss; it is also a text about the body and the passage of time, about writing history, about memory and its repression. Its anonymous first-person narrator, an East German palaeontologist, has retreated from her contemporary society to recall memories of a passionate, clandestine and ultimately fatal love affair with a West German natural scientist, which was played out against the tumultuous backdrop of Berlin in the immediate post-Wende period. Repression is at work on a grand scale in *Animal triste*; the full extent of the trauma at its source is revealed only on the final pages of the text. *Animal triste* anticipated a central concern of *Pawels Briefe*, published in 1999: the interplay of forgetting and remembering. Maron's family story,

Introduction

which the author describes as her most personal text,[21] unfolds against the turbulent backdrop of twentieth-century German history, extending from 1930s Berlin to her grandfather Pawel's execution at Nazi hands, from childhood and youth in the GDR to the post-unification period. Chapter Five, 'Exposing the Gaps in Memory: Forgetting and Remembering in *Pawels Briefe*', examines the generational memory gaps that inform Maron's family story. Her attempts to access the final years of her grandparents' life are themselves refracted through conflicting memories of life in the GDR. In a theoretical landscape concerned with individual, collective and cultural memory discourses, *Pawels Briefe* is an important East German contribution to current debates on memory and its repression. Chapter Five also explores the use of montage, in particular the interplay of image and text, in Maron's attempts to recover the past. With the aid of rediscovered photographs and letters, she effects an imaginary reconstruction of her family biography, which historical forces had so brutally ruptured.

The rupture of individual biographies also emerges as a seminal theme in Maron's most recent novels, which form the focal point of Chapter Six, 'Lebensentwürfe, Zeitenbrüche: Biographers and Biographies in *Endmoränen* and *Ach Glück*'. Significantly, the scathing criticism of the GDR, prevalent throughout her writing, is no longer evident. Instead, the heady optimism of unification has ceded to a sobering portrayal of post-unification reality. The protagonist Johanna is a historical biographer who struggles with the insignificance of her professional and private biography in a post-GDR age.

In his essay 'Darstellung, Ereignis und Struktur', the historian Reinhart Koselleck raised awareness of deeper structures inherent in the historical process.[22] His understanding of history as a complex interplay of event and overarching, diachronic structures offers a useful paradigm with which to read and reread Maron's texts. The dialectic of event and structure lies at the very heart of her writing as she unifies in her texts the disparate experience of the socialist structure within a personally narrated life. Her oeuvre thus testifies to the difficulties facing writers from the GDR, emerging from a system whose deeper structures continue to shape their identity and their writing.

---

21 Deirdre Byrnes, Interview with Monika Maron, Berlin-Schöneberg, 29 June 1999.
22 Reinhart Koselleck, 'Darstellung, Ereignis und Struktur', in *Vergangene Zukunft: Zur Semantik geschichtlicher Zeiten*, 3rd edn (Frankfurt am Main: Suhrkamp, 1995), pp. 144–57. The volume was first published in 1979.

In an interview conducted five years after the fall of the Berlin Wall, Maron expressed a desire to break away from the GDR in her writing: 'Loslösung von der Fixierung auf dieses Staatsgebilde DDR.'[23] In this study I will show that, despite such assertions and despite the re-contextualisation necessitated by the collapse of the GDR, it seems impossible to prize apart her texts from the highly politicised context in which they were composed. It is precisely this inextricable bind which makes her work so interesting for contemporary readers. Rereading her texts in a post-Wende light, I will explore the complexity of Maron's relationship with the state from which she emerged and consider how this complexity manifests itself in her writing before and after 1989.

---

23 Martin Doerry and Volker Hage, 'Ich hab' ein freies Herz: Monika Maron über Autoren in der Politik und die Zukunft des VS', *Der Spiegel*, 25 April 1994, pp. 185–92 (p. 192).

CHAPTER ONE

Writing Herself out of the System: The Early Texts

Monika Maron began her writing career as a journalist. Josefa Nadler, the protagonist of her debut novel *Flugasche*, is also a reporter, based in East Berlin and working for the *Illustrierte Woche*. In this chapter I will examine how Maron effected the transition from the diplomatic manoeuvres of reportage to deliberate flouting of stylistic convention, regardless of the consequences, in her earliest fictional writing.

In the early 1970s Maron was a reporter for the popular women's weekly *Für Dich*,[1] before moving to the *Wochenpost*, where she worked from 1974 until 1976. Her contributions to this influential East German weekly are significant for a number of reasons. Although largely neglected by critics to date, this corpus represents a crucial phase in her relationship to the political system. During her three years at the *Wochenpost*, she negotiated those journalistic conventions which curtailed expression in the GDR press. She remained determined to depict conditions and voice criticism, yet all the while operating within sharply demarcated, albeit unspoken limits.

The limits of journalistic expression and the official formulations demanded by the GDR press are also explored in *Flugasche*. Josefa Nadler's unwavering commitment to furnishing a truthful report of environmental pollution in the town of B. results in her exclusion from the prevailing discourse system. The dream-like sequences and nightmarish visions that dominate her subconscious in the aftermath of her retreat from the newspaper serve as a powerful counter-text to the official modes of expression. This chapter will

---

1   In his article 'Publikumszeitschriften und ihre Leser', Dieter Löffler provides detailed analysis of *Für Dich*'s content and its readership. Favourite rubrics included health issues, the environment and foreign affairs. Its readership was composed predominantly of professional women in their twenties and thirties. 'Publikumszeitschriften und ihre Leser', in *Zwischen 'Mosaik' und 'Einheit': Zeitschriften in der DDR*, ed. by Simone Barck, Martina Langermann and Siegfried Lokatis (Berlin: Links, 1999), pp. 48–60.

offer a rereading of Maron's earliest texts in terms of conflicting discourse systems. I will foreground the manner in which the young journalist Monika Maron negotiated those compromise manoeuvres which were a prerequisite for publication and an essential aspect of a politicised GDR press. Her fictional counterpart Josefa Nadler goes further still and writes herself out of the prevailing political and discourse system.

Maron's Articles for the *Wochenpost*

The *Wochenpost* was one of the most influential newspapers in the GDR. Readers' letters, which the journalist Klaus Polkehn intersperses throughout his comprehensive history *Das war die Wochenpost: Geschichte und Geschichten einer Zeitung*, contain descriptions of frenetic mass purchase and reveal the extent of the newspaper's popularity:

> Punkt 8.00 Uhr wurde geöffnet. Die Menschen stürzten hinein, griffen sich einen Einkaufswagen, und mindestens 90% von ihnen rasten zum Zeitungsregal, auf dem auch ein hoher Stapel *Wochenpost* lag. Und nun begann eine regelrechte Schlacht um diese Zeitung [...] Binnen Minutenfrist war der Stapel weg.[2]

A member of the editorial team from the newspaper's inception, Polkehn offers a detailed insight into the workings of the GDR press. Founded in 1953, the *Wochenpost* was an important weekly from the outset. By 1971 its circulation figures had surpassed one million and it retained this popularity

---

[2] This excerpt from a previously unpublished reader's letter, dated 1987, is reproduced in Klaus Polkehn's history of the newspaper *Das war die Wochenpost: Geschichte und Geschichten einer Zeitung* (Berlin: Links, 1997), p. 113. The description of feverish purchase is echoed in several other readers' letters, spanning four decades, from the newspaper's inception until its discontinuation in 1997, and also reproduced in the text. Quotations from the text will be followed in parentheses by the words *Das war die Wochenpost* and the relevant page number.

until the Wende (*Das war die Wochenpost*, p. 109).³ A 1972 survey revealed that its core readership was composed of state employees, students and skilled workers.⁴

Although published by the SED-owned publishing house Berliner Verlag, the intellectual climate was clearly more progressive than in other GDR newspaper offices. Maron herself is unequivocal in this regard. In a radio interview that she gave in 1999 – an interview to which I shall return on a number of occasions during the ensuing analysis of her newspaper contributions – she explains why writing for the *Wochenpost* was a far better experience than her time spent working for the women's magazine *Für Dich*, 'weil die Leute, die dort arbeiteten, also auch die Chefredakteure, nicht für die Unwahrheit ausgegeben hatten, was die Wahrheit war.'⁵ Polkehn credits Kurt Neheimer, *Wochenpost*-editor from 1967 until 1982, as playing a particularly influential role in fostering such a positive working environment. He goes on to describe the formation of a central group of reporters in the early 1970s. Significantly, he cites Maron as belonging to this elite of tenacious researchers and brilliant journalists who contributed well-written and informative reports, 'die in den anderen DDR-Medien fehlten' (*Das war die Wochenpost*, p. 65). Turning at this juncture to Maron's contributions to the *Wochenpost*, a dual discourse quickly emerges: the journalist oscillated between light-hearted, ostensibly innocuous columns on daily life in the GDR and incisive factual reports that articulated an underlying discontent with environmental and working conditions.⁶

---

3   In his final chapter Polkehn chronicles the rapid decline of the newspaper in a unified Germany. It was taken over by the Hamburg-based *Woche*. The final *Wochenpost* supplement to the *Woche* appeared on 13 May 1997.
4   Polkehn devotes a chapter to the newspaper's readership: 'Wer las die *Wochenpost*?' (pp. 109–16).
5   Walter Krause, 'Zwischentöne', Gespräch mit Monika Maron, Deutschlandfunk, 7 February 1999. Quotations from this interview will be followed in parentheses by the word 'Zwischentöne'.
6   The ensuing reading of Maron's contributions to the *Wochenpost* has as its point of departure my article 'Monika Marons Beiträge zur *Wochenpost*: Eine Analyse', which was published in *Denkbilder: Festschrift für Eoin Bourke*, ed. by Hermann Rasche and Christiane Schönfeld (Würzburg: Königshausen & Neumann, 2004), pp. 248–56.

The Articles on Page Eighteen

Polkehn underscores the idiosyncratic character of page eighteen, itself something of an institution at the *Wochenpost*. By his own admission, the page was more than a little unconventional: 'eine Seite, die in vielfacher Hinsicht aus dem Rahmen fiel [...] immer vergnüglich, oft sehr lustig' (*Das war die Wochenpost*, p. 231). It had a very specific remit, as described by Rolf Pfeiffer, the editor responsible for the page from its inception in 1973 until 1991, and himself a regular contributor to the column:

> Der Hauptakzent bei der Gestaltung dieser Seite muß darauf gerichtet sein, die von anderen Medien unterbewerteten oder nicht beachteten Themen aufzugreifen, in ihrer 'Randerscheinung' Typisches aus dem DDR-Alltag aufzudecken, ihnen eine neue Sicht abzugewinnen und den Lesern auf unterhaltsam-verbindliche Art Wissen zu vermitteln. (*Das war die Wochenpost*, p. 231)[7]

Page eighteen was to be at once entertaining and informative, affording its readers new perspectives on daily life in the GDR. Polkehn notes that many of the articles on page eighteen appeared under the rubric 'Three days as ...'; the contributors spent time in various workplaces and recounted their experiences. The relative freedom enjoyed by these journalists was envied by their peers, to whom 'die ungeliebten Pflichtstücke' (*Das war die Wochenpost*, pp. 232–33) were assigned.

By assuming various roles, Maron provided the new insight encouraged by Pfeiffer. 'Im Laden an der Ecke' (24 May 1974), for example, chronicles the three days she spent stocking shelves and observing customers in her local supermarket. 'Hinter dem Tresen' (24 January 1975) details her experiences as a hotel receptionist. In 'Als Wurschtmaxe auf dem Alex' (11 October 1974), Maron recounts her experiences of working in a fast food stall on Alexanderplatz. 'Mit Eis und Brause unterm Turm' (25 October 1974) sees her cast in the role of ice-cream seller and she takes obvious delight in observing the details of ordinary life. In the light-hearted article 'Wir und der Hut' (2

---

[7] Polkehn formulated this description of page eighteen's role in November 1982, on the occasion of the four hundredth edition of the page. However, even a cursory glance at earlier articles on page eighteen reveal a commitment to informing and entertaining the readers, while reporting on everyday life in the GDR.

April 1976), she studies the behaviour of customers in the hat department of a shopping centre on Alexanderplatz. '"Liebes Brautpaar ..."' (26 December 1975), Maron's account of the two days she spent observing proceedings in an East Berlin registry office, opens in ironic fashion as she debunks the concept of marriage: 'Manche lassen sich sogar scheiden, nur um den gleichen Mann oder die gleiche Frau noch einmal heiraten zu dürfen, so schön finden sie das Hochzeitmachen.' These contributions offer her individualistic, gently ironic perspective on daily life in the socialist community.

The didactic function of the GDR press was clear, even in the humorous articles on page eighteen. Polkehn foregrounds this dual role when he writes of the 'Spannungsfeld, in dem die *Wochenpost* jahrzehntelang gearbeitet hat. Die Redaktion sollte und wollte ein unterhaltsames und vergnügliches Blatt machen, und sie mußte zugleich die Beschlüsse der Partei verkünden. Sie wollte den Lesern Wissen – auch politisches Wissen – vermitteln'.[8] On page eighteen Maron fulfilled the dual function, as envisaged by Pfeiffer, of entertaining and educating her readership: her light-hearted articles were flanked by columns providing statistics on the educational, political and economic achievements of the socialist state. In 'Durch die Hintertür' (17 January 1975), Maron recounts her experiences as a chambermaid in a Berlin hotel. The accompanying text in the margin details measures already undertaken to improve working conditions for chambermaids and also anticipates future plans. Reference to envisaged progress within the socialist state testifies to the obligatory insertion of a teleological metanarrative, itself a constant presence and prerequisite for publication in the context of a highly politicised GDR press.

Education is a theme in four of Maron's contributions to page eighteen. Her article 'Erzieh' mich mal' (25 April 1975) is devoted to the three days she spent working in a kindergarten. The opening quotation in the margin, an excerpt from the 1967 Education Plan, envisages the kindergarten fulfilling those tasks assigned to it by the socialist community, in particular the all-round development of the children in its care. In the course of the article Maron articulates her reservations about authoritarian education and reflects upon dysfunctional families. She is full of admiration for the kindergarten teacher.

---

[8] Klaus Polkehn, 'Ein Nischenblatt?: Die *Wochenpost* als "sozialistische Familienzeitschrift"', in *Zwischen 'Mosaik' und 'Einheit': Zeitschriften in der DDR*, pp. 61–68 (p. 62).

'Ich werde eingeschult' (29 August 1975) charts her young son's preparation for and first days in primary school and the changes this transition brings to her life also. 'Ein Mann im Hort' (9 July 1976) is a glowing portrait of Herr Maurer, a pragmatic and inspiring carpentry teacher whose pedagogical programme involves preparing his charges for the world of work. He eschews the authoritarian approach, 'kein pädagogisches Entweder-Oder, keine Autoritätsangst', viewing his role in terms of advancing the socialist community: '[Er] fühlt [...] sich als Beauftragter der sozialistischen Gesellschaft zur Betreuung unserer Nachkommen, einer der sinnvollsten Berufe, die sich denken lassen.'

'Neptunfest' (26 September 1975), Maron's article about a ritual performed at a children's summer camp on the Baltic coast, caused an outcry in political circles. The article captured the children's fear when confronted with the masked figure of Neptune, accompanied by his minions, who dragged their reluctant peers into the water to be 'baptised'. What was presumably an exercise in forging relationships and promoting a sense of belonging to the group descended into an unnerving spectacle. Maron registered the disconcerted reaction of adult spectators also: 'beklommen, unsicher, ablehnend. Die Szene erinnerte an Krimis oder Filme mit dem Vermerk: nicht jugendfrei.' Polkehn recalls that Margot Honecker, the GDR Minister for Education, launched a scathing attack on the article: its author, she claimed, had defamed the socialist achievement of facilitating a summer holiday for as many children as possible. Within the parameters of page eighteen Maron thus succeeded in criticising an aspect of socialist education. Her tactical manoeuvring is recognised by Polkehn: in the guise of an ostensibly light-hearted foray into the realm of mythology, she denounced an antiquated educational practice in the GDR.[9]

Maron's distinctive voice resonated throughout her contributions to page eighteen. Sometimes self-deprecatory, occasionally critical, often gently ironic, these articles expressed her fascination with the idiosyncratic aspects and apparently insignificant details of life in the socialist state.

---

9 Polkehn observes: 'Die Kritiker hatten schon sehr richtig erkannt, daß hier Relikte einer überholten Pädagogik aufgespießt wurden, und sei es unter der harmlosen Überschrift "Neptunfest"' (*Das war die Wochenpost*, p. 235).

'Die Grenzen ausprobieren': The Articles on Pages Four and Five

The compromise manoeuvres, already intimated in the preceding analysis of page eighteen, became far more pronounced in Maron's reports on economic and working life. The very arrangement of these articles on pages four and five is significant: they were flanked by columns that inundated the reader with statistics pertaining to the political and economic climate and provided appropriately rousing quotations from Marx, Lenin and Honecker. Socialist history was thus inscribed into these reports, together with repeated reference to future plans.

In 'Musketiere in Arnstadt?' (29 March 1974), Maron researches local government politics in one of the oldest towns in the GDR, describing the councillors as musketeers of communism. 'Der Marktplatz in Greifswald' (20 December 1974) ends in an equally positive manner with the reporter reflecting upon the proposals for town planning. Her optimistic tone continues in 'Traktoristen' (20 September 1974) as she considers what has become the norm for agricultural collectives in the GDR: 'Anbauflächen von 60–80 Hektar, 70,8 Prozent aller Beschäftigten in der Landwirtschaft mit abgeschlossener Berufsausbildung [...] ein Auto in der Garage, wo früher kaum eine Kuh im Stall stand, Urlaub im Sommer und Schichtarbeit und nicht zuletzt der Kreisbetrieb selbst.' Having emphasised current achievements, she concludes her report with reference to plans for the following year. Such future orientation was itself characteristic of these articles in which the aforementioned socialist teleology was inscribed.

Once again education emerges as an important theme. 'Ist Geld die Hauptsache?' (9 August 1974) is Maron's laudatory report on the mechanics and electricians of a machine combine in East Berlin. They display an understanding of political and economic processes and of the potential of education and knowledge therein. 'Bauen lernen' (24 September 1976), Maron's equally positive account of apprentices in an East Berlin building collective, opens with a quotation from Erich Honecker's speech at the Tenth FDJ Congress, where it was decided to involve young people directly in the building of the capital because this activity would promote desirable characteristics distinguishing 'die künftigen Erbauer des Kommunismus'.[10] Conspicuous in her report is the

---

10   As the official youth movement in the GDR, the *Freie Deutsche Jugend* sought to educate young people in the spirit of socialism.

author's undisguised admiration for those apprentices who have the courage to express their opinions. Conversations with these young people illustrate the lasting influence of the master craftsmen: 'Sie hinterlassen ihre Spuren in den Persönlichkeiten', Maron observes. Her article 'Der Prellbock' (15 November 1974) is a portrait of two such masters. The accompanying column quotes from the law gazette, dated 20 July 1973, and provides a detailed list of their responsibilities, including the cultivation of 'allseitig gebildete sozialistische Persönlichkeiten', the promotion of intellectual and cultural life, the improvement of living and working conditions, and the education of their apprentices in the spirit of socialism. 'Das Schiff auf der Insel' (1 February 1974) is Maron's laudatory account of an East Berlin youth club that is also a forum for political discussion. The exclusively positive focus of the article is mirrored in the journalist's choice of vocabulary when she praises the idyllic location, ordered environment and friendly atmosphere.

Within such parameters it was evident that any criticism had to be camouflaged in a language of socialist progress and productivity. In a radio interview Maron spoke of the boundaries that restricted journalistic practice in the GDR and of her determination to push these boundaries to the very limit:

> Aber natürlich konnte ich auch nicht schreiben, was ich wollte. Aber […] ich bin mit fast jedem Artikel, den ich geschrieben habe, an die Grenze dessen gegangen, was möglich war. Die waren nicht immer weit, die Grenzen, aber man mußte es halt ausprobieren. ('Zwischentöne')

Nowhere is this desire to transgress limits more apparent than in Maron's three articles on Bitterfeld, the East German industrial town that was to gain notoriety as a source of environmental pollution. 'Eva in Bitterfeld' (1 August 1975) is a portrait of twenty-three-year-old Eva Wisotzki who works in the chemical plant. Once again the introductory quotation in the accompanying column establishes a very positive tone by referring to the Party's primary intention of promoting the creative talents of young people in the GDR and facilitating their development as 'sozialistische Persönlichkeiten'. The first paragraph of Maron's report is equally positive in its description of Eva as a friendly, reliable and diligent worker. However, the second paragraph immediately shatters any illusions: Bitterfeld is described as an old, grey and filthy town, 'in Chemienebel gehüllt, die der Wind seit 81 Jahren vom Werk über die Wohnhäuser Bitterfelds weht.' Maron describes the pervasive presence of the fine, white dust throughout the plant, the dreadful smell and the intolerable heat. This is a town whose inhabitants speak openly about their problems, 'weil sie ohnehin nicht zu verbergen sind, weil sie als Ruß und Abgase auf die Stadt fallen.' In conversation with Maron, the factory manager seems genuinely regretful at the workers' reluctance to question the situation. He wonders aloud if individual ideas are being promoted at all. Eva is a model worker who is praised by family and colleagues alike; the only criticism levelled against her is a placid nature, her acceptance of what are clearly inadequate working and environmental conditions:

> Mir fällt auf: Wenn Eva Wisotzki von den Unzulänglichkeiten ihrer Stadt spricht, so weder wehklagend noch zornig, sondern lächelnd, mit spöttischem Stolz fast, in gleicher Art, in der sie lächelt, wenn Fremde bei 40 Grad in der Meßwarte stöhnen oder beim Spaziergang über die Rußteilchen auf ihren weißen Hemden schimpfen. 'Daran gewöhnt man sich', sagt sie, und ihr Lachen ist der Beweis: das stimmt.

In one of her final articles for the *Wochenpost*, Maron returns again to Bitterfeld. In an interview she remarked that even in those articles which dealt with economic issues, she was far more interested in the human dimension. She explained the significance of Bitterfeld for her journalistic pieces: 'Ich sollte erklären, was der Beruf eines Techologen ist oder so, dann habe ich diese Themen nach Bitterfeld verlegt, weil mich das dann irgendwann fasziniert hat, dieser Ort, nachdem ich das erste Mal da war' ('Zwischentöne'). 'Was macht der Technologe?' (7 May 1976) is a portrait of the technician Detlef Schmidt. The accompanying column opens with a suitable quotation from Erich Honecker about the influence of technology on productivity. This is followed by statistics pertaining to increased productivity in Bitterfeld. Maron accompanies Schmidt around the plant over a three-day period; she does not refrain from detailing her overwhelmingly negative first impression: '[ich] stehe [...] in der Halle, in weißen Staub gehüllt: in Nase, Hals und Bronchien brennt es erbärmlich, ich stürze aus der nächsten Tür.' In response to the visiting reporter's question as to how the workers can physically tolerate such an environment, Schmidt offers the explanation that they become accustomed to it; the conversation then turns to his plans for a new, technologically advanced plant that would lead to increased productivity and improved working conditions: 'Die Kollegen würden kaum noch mit dem

Staub in Berührung kommen, bekämen keine roten Köpfe mehr und keine Kopfschmerzen, sagt er und betrachtet noch einmal das Viereck, als gäbe es etwas zu sehen.' Maron, however, remains underwhelmed: 'Ich finde nichts als nackten Boden, Sand und Steine.' Bitterfeld, it seems, is located at the hub of technological innovation, yet the reporter's doubts continue to echo throughout this apparent hymn to progress.

'Drachentöter'

'Drachentöter' constitutes Maron's most damning indictment of environmental pollution in Bitterfeld. This 'Reportage aus Bitterfeld' was all the more daring given that it was one of her earliest contributions to the *Wochenpost*.[11] The fourth page of the issue dated 21 June 1974 is dominated by a forbidding photograph of chimneys billowing smoke into a darkened, polluted sky. The statistics in the margin, usually so positive in tone, provide a litany of the town's environmental and health problems, which originated with the plant's inception at the turn of the century. The dramatic opening paragraph sets the scene:

> In B. steigt nur aus, wer hier aussteigen muß, wer hier wohnt oder arbeitet oder sonst hier zu tun hat. Die, die weiterfahren, sehen durch die Fenster ihres Zuges bedenklich oder betroffen in den Himmel über der Stadt, den diesigen, nebligen Himmel, den die Sonne nicht durchdringt, den Schornsteine durchbohren, in dem weithin sichtbar eine aprikosenfarbige Flagge aus Stichoxiden weht. Ein Chemie-Himmel.

Prior to her discussion with Enders, the official responsible for environmental protection, Maron considers the irony of this concept in such a polluted landscape. Although her reservations are instantly relativised by encouraging reference to the government's production plan, it is clear from the outset that she has no intention of concealing the extent of environmental pollution.

---

11 In *Bitterfelder Bogen*, published in 2009, Maron describes her return to the town that played such an important role in her early writing career. She recalls her visit there as a young reporter and her feelings of shock, shame and anger at the extent of environmental pollution. Once a 'Synonym für marode Wirtschaft, vergiftete Luft und verseuchten Boden' (*Bitterfelder Bogen*, p. 28), Bitterfeld has been transformed and is now a leading producer of solar energy.

The incidences of bronchitis and respiratory illness are five times higher in Bitterfeld than in other German cities. Maron announces to Enders her intention of writing about the one hundred and eighty tons of ash that rain daily upon the town.

In the aforementioned radio interview with Walter Krause, Maron spoke extensively about her journalistic career. She alluded to the tacit understanding between journalists in the GDR and a readership very much aware of the restrictions curtailing expression: 'Es gab so Vereinbarungen [...] [Der Leser] wußte [...], ach jetzt muß sie das mal schreiben, sonst wird der Rest nicht gedruckt werden' ('Zwischentöne'). Analysis of 'Drachentöter' reveals Maron's adherence to several journalistic conventions determining publication: these include reference to prophylactic movements and to future plans and the inclusion of the obligatory positive ending. The visiting reporter is visibly appalled at environmental conditions, prompting Enders to change the topic of conversation from the present situation to future plans, 'vom Ist-Zustand auf den Soll-Zustand', emphasising, in particular, the imminent closure of the old power plant: 'Der größte Aschespucker von Bitterfeld, der Drache, der seit sechzig Jahren Rauch und Schmutz über die Stadt faucht, soll getötet werden. Der Drache heißt: Kraftwerk Süd.'

The section entitled 'Die schmutzige Erbschaft' details the history of the chemical industry in Bitterfeld, dating back to 1894. Enders talks about the legacy of capitalism, but it is the visiting reporter who asserts that the town's rebirth as a centre for the chemical industry was simultaneously the death knell 'für ein menschenwürdiges Leben in dieser Stadt.' Attention turns again to environmental concerns: the reader learns that there are no less than twenty-five separate locations in Bitterfeld where the level of pollutants in the air is measured. Although very enthusiastic about the imminent closure of Kraftwerk Süd, Enders wonders aloud if, in fact, it would have been better to halt production completely. The section 'In der Höhle des Drachen' describes the working environment in the old plant. Maron engages in a further journalistic manoeuvre when her allusion to the inadequate conditions and insufficient number of stokers is qualified by referring to the efficacy of the collective and to the rewards of the socialist work ethic: 'In der Höhle des Drachen, dieses dreckschleudernden Ungetüms des Kapitalismus, haben Menschen Beziehungen zueinander gefunden, ohne die sie nicht mehr leben und arbeiten wollen [...] sozialistische Beziehungen.'

The effect of Maron's critique is also relativised somewhat through the addition of the prerequisite positive ending. The information in the accompanying column on page five has a positive focus. A quotation from the SED's Five-Year Plan (1971–75) foregrounds environmental issues as a primary concern for the government. This is followed by an excerpt from the 1974 programme for the improvement of living and working conditions in Bitterfeld. There is reference to long-term building projects and plans to improve the town's infrastructure. Although Maron begins her article in a forthright manner, the final paragraph contrasts with this uncompromising tone. The emphasis has been placed firmly upon productivity: two percent of the GDR's national income originates in Bitterfeld. The visiting journalist concludes her report on an ostensibly optimistic note:

> Die Frage: Was zuerst? mußte in der Chemiestadt lange mit dem Wort Produktion beantwortet werden. Trotzdem oder besser: Gerade durch diese zwei Prozent wurden die Möglichkeiten geschaffen, dem Drachen seine Köpfe abzuschlagen, die Umwelt zu schützen und zu verändern und auch aus einer Chemiestadt eine saubere Stadt zu machen, die keinen Ersatzhimmel braucht.

Maron is clearly engaged in a compromise manoeuvre, a fact recognised by Polkehn who describes the concluding sequence as a concession to the political authorities: 'Eine Konzession an die ZK-Beckmesser, die die *Wochenpost* ohne den halbwegs optimistischen Ausklang gnadenlos attackiert hätten' (*Das war die Wochenpost*, p. 214). A close reading of 'Drachentöter' reveals a critical subtext present beneath the necessary overlay of set pieces. Throughout the article the attention of Maron and her readers was repeatedly deflected from the harsh reality of environmental pollution to positive plans for the future. The reporter may have been determined to expose conditions in Bitterfeld, but such criticism had to be camouflaged in a discourse of progress, productivity and the merits of socialism.

'Drachentöter' is a pivotal article for another reason also: it was to serve as a blueprint for Maron's debut novel. Analysis of the thematic and stylistic parallels between the article and *Flugasche* reveals a blurring, consciously or otherwise, of the boundaries between genres. The ominous statement with which Maron opens her 'Reportage aus Bitterfeld' is faithfully reproduced in *Flugasche* as Josefa agonises over the beginning of her article about the power plant: 'In B. steigt nur aus, wer hier aussteigen muß, wer hier wohnt oder arbeitet oder sonst hier zu tun hat.'[12] The influence of 'Drachentöter' becomes even more apparent on a thematic level: the novel articulates the difficulties encountered by Josefa in her professional and private life as she attempts to provide a truthful account of environmental and working conditions. Like Maron, the visiting journalist Josefa is accompanied around the power plant. The reservations articulated by Enders, for example about the environmental repercussions of increased productivity, are tempered by repeated reference to future plans; his fictional counterpart Alfred Thal, press secretary to the plant's director, does nothing to hide his scepticism about such plans because expectations have been thwarted before. In both article and novel the new building is being painted a light blue as an 'Ersatzhimmel', a disturbing image that serves to reinforce the bleakness of the Bitterfeld landscape. Characteristic of both texts is the reference to the 'Bitterfelder Blick' practised by the inhabitants, who walk 'mit zusammengekniffenen Lidern' (FA, p. 16) through the polluted town. Maron describes the old power plant as a filthy, capitalist monster; her fictional counterpart is overcome by the need to escape the oppressive working conditions of what she terms an 'Ungetüm' (FA, p. 20). Maron is aware not only of how inappropriate her questions seem in the context of such inadequate working conditions, but also of the stereotypical journalistic role. In 'Drachentöter' she registers 'die skeptischen Blicke der Männer und Frauen angesichts des Reporters, der wieder einmal nach Heldentaten sucht', thus anticipating a similar scenario in *Flugasche*. Josefa feels frustrated by the token questions and answers demanded by the official discourse system. As she explains to her colleague and mentor Luise: 'Und dann, Luise, hatte ich genug von dem peinlichen abgekarteten Arbeiter-Journalisten-Spiel' (FA, p. 50).[13] The story of the eponymous dragon-slayer is

---

12　Monika Maron, *Flugasche: Roman* (Frankfurt am Main: Fischer Taschenbuch Verlag, 1995), p. 32. *Flugasche* was first published by S. Fischer in 1981. I will be referring to the paperback edition. Quotations from the text will be followed in parentheses by the abbreviation FA and the relevant page number.

13　Such a portrayal contrasts with the ideals of the *Bitterfelder Weg*, a government initiative that was intended to foster links between intellectuals and workers. The first Bitterfeld Conference took place in 1959; a second followed five years later. The aim of this movement, propelled by cultural policy dictates, was twofold: writers were encouraged to visit factories and report on conditions there, while workers were encouraged to write, as is clear from the catchphrase 'Greif zur Feder, Kumpel: Die sozialistische Nationalliteratur braucht dich!'

later recounted in *Flugasche*, providing further evidence of the way in which the report anticipates its quasi-fictional counterpart. Thal explains to Josefa that one of the chemists had composed a fairy tale for his daughter in which the power plant was depicted as a seven-headed dragon, 'jeder Schornstein ein Kopf' (FA, p. 134). Thal admits that publication of the fairy tale in the factory's newspaper had caused controversy in official quarters – perhaps Maron's veiled allusion to the difficulties she encountered at the *Wochenpost* in her attempts to provide a truthful account of her experiences. By the time she came to write *Flugasche*, she was no longer prepared to shroud her criticism in a discourse over which she had, at best, limited control. The move from journalism to fiction afforded her the freedom necessary to flout, even transgress conventions and to criticise in a more overt manner than journalistic restrictions could ever allow, even if such a depiction simultaneously undermined any opportunity for publication in the GDR.

Flugasche

The death of Karl Maron in 1975 was to have a major effect on his stepdaughter. In her family story *Pawels Briefe*, published more than two decades later, she recalls her enormous sense of liberation and relief. Hella gave her the inheritance to which she would have been entitled, had she been Karl Maron's real or adopted daughter. Maron was to recall this period as one of limitless opportunities: she bought a car, learned to drive, resigned from the *Wochenpost*, and began to write her debut novel (PB, pp. 192–94).

By this time she had grown increasingly frustrated and disillusioned with the restrictions of journalistic discourse: 'Es ging mir die Kraft aus, dieses Spiel weiterzuspielen.'[14] Although she had completed the text by 1978, several years were to elapse before it secured a readership. *Flugasche* was first published in 1981 by the S. Fischer Publishing House in West Germany. At the Leipzig Book Fair of the same year Klaus Höpcke, Deputy Minister for Education and the Arts in the GDR, insisted that the novel could have been published

---

14 Interview with Deirdre Byrnes, Berlin-Schöneberg, 29 June 1999.

Writing Herself out of the System: The Early Texts 31

in East Germany, had the author been willing to amend her text to provide a much more positive depiction of working life.[15] In 1988 plans for publication in the GDR, on this occasion by the Aufbau Publishing Company, were again thwarted. Elmar Faber, Head of Publishing, justified his decision by referring to the 'unsavoury' correspondence in the *Zeit* between Maron and the West German journalist Joseph von Westphalen.[16] The objections to her published correspondence with von Westphalen during a ten-month period from July 1987 to March 1988 may have derived in no small part from the foregrounding in her letters of the gaping discrepancies between East and West Germany.

Upon publication in West Germany, *Flugasche* was immediately hailed as the first novel from the GDR to deal with environmental issues.[17] While the text represented a significant contribution to the literary presentation of this problem, the author herself called into question its reception as an environmental novel and placed the focus on a very different aspect:

> Ich wollte eigentlich über den Konflikt schreiben, was passiert, wenn ein Einzelner sich einmischen will in etwas, von dem er meint, er müsse sich einmischen, also über unsere allgemeinen Bedingungen, die wir da hatten, und insbesondere in einem Beruf wie dem des Journalisten, der verpflichtet ist, der Öffentlichkeit mitzuteilen, was er da vorgefunden hat. ('Zwischentöne')

Significantly, she discussed the protagonist's personal dilemma in terms of journalistic responsibilities. The reading of *Flugasche* that I will advance in this section considers the depiction of journalistic practice in the text and

---

15   In 'Verordnetes Schweigen' (*Frankfurter Allgemeine Zeitung*, 14 April 1981, *Literaturbeilage*, p. L2), the reviewer Uwe Wittstock refers to Höpcke's speech at the Leipzig Book Fair. He points to the parallels between Maron's situation and that of her fictional counterpart.
16   In his article 'Alles zu wenig, alles zu spät: Steht die Kulturpolitik der DDR vor einer Wende?' (*Die Zeit*, 17 June 1988, p. 38), Volker Hage describes the succession of thwarted publication attempts.
17   In his review 'Wo die Bronchien schmerzen' (*Die Welt*, 24 March 1981, p. 23), Jörg Bilke described Maron's text as the first environmental novel from the GDR and reacted to Höpcke's criticism by insisting that the primary focus was not work but environmental pollution. Commenting more than a decade later and in a post-Wende context, Thomas Fox claimed that Maron's 'treatment of environmental issues [...] provided the novel with its most innovative aspect within GDR literary history.' *Border Crossings: An Introduction to East German Prose* (Ann Arbor: University of Michigan Press, 1993), p. 282.

Josefa's determination to fulfil her responsibilities, regardless of the consequences. Although critical attention has focused on the novel's scathing depiction of pollution, a small number of critics have recognised the importance of journalism as a theme. One of the most significant contributions in this regard comes from Alexandra Schichtel who reads *Flugasche* as 'Marons endgültige Abrechnung mit ihrem früheren Beruf.'[18] In what follows I will extend Schichtel's analysis by considering what she rightly sees as the clichéd, conformist nature of reportage in the GDR within the context of conflicting discourse systems.

The perceptive reader was aware of the compromise manoeuvres, such as the inclusion of the obligatory uplifting ending, which were necessary to ensure publication in the GDR. As Maron explained in an interview: 'Dazu hatte man die Hoffnung, daß der halbwegs vernünftige Leser wußte, daß kein Text anders erscheinen konnte.'[19] She was cognisant of the fact that her debut novel would transgress such boundaries: 'Der Roman ist eigentlich die andere Variante: Also, was wäre passiert, wenn ich nicht halbwegs vernünftig gewesen wäre? Das, was ich in dem Buch beschreibe, ist mir eigentlich erst mit dem Buch passiert.'[20] In response to a colleague's question as to which version of events she has decided to write, the protagonist of *Flugasche* remains adamant: 'Ich schreibe aber die unvernünftige' (FA, p. 58). In the following analysis I will explore the various forms of discourse present in the text, beginning with the regulated system of communication, including inscription of the socialist master text, which is so vehemently rejected by Josefa, then moving to consider the alternative discourse of the imaginative realm. I use the term 'alternative discourse' to mean not only a different kind of language, but also a different mode of thinking and perception and, as such, a potent counter-text.

---

18   Alexandra Schichtel, 'Monika Maron: Flugasche (1981)', in *Zwischen Zwang und Freiwilligkeit: Das Phänomen Anpassung in der Prosaliteratur der DDR* (Opladen: Westdeutscher Verlag, 1998), pp. 143–59 (p. 144).
19   Michael Hametner, 'Von Opfern, die Täter wurden', in *Börsenblatt für den Deutschen Buchhandel*, 26 June 1992, p. 42. Quoted in Schichtel, p. 145.
20   Hametner, p. 42.

'Dressierte Hofhunde': Journalism and Journalists in Flugasche

Flugasche charts the difficulties Josefa encounters in her attempts to inform her readership of environmental and working conditions at the power plant in B. as she has experienced them: 'die Verhältnisse zu beschreiben, wie sie vorgefunden wurden' (FA, p. 73). Journalistic discourse in the GDR was governed by thematic and stylistic restrictions and by political expediency. Even before her first trip to the power plant, Josefa reflects upon the utterly predictable nature of GDR newspaper articles. If the title of her assignment had read 'Porträt über den Arbeiter Soundso', instead of 'Reportage über B.' (FA, p. 13), she knows that she could have dispensed with the visit altogether and merely produced a standard portrait, indistinguishable from the many already written. Josefa mentally formulates a portrait of 'worker so-and-so', who has become such a cliché that he is not even individualised by name. The worker, for his part, is also aware of the conventions to which both sides must adhere: 'er weiß: Was immer ich an ihm finde, ich werde Gutes schreiben' (FA, p. 13). He delivers an appropriate response: 'der Kollege Soundso [...] erzählt von seinem Kollektiv, seinem guten Meister, seiner guten Ehe' (FA, p. 13). This positive focus is itself reminiscent of those portraits which frequently featured on pages four and five of the *Wochenpost*, some of which I analysed earlier in the chapter. Willing to engage in compromise manoeuvres in the absence of any alternative, even Josefa's mentor Luise is frustrated when an article is rejected because it is not sufficiently optimistic in tone. The ridiculous official commentary reads: 'die Dorfbewohner müßten ihre Häuser und Stachelbeersträucher mit mehr Optimismus verlassen, als im Text zu finden sei' (FA, p. 76). The clichéd nature of communication in the offices of the *Illustrierte Woche* is also clear from Josefa's description of an editorial meeting at which her contentious article is to be discussed; she realises to her amazement that her colleagues are capable of regurgitating 'stereotype Floskeln' (FA, p. 44) without even breaking into a smile.

Appalled at the antiquated machinery and polluted atmosphere of the power plant, the visiting journalist berates herself for her naive acceptance of the exclusively positive reports on the GDR chemical industry, with their repeated reference to new products and economic plans. She adds the cynical comment that there is never any mention in these articles of the 'Aschekammern, die das Schlimmste sind' (FA, p. 21). Rebelling against her pre-determined role, Josefa encourages the stoker Hodriwitzka to press for the closure of the old plant and asks decidedly uncomfortable and unexpected questions about the workers' unwillingness to defend themselves. Upon learning in the course of her second visit to B. of the stoker's death in mysterious circumstances, Josefa begins to doubt her ability to effect change and feels an increasing disillusionment with what she terms the tangential existence of the journalist: 'Alles wurde an seiner Peripherie gestreift, und schon in der Berührung bewegte sie sich vom Schnittpunkt fort, ihrer Existenz gemäß' (FA, p. 132).

Josefa's frustration also stems from the imperative to adopt those writing strategies that were an essential prerequisite for publication in the GDR. Her boyfriend Christian, very much aware of the 'Spielregeln' (FA, p. 191) operating in her professional domain, advises her to write two versions of her visit to the power plant: 'Die erste, wie es war, und eine zweite, die gedruckt werden kann' (FA, p. 24). His proposed solution, dismissed by the protagonist as a cynical renunciation of truth, illustrates once more the compromise manoeuvres that were an intrinsic aspect of journalistic discourse in the GDR. Christian insists that his suggestion, even if rejected by Josefa as 'Schizophrenie als Lebenshilfe' (FA, p. 24), is still better than her practice of 'Selbstzensur: rechts der Kugelschreiber, links der Rotstift' (FA, p. 25).[21] Writing conventions have etched themselves so indelibly in their minds that Josefa and her colleagues automatically censor their own work. In conversation with Luise, the protagonist alludes to this fact when she observes that journalists delete at least half of what they write, in the knowledge that others are more than willing to censor their material. Her analogy 'Wir benehmen uns wie dressierte Hofhunde, die letztlich nur ihre eigene Kette bewachen' (FA, p. 74) conveys not only the external pressures but also the self-imposed restrictions under which she and her colleagues write.

---

21 In his comprehensive history of the *Wochenpost*, Polkehn alludes at various points to self-censorship: 'Mit dem Prinzip der Selbstzensur hatte der DDR-Journalist zu leben, wollte er nicht den Beruf wechseln. Das Fatale daran war, daß es auf die Dauer jede schöpferische Initiative ersticken mußte, weil schließlich jeder seine eigene Schere im Kopf hatte, vom Chefredakteur bis zum Hilfsredakteur' (p. 83). An extract from an issue dated 10 November 1989 heralds the end of self-censorship: 'Wir wollen nicht länger Seiltänzer sein. Wir wollen die Schere aus dem Kopf haben' (p. 349).

In a central passage Josefa struggles to formulate her impressions of B. As a possible opening sentence she considers Thal's observation that B. is the filthiest town in Europe, but is aware that her superiors at the newspaper will invariably reject this suggestion. Her ironic comment 'Die dreckigste europäische Stadt ausgerechnet in einem sozialistischen Land. Wenn wir uns schon die traurige Tatsache leisten, so wenigstens nicht ihre öffentliche Bekanntmachung' (FA, p. 32) indicates the extent to which journalists in the GDR were constrained by political expediency. She eventually decides upon the formulation 'In B. steigt nur aus, wer hier aussteigen muß, wer hier wohnt oder arbeitet oder sonst hier zu tun hat' (FA, p. 32), replicating, as noted earlier in this chapter, the first sentence of Maron's seminal article 'Drachentöter'.

Josefa considers how control of the written word can culminate in control of thought: 'Nichtdruckbares wird nicht zu Ende gedacht. Es ist nur ein kurzer Weg von undruckbar zu undenkbar' (FA, p. 32). She is aware that she, too, is in danger of becoming implicated in the official mode of thinking: 'Vielleicht trennen mich nur einige Jahre von ihnen, die Jahre, in denen der *Un*-Mechanismus endgültig einrastet und mir das *Un*druckbare, das *Un*aussprechliche, das *Un*denkbare zur *Un*wahrheit werden wird' (FA, p. 33). The increasingly stultifying list – the unprintable, the inexpressible and the unthinkable – culminates in the very antithesis of Josefa's striving for complete und uncompromising expression: the concept of Untruth. Although guilty in the past of disguising the truth 'hinter schönen Sätzen' (FA, p. 34), her impassioned response to conditions at B. and her intensive work on the manuscript mean that she is now incapable of disseminating untruths.

The intellectual and emotional stultification in Josefa's professional domain has lasting repercussions, as Maron's portrayal of journalists in the novel illustrates. Fred Müller, for example, is an alcoholic who, in a drunken outburst, expresses revulsion at his daily routine and working environment. Rudi Goldammer is a nervous figure who avoids confrontation, burdened by his past as prisoner and overseer in a concentration camp: 'Als Kapo im Konzentrationslager hatte Rudi über Leben und Tod entschieden' (FA, p. 123). He suffers from a variety of psychosomatic illnesses, the body's symptomatic response to a restrictive environment. Jauer is a particularly disturbing figure who has returned to the newspaper offices after a period of psychiatric treatment. Josefa is disconcerted by the vacant expression in his eyes and the thin red scar on his forehead, indicative of sinister, ostensibly therapeutic methods. His mode of expression, too, has been altered and his speech is strewn with psychiatric terminology. Portrayed as a host of eccentric, bewildered and troubled characters, Josefa's colleagues bear the physical, emotional and even linguistic scars of a society in which truthful expression is consistently denied.

Flugasche is a scathing portrayal of journalistic practice in the GDR: the utter predictability of articles, the formulaic language, the self-censorship and endless compromise manoeuvres, and the lasting repercussions of incessant untruths. Josefa is completely unwilling to accept the continuous compromising of truth, the 'kastrierte Wahrheit' (FA, p. 36) of her professional environment. In her determination to furnish a truthful account of conditions at B., she writes herself out of the prevailing discourse system.

An Alternative Discourse

In this section I will analyse the dream-like sequences and increasingly nightmarish visions that begin to dominate Josefa's subconscious as the novel unfolds. Conflicting discourses emerge, particularly in the second part of the text, with the imaginative realm providing a potent counterpoint to a highly restrictive external reality.

Escape from this claustrophobic environment comes in the form of visions of flying. The first such flight occurs after Josefa has delivered her controversial manuscript to Luise. The protagonist envisages floating above the streets of East Berlin. Reference to the mythical figure of Daedalus indicates Josefa's awareness of the dangers inherent in flying too close to the sun, in daring to seek imaginative respite from what Martin Kane describes as 'the deadening routine of everyday reality.'[22] Allusion to Daedalus is followed immediately by the motto 'Brüder, zur Sonne, zur Freiheit; Brüder, zum Lichte empor' (FA, p. 71). Interestingly, these are the opening lines of a famous workers' song; used in this setting, with sarcastic effect, they underscore the absence of freedom and are an example of Maron's subversive intertextuality.[23]

---

22   In his essay 'Culpabilities of the Imagination: The Novels of Monika Maron', Martin Kane reads Josefa's retreat into the imaginative realm as a form of protest against societal constraints. *Literature on the Threshold: The German Novel in the 1980s*, ed. by Arthur Williams, Stuart Parkes and Roland Smith (New York: Berg, 1990), pp. 221–34 (p. 227).
23   The original text of this proletarian song was written in 1895–96 by the Russian revolutionary and poet Leonid P. Radin during a period of imprisonment in Moscow. The German conductor Hermann Scherchen heard the song for the first time as a prisoner of war

A psychological reading of this sequence would invariably begin with Freud's classic account of dreams of flying, which he includes in the group of most familiar dreams relating to infantile experiences and reproducing impressions of childhood.[24] Josefa encounters a young man whom she addresses as Pawel, the first name of an influential figure from her own childhood, her maternal grandfather Pawel Iglarz. The flight of Pawel and Josefa is an image of harmony, contrasting with the dissonance and strife of the working environment from which the protagonist has sought respite, if only in her imagination. Her request 'Sag mir noch mehr von den schönen Sätzen' (FA, p. 72) illustrates an appreciation of the poetic language of Pawel, a language conspicuously absent from Josefa's professional milieu, where melodious sentences are nothing more than stock phrases designed to camouflage decidedly uncomfortable truths. Pawel's description of a burgeoning natural landscape points to the presence of an important intertextual reference – the Old Testament *Song of Songs*. In suitably poetic terms Pawel describes the approach of spring: 'Denn siehe, der Winter ist vergangen, der Regen ist weg und dahin. Die Blumen sind hervorgekommen im Lande, der Lenz ist herbeigekommen, und die Turteltaube läßt sich hören in unserem Lande' (FA, pp. 71–72). Josefa, too, quotes from this biblical source in a passage that reflects her increasing emotional estrangement from Christian and feelings of isolation in her professional domain: 'Ich suchte ihn, aber ich fand ihn nicht; ich rief, aber er antwortete mir nicht. Es fanden mich die Hüter, die in der Stadt umgehen, die schlugen mich wund, die Hüter auf der Mauer nahmen mir meinen Schleier' (FA, p. 72). The insertion of lyrical passages from such non-approved sources is further indication of Maron's subversive use of intertextuality.[25]

---

and wrote the German version in 1918. It subsequently became one of the most popular workers' songs in the GDR and was frequently sung at marches and demonstrations.

24 Freud describes typical dreams as follows: 'Ziemlich übereinstimmend hat sich aber die Deutung verschiedener Traumformen gestaltet, die man als "typische" bezeichnet hat, weil sie bei so vielen Personen mit ganz ähnlichem Inhalt wiederkehren. Es sind dies die bekannten Träume vom Herabfallen von einer Höhe, vom Zahnausfallen, vom *Fliegen* und von der Verlegenheit, daß man nackt oder schlecht bekleidet ist.' 'Traumreize und Traumquellen', in *Gesammelte Werke: Chronologisch geordnet*, ii und iii: *Traumdeutung und Über den Traum* (London: Imago Publishing, 1942), pp. 22–45 (p. 40).

25 A more detailed exploration of the intertextuality of Maron's writing will be provided in Chapter Four.

The protagonist's meeting with Luise to discuss the contentious manuscript marks an abrupt return to reality. Although Josefa tries to convince herself that there is nothing sensational about her report, she realises that its submission will have serious repercussions: reason enough to fly, as she wryly observes. In this context her desire to fly is a response to a restrictive state apparatus and her insistence upon imaginative freedom an assertion of autonomy.

The second part of *Flugasche* opens with a direct reference to the escape route that dreams provide. Significantly, they offer welcome respite from the seemingly endless conversations taking place all around Josefa: 'Fluchtweg [...] aus den vielen Reden, die um sie herum geführt wurden und die sie selbst führte' (FA, p. 145). In this section of the book the subconscious is the site of disturbing, violent images. The repressed aspects of the protagonist's external reality resurface upon her retreat: 'Josefa war erschrocken über das Grauenhafte, das es gab, das es geben mußte, da es in ihr war, zusammengefügt aus Tatsächlichem, das mehr Raum brauchte als ihren Kopf und das sich als scharfer Extrakt in ihr niedergelassen hatte, wie sie glaubte' (FA, p. 145).

Josefa's sense of powerlessness in her professional environment is also mirrored in her passivity vis-à-vis those figures populating her imagination and who assign to her 'die Rolle einer Bedrängten [...] und wollte sie die nicht spielen, blieb ihr nur die Möglichkeit, sich mit der Rolle eines Zuschauers zu begnügen' (FA, p. 146). She is cast in the role of observer. The emphasis on performance is particularly evident in what Renate Kraft has termed the 'Lila Traum'.[26] This dream occurs as the discussions about Josefa's future become increasingly intense. Her distress is articulated in disturbing images of decay. Two old women appear on stage. The eyes of the older woman are sunken into her skull; the hands of her daughter are wrinkled and deformed. The stage is bathed in a single colour – purple. Against this backdrop a power struggle is unfolding. Even before the younger woman speaks, her mother beats her about the head with a stick. The daughter's complaint that she is unable to read or write is greeted with a further vicious assault from the mother who, having broken a purple glass on her daughter's head, takes a shard from the

---

[26] Renate Kraft, 'Was der Schlaf der Vernunft gebiert ...: Über die Funktion der Träume in Monika Marons Roman "Flugasche"', *Frauen in der Literaturwissenschaft*, 25/26 (1990), 34–36 (p. 34).

floor and cuts open her hand. The struggle continues as the daughter retaliates, attacking 'wie ein wütender Wolf' (FA, p. 148).

In the context of conflicting discourse systems, this purple dream fulfils an important role. Although the older woman accuses her of lying, the daughter insists that the room is, in fact, purple. There are parallels with Josefa's situation: despite the pressure to conform, she is determined to depict conditions as she has experienced them, even if this entails writing herself out of the prevailing discourse system. The daughter is punished, as Antonia Grunenberg points out, for naming things correctly.[27] She is no longer content with her 'Bilderbücher[n]' (FA, p. 148); Josefa, for her part, has tired of the prescribed images and formulaic phrases of GDR journalism. Just as the daughter struggles to overcome illiteracy and express herself, Josefa seeks a forum in which truthful expression is facilitated. In both real and subconscious worlds, writing is presented as a form of female empowerment.

The scene ends with the arrival of a mysterious figure dressed in black, at which point Josefa is wakened by her crying son. Significantly, the figures remain frozen in the closing frame, indelibly etched upon her subconscious. In this respect, *Flugasche* anticipates Maron's second novel *Die Überläuferin*. Following the final 'Zwischenspiel' – one of four satirical interludes in the text – Rosalind vows to erase the uninvited guests from her memory, but this proves to be impossible: 'Sie waren hier, in ihrer Wohnung, zum Denkmal erstarrt'.[28] In both instances the grotesque figures become lifeless but lasting reminders of the existence from which the protagonists have sought respite, if only in their imagination. Complete escape from society and, more importantly, from their discursive positions within it, seems impossible.

In the aftermath of her retreat from the newspaper, Josefa is subject to increasingly violent dreams: 'blutrünstige Phantasien, gespielt von schaurigen Gestalten und teuflischen Fratzen, die sie quälten und die sie noch verfolgten, wenn sie die Augen öffnete' (FA, p. 209). One particularly chilling encounter

---

27 Antonia Grunenberg, 'Der Traum als Heilmittel gegen die verordnete Infantilität – "Flugasche" von Monika Maron', in *Aufbruch der inneren Mauer: Politik und Kultur in der DDR 1971–1990* (Bremen: Edition Temmen, 1990), pp. 209–15 (p. 211).
28 Monika Maron, *Die Überläuferin: Roman* (Frankfurt am Main: Fischer Taschenbuch Verlag, 1995), p. 180. The novel was first published in 1986. I will be referring to the paperback edition. Quotations from the text will be followed in parentheses by the abbreviation ÜB and the relevant page number.

is described in graphic detail. A man and a woman stare at one another across a table. The woman's desire to travel to the ocean anticipates Maron's 1982 story 'Das Mißverständnis', in which an anonymous female character wishes to journey to the fantasy land of 'Nordsüden'. In both instances the journey fails to materialise and comes to symbolise the futility of individual aspirations. In Josefa's dream the promise of new beginnings, heralded by the woman's pregnancy, is brutally dashed as the scene unfolds. The man has only one leg. Repulsed at the sight of his scarred stump of leg, the woman refuses to sleep with him; he responds by beating her savagely, the scene culminating in his raping her to death. Grunenberg is correct in her critique of the scene's 'Holzhammersymbolik', strewn, as it is, with clichéd images such as bleeding eyes and missing limbs.[29] However, it remains a powerful articulation of Josefa's distress and vulnerability, occurring at that point in the text when the discussion among her colleagues about her behaviour and her professional future is reaching its height. Surprisingly, the protagonist does not experience the brutal encounter as a nightmare; instead she revels in its gory details when she relates the dream to Christian. Pondering the full import of his question 'Woher kennst du diese Wut?' (FA, p. 213), Josefa realises her capacity for rage, even if this anger can only be expressed subliminally.

The penultimate sequence is perhaps the most enigmatic of all. Josefa remains in her apartment rather than attend the meeting at which her future as a journalist is to be decided. The scene opens with a series of positive images: the imminent blossoming of the buds on the tree in front of the window, a thrush flying through the morning sky. At the sight of the bird in flight, Josefa embarks upon a final journey into an imaginative realm teeming with obscure images. The white spot on the thrush's back becomes, in her imagination, a doll wearing a bridal costume. Contrary to expectation, however, the delicate fabric and white colour do not symbolise purity; instead the bride is a poisonous creature: 'Bring sie zu ihrem Bräutigam, damit er stirbt an ihrem Gift und eingeäschert wird in ihrer Glut. Flieg schneller, schwarzer Leichenvogel' (FA, p. 242). As the flight continues, the bride assumes autonomy. Removing the veil from her face, she holds it to the wind in a defiant gesture and begins to fly independently. This image of non-conformity and of female empowerment strengthens the protagonist's resolve. When Luise telephones, she remains adamant: 'Sag ihnen, daß ich nicht komme, daß ich überhaupt nicht mehr

---

29 Grunenberg, p. 214.

komme' (FA, p. 243). Josefa persists in pitting her individual voice against the might of the collective. Her withdrawal is powerful testimony to the sacrifices that she is prepared to make in the interests of journalistic and personal integrity. She remains in her room rather than attend the meeting at which her professional future is to be decided.[30] In the final sentence of the text, the reader learns that on same afternoon when the staff of the *Wochenpost* has convened to discuss the behaviour of their wayward colleague, the government decides to close the old power plant at B. Josefa has effected change, albeit at the expense of her career.

For Josefa, the prevailing discourse system stifles any creative impulses: 'langsam stirbt er [unser armer gebremster Mensch] ab', she comments, adding that authentic expression is possible only in the realm of dreams and fantasy: '[er] wagt sich nur noch in den Träumen hervor' (FA, p. 79). Dream-like sequences cede to disturbing images as the story unfolds, providing an alternative discourse that erupts from, interrupts and subverts the linear narrative. These passages may be read as an example of what Wolfgang Emmerich has termed the 'Mobilisierung von Phantasie' ('Für eine andere Wahrnehmung', p. 17), to which I referred in my introductory chapter – a privileging of the imaginative realm. Visions of flying, representing at once liberation and escape, give way to more nightmarish sequences, which mirror the protagonist's inner turmoil and seem to indicate that complete release from a highly politicised external reality is impossible.

Conclusion

Maron's earliest texts are concerned with forms of discourse. Writing for the *Wochenpost*, she negotiated the compromise manoeuvres that were an intrinsic part of journalistic practice in the GDR. Page eighteen offered a certain freedom to focus on the quotidian aspects of life in the socialist state; the

---

30 In Maron's second novel *Die Überläuferin*, the bedroom also functions as a private space into which the protagonist retreats. Rosalind's room is the point of departure for her defection into the realm of fantasy and the space to which she returns at the end of the novel.

articles on pages four and five, by contrast, reported on economic issues and working life in the GDR of the mid-1970s. 'Drachentöter' emerged as a pivotal article, scathing in its indictment of Bitterfeld, yet all the while adhering to journalistic conventions.

Flugasche provided the author with a forum where she exposed the formulaic language and set pieces of the GDR press. Bound by publication imperatives, the young journalist Monika Maron may have tested, but was ultimately unable to transgress the official modes of expression. Committed from the outset to a truthful and complete account of conditions at B., her fictional alter ego Josefa Nadler writes herself out of the prevailing discourse system and retreats into an explosive and emotionally charged inner landscape. The imaginative realm reads as a subversive counter-text to the scripted existence of life in the GDR.

In conclusion, the struggle for authentic expression shapes Maron's earliest texts. This struggle takes the form of withdrawal and radical transgression in her second novel *Die Überläuferin*, as I will demonstrate in the next chapter.

CHAPTER TWO

Transgressing in Style: *Das Mißverständnis* and *Die Überläuferin* as Counter-Texts

In his essay 'Für eine andere Wahrnehmung der DDR-Literatur: Neue Kontexte, neue Paradigmen, ein neuer Kanon', published in 1992, the literary historian Wolfang Emmerich called for a fresh approach to GDR literature. By focusing on aesthetic elements, this type of literary criticism had the potential to liberate texts from the constraints of the sociopolitical approach, the 'umfassende und allseitige Politisierung' (*Literaturgeschichte*, p. 17) that had dominated literary criticism up to 1989 and that Emmerich later described as 'der vielleicht entscheidende Pferdefuß der DDR-Literatur-Forschung' (*Literaturgeschichte*, p. 17). For Emmerich, stylistic breaches in the form of disruption to the linear narrative, intertextuality, polyphony, multiple narrative perspectives, and, in particular, the unleashing of imaginative impulses all contribute to literature's role as counter-text: 'Die bessere DDR-Literatur löst sich vom Offizialdiskurs und entwirft Literatur als "Gegentext", als Subversion des Leitdiskurses' ('Für eine andere Wahrnehmung', p. 17). This chapter will explore how Maron provides in *Das Mißverständnis*, published in 1982, and in her 1986 novel *Die Überläuferin* powerful counter-texts to the scripted existence of life in the GDR.

As demonstrated in the previous chapter, the protagonist of Maron's debut novel *Flugasche* wrote herself out of the prevailing discourse system. The journalist Josefa Nadler renounced participation in her society and its stifling language by withdrawing from her professional milieu and retreating into the imaginative realm. Maron takes this concept of withdrawal further still in her second novel *Die Überläuferin*: the protagonist's rejection of her society assumes the drastic form of complete physical paralysis and leads to a phantasmagoric, increasingly nightmarish journey into a turbulent inner landscape. *Das Mißverständnis: Vier Erzählungen und ein Stück* is situated uneasily between these two novels. Teeming with obscure images, the collection of four short stories and a play is further instance of a challenging counter-text. Writing against the prevailing discourse in this manner meant writing outside of the political and literary system: all of these texts were denied publication in the GDR.

In his entry for the *Kritisches Lexikon zur deutschsprachigen Gegenwartsliteratur*, Eckhard Franke establishes a direct and convincing correlation between Maron's increasing recourse to fantastical elements and the stagnant and stultifying confines of the GDR in the 1980s.[1] This chapter will explore the fantastical topography that Maron created in these texts from the 1980s. I will illustrate how the imaginative realm offered a powerful alternative discourse, even if complete escape from the physical and psychological confines of the GDR remained impossible. I use the term 'alternative discourse' to mean not only a kind and use of language that is far removed from the restrictive form of communication with which the characters become increasingly frustrated, but also a different mode of thinking. *Das Mißverständnis* and *Die Überläuferin* provide examples of the 'Mobilisierung von Phantasie' ('Für eine andere Wahrnehmung', p. 17), the development of imaginative impulses which Emmerich urges critics to consider in an attempt to look beyond the political dimension of writing within – and against – the GDR.

As anticipated in *Flugasche*, the quest for identity in the form of authentic expression came to define Maron's writing in the final decade of the GDR. The struggle for authentic expression took the form of withdrawal, stylistic experimentation and radical transgression in *Das Mißverständnis* and *Die Überläuferin*, as this chapter seeks to demonstrate.

Das Mißverständnis

Misunderstandings and miscommunications abound in *Das Mißverständnis*. The very title of the collection points to the impenetrability of these texts which at once disconcert and challenge the reader. In the opening story an anonymous female character and her reluctant male companion set off on a journey to Nordsüden, but never reach their destination. The land of

---

[1] Eckhard Franke and Roman Luckscheiter, 'Monika Maron', in *Kritisches Lexikon zur deutschsprachigen Gegenwartsliteratur*, March 2005.

Das Mißverständnis and *Die Überläuferin* as Counter-Texts

Nordsüden is thus a symbol of unattainability; the coming together of polar opposites, as expressed in the name, remains an illusion. In 'Annaeva' the female protagonist leaves behind a monotonous existence; rejecting 'den ganzen langen Scheintod bis zum Tod',[2] she journeys through the desert in search of her true identity. 'Herr Aurich', the only text of the collection in which Maron refrains from stylistic experimentation, is a satirical portrait of a middle-aged communist bureaucrat. 'Audienz' charts the bizarre encounter between Rosalind and a handsome, seductive psychiatrist who assumes the role of God. In the play 'Ada und Evald' Maron introduces an array of strange characters: the romantic Ada, hopelessly in love with the failed and self-absorbed poet Evald, Suizi, who contemplates suicide and has a noose permanently around his neck, the philosopher X, the preacher, and the enormous Clairchen, who also features in *Die Überläuferin*.

I will begin my analysis of *Das Mißverständnis* by considering the depiction in the texts of a highly oppressive reality from which the various characters withdraw. I will also examine the deadening language that defines this external reality before moving to consider the subversive counter-text that Maron creates. This alternative discourse harnesses the senses and privileges the imaginative realm, even if complete escape proves to be unattainable.

'Scheintote Gegenwart': Life in the GDR

In the opening story of the collection, the female protagonist convinces her male companion to leave Greenland and embark upon a journey with her. A stark, snow-covered landscape and the complete absence of colour symbolise the monotony of existence; the woman explains to her doubting companion that the land of Norsüden, by contrast, celebrates colour and would provide an antidote to the sterile environment in which they live: 'Und nichts ist da weiß, jedes Ding hat seine Farbe, weiß ist verboten' (MV, p. 26). She was once a postwoman until the inhabitants of Greenland stopped writing letters

---

[2] Monika Maron, 'Annaeva', in *Das Mißverständnis: Vier Erzählungen und ein Stück* (Frankfurt am Main: Fischer Taschenbuch Verlag, 1993), pp. 33–45 (p. 38). The collection was first published in 1982. I will be referring to the paperback edition. Quotations from the text will be followed in parentheses by the abbreviation MV and the relevant page number.

altogether, this cessation perhaps symbolic of an inability to communicate in a stultifying environment. In place of such correspondence, killing has become a regular occurrence: 'das Töten als neue, allgemein übliche Form der Kommunikation' (MV, p. 21). The 'tägliche Monotonie' (MV, p. 21) of life in Greenland, a barely-concealed reference to the GDR, stifles its inhabitants: 'Eine graue Lethargie hatte sich auf das Volk von Grönland gelegt' (MV, p. 21). Rejecting a life 'von unendlicher Langeweile' (MV, p. 21), the woman seeks escape from the pervasive boredom.

Seeking release from a similarly lethargic existence, Annaeva awakes one morning, 'wieder müde und lustlos' (MV, p. 33), and decides to leave the city behind. A voracious reader, she had come to play out her life vicariously between the covers of books, but even this form of escape merely confirmed the superfluity of her existence: 'Sie selbst nichts als ein Plagiat der Bücher. In ihnen war ihr Leben längst beschrieben, vollendet, gefeilt und geschliffen; sie mußte es nicht mehr leben (MV, p. 36). Annaeva's flight into the desert expresses a desire to feel alive – 'Sie suchte Beweise ihrer lebendigen Existenz' (MV, p. 36) – and a deep-seated need to discover who she really is: 'Ich setze meine Füße und komme vorwärts, mein Ziel ist so weit wie der Horizont [...] unter mir ist die Erde, über mir ist der Himmel, dazwischen bin ich' (MV, p. 35).

The third story charts the slow demise of the model communist Erich Aurich. He suffers a stroke and is politely requested to retire. His feelings of self-importance are revealed to be nothing more than an illusion, as he learns when he phones his former workplace only to discover that he has already been forgotten: 'So stand es also. Möglich, daß es ihn gegeben hat. Demzufolge ebensogut möglich, daß es ihn nicht gegeben hat' (MV, p. 74). This passage underscores the functionality of a political state that considers its loyal employees to be utterly dispensable. Registering his complete insignificance, a shocked Aurich wonders: 'Und wo soll er gewesen sein in den dreißig Jahren [...], in denen er sich geopfert hat für die anderen bis fast zum Tode' (MV, p. 74).

In the play with which the collection concludes, we first encounter Ada, one of the two female characters, in her cell. This claustrophobic setting mirrors confinement within the political state. Peopled by characters that are in a permanent state of waiting, the play has Beckettian overtones. Ada waits patiently for the arrival of her lover Evald. Suizi, for his part, waits for Ada.

Her cry 'Ich will, daß etwas passiert' (MV, p. 103) expresses the desire for action that is so important to many of Maron's later protagonists.[3] Just as the woman in the title story aborts her proposed trip in the frustrating final line 'Komm, laß uns nach Hause gehen und auf einen besseren Tag warten' (MV, p. 29), waiting in 'Ada und Evald' is an ultimately futile endeavour: 'weil der Mensch liebt, was sich ihm entzieht' (MV, p 100). In the play's penultimate scene Ada is once again alone, contemplating an existence that she describes in the bleakest of terms as a living death: 'Meine scheintote Gegenwart' (MV, p. 122).

'Ein Leben in Riten und Floskeln': Empty Language and Failed Communication

The deadening reality of the existence portrayed in *Das Mißverständnis* stultifies any meaningful communication. While the woman and the man in the title story do engage in conversation, the dialogue is fragmented and interwoven with their thoughts. The man, who administers the royal coffers, is reluctant to leave Greenland. His speech contains the repetition of such enigmatic phrases as 'Alles ist ein Prozeß, und ich habe keine Schuld' (MV, p. 25). The woman is the more dominant partner in the exchange and seeks to convince him of the attractions that Nordsüden holds. Ultimately, however, their attempts at communication fail. They abandon their journey; the stasis of life in Greenland still remains.

Annaeva flees not only from the pervasive lethargy of her surroundings, but from the empty rituals and clichés that serve to reinforce the rigidity of life in the political state: 'ein Leben in Riten und Floskeln, Lehrsätze mit Gesetzesanspruch wider die Erfahrung' (MV, p. 38). A model communist bureaucrat, Erich Aurich has perfected this dogmatic form of expression. Imbued with a sense of his own self-importance, he takes his bureaucratic role very seriously indeed: 'Ihm war die Verantwortung als etwas Schweres,

---

3 Rosalind Polkowski, the protagonist of Maron's second novel *Die Überläuferin*, dreams of action, while her successor in *Stille Zeile Sechs* becomes a perpetrator of sorts during increasingly emotive exchanges with the communist functionary Herbert Beerenbaum.

zugleich Erhebendes in den Körper eingewachsen [...] ein Teil seiner selbst war sie geworden' (MV, p. 65). Aurich sees himself as fitting within a strictly ordered political and social hierarchy: 'die kleinere Herrn Aurich zugeteilte Welt, die ihm immer pyramidenförmig erschienen war, und in der er gleich unter der schmalen Spitze seinen festen Platz gefunden hatte' (MV, p. 59). Maron paints a satirical portrait of a communist whose ego is so inflated that his grandiose plans for a glittering political future blind him to his mediocrity. He has internalised the ultimately meaningless language of his professional milieu to such an extent that he remains blissfully unaware of his utter dispensability – a further instance of misunderstanding.

That attempts to communicate are inevitably fraught with misunderstandings seems to be a central tenet of Maron's collection. The failure to communicate is also an important theme in 'Ada und Evald'. Evald is a struggling and self-absorbed poet, sarcastically described by X as a talentless genius: 'Evald, das talentlose Genie, zerrt sich die Verse aus dem Leib, die nicht darin sind. Für einen Tropfen Nachruhm' (MV, p. 105). In a seminal scene the romantic idealist Ada dreams of 'Wortdiebe' (MV, p. 115); she describes language as a changing landscape in which words assume greater or less importance over time: 'Das sind die Zeiten großer Veränderungen in der Menschengeschichte, in denen der veränderte Geist der Menschen die sprachliche Landschaft umgestaltet, sie verschönt oder sie verwüstet' (MV, p. 116) Hope, once such an important word, 'vergleichbar einem hohen Berg' (MV, p. 116), has lost its significance and is now a 'Sandhaufen, den der Wind langsam abträgt' (MV, p. 116). Despite the nefarious rule of the word thieves, who stifle meaningful communication and self-expression, Ada clings to the word 'Hoffnung'. Her dream concludes with a chorus singing:

> Freiheit, Sehnsucht, Hoffnung, Glück.
> Wir holn die gestohlenen Wörter zurück. (MV, p. 120)

By reclaiming the words freedom, desire, hope and happiness, Ada insists upon a more authentic form of expression, which forms an essential counter-text in the play and throughout the volume.

'Früher war ich ein Vogel': *Das Mißverständnis* as Counter-Text

Determined to liberate themselves from the constraints of an oppressive external reality and its atrophied language, the female characters in *Das Mißverständnis* seek an authentic form of expression. A hopeful Ada advocates the importance of 'Sehnsucht' (MV, p. 120); Clairchen provides the most obvious example of female sensuality in the volume. Coupled with fantastical elements, this sensual dimension contributes to the creation of a subversive counter-text in *Das Mißverständnis*.

The very opening sentence of the collection harnesses the senses: 'Über Grönland wehte ein staubiger Wind, der nach Brombeeren roch' (MV, p. 7). Alice Bolterauer offers a convincing analysis of this opening passage:

> Der Dezimierung der äußeren Empfindungen – hier in Grönland ist alles weiß und kalt – korreliert die Reduktion der inneren Empfindlichkeit: Trauer und Freude hören auf, sich Ausdruck zu verschaffen. In diese Szenerie einer weitgehenden Anästhetisierung bricht die Wucht einer Sinneswahrnehmung, die gleichermaßen unwahrscheinlich ist, wie sie als Versprechen erscheint: ein Duft nach Brombeeren, der Geruch einer blühenden, lebendigen, farbenfrohen Natur, dessen Wahrnehmung zum Versprechen eines anderen Seins wird und der als Impuls, aufzubrechen, fungiert.[4]

Bolterauer traces the new form of perception embraced by the female protagonist. This perception entails an awakening of the senses and is captured in the aroma of blackberries that seems so attractive to her. It is only through communion with nature that the female protagonist of the second story can explore her identity. Even before Annaeva leaves the city behind, she seeks respite in the natural world:

> Am liebsten war ihr Gewitterregen, der sie bis auf die Haut durchnäßte. Sie ging durch die dunklen, leergespülten, nur hin und wieder vom Blitz erhellten Straßen, ließ sich vom Donner wie von Hammerschlägen treffen, ließ den Wind tief in ihr Fleisch schneiden. (MV, p. 36)

---

[4] Alice Bolterauer, '"Brombeergeruch" und "Vogelfedern": Die Erfahrung von Gegenwart in Monika Marons Prosatext *Das Mißverständnis*', in *Monika Maron in Perspective: 'Dialogische' Einblicke in zeitgeschichtliche, intertextuelle und rezeptionsbezogene Aspekte ihres Werkes*, ed. by Elke Gilson, German Monitor, 55 (Amsterdam and New York: Rodopi, 2002), pp. 21–33 (p. 24).

Annaeva is awakened from her lethargy. The description of rain on her skin anticipates similar exhilaration experienced by the protagonist Rosalind Polkowski in the closing sequence of *Die Überläuferin*. In *Das Mißverständnis* communion with nature is taken to extremes in the figure of Clairchen who communicates with and dreams of marriage to a chestnut tree.

'Früher war ich ein Vogel', the woman announces in the opening story, 'Ich kann mich nicht erinnern, nur manchmal träume ich, daß ich fliege. Dann sehe ich Farben, die es in Grönland nicht gibt' (MV, p. 12). We are reminded of Josefa's visions of flying, which served in *Flugasche* as counter-text to a prosaic external reality; in *Das Mißverständnis* the reader embarks with the characters on a series of fantastical journeys. The stories are strewn with obscure images. The play 'Ada und Evald' has surrealist overtones, including the unnerving presence of puppets resembling some of the characters and whose heads are disassembled and reassembled at various points in the text. Its debut performance in Wuppertal garnered mixed reviews, with audience and critics alike at a loss as to how it should be interpreted.[5]

Maron's stylistic experimentation in this collection certainly challenges the reader. The texts are often fragmented. Dialogues are frequently interrupted by streams of consciousness. Entire sequences remain resistant to interpretation. Significantly, images of violence, destruction, death and decay feature prominently. Killing has become a routine activity for the inhabitants of Greenland. In 'Ada und Evald' the preacher announces the imminent destruction of the world: 'Glaubt an die Zerstörung, glaubt an die Erschaffung des Nichts' (MV, p. 114). In the final scene of the play, we learn that Clairchen has committed suicide by hanging herself from the chestnut tree. The stark reality of physical decay is depicted in Maron's portrait of a middle-aged communist: 'Herr Aurich schrumpfte. Um Hals und Bauch hingen ihm fleischlose Hautlappen, durch die transparenten Schläfen schimmerte blaue Verwundbarkeit' (MV, p. 58). After twenty days wandering in the desert, Annaeva, too, is a reduced figure. Her death is foreshadowed when she dreams of swarms of flies feeding on the decaying corpse of Ferdinand who died attempting to cross the desert. The closing sequence anticipates a similar end for Annaeva:

---

5   Rea Brändle, for example, highlights the challenging nature of the play, describing it as 'eine Herausforderung und zugleich ein phantastisches Angebot' ('Erkundungsfahrten zu neuen Fragen', *Tages-Anzeiger Zürich*, 2 June 1986).

> Ich kann liegen bleiben und auf meine Zukunft warten, die ich selbst bin; die zwei, die
> ich bin, streiten lassen, bis ich selbst Niemand bin, der auf mich wartet.
> Und fressen mich die Raben
> dann werd ich nicht begraben. (MV, p. 45)

The presence in the text – and in the minds of the various characters – of such disturbing images indicates a turbulent inner landscape, reflecting on a subconscious level the violence and oppression of the external reality from which they seek to escape.

Bolterauer interprets the counter-text that Maron creates in the title story as a realm where an authentic life becomes possible:

> Das, was als Gegenentwurf zu diesem Sein der Monotonie, der Einsamkeit und der Kälte fungiert, ist [...] eine Vorstellung zu einem anderen Sein [...], das über die Negation des Bestehenden und Selbstverständlichen hinaus auch als Ort eines authentischen Lebens gedacht werden kann.[6]

The search for an authentic life and an authentic form of expression comes to define Maron's writing in the final decade of the GDR. In *Die Überläuferin* this search continues and again involves retreat into the imaginative realm.

Die Überläuferin

With its fragmented structure, multiple narrative perspectives and complete disregard for chronology, Maron's second novel is a challenging, disconcerting text. Thomas Beckermann underscores the stylistic transgressions at work when he describes it as a 'radical book: it relies entirely on imagination, language and form, it shuns proximity to recognizable reality and yet it strives with utmost accuracy to narrate movement in a time of deadly stasis.'[7]

---

6   Bolterauer, p. 28.
7   Thomas Beckermann, '"Die Diktatur repräsentiert das Abwesende nicht": Essay on Monika Maron, Wolfgang Hilbig and Gert Neumann', in *German Literature at a Time of Change 1989–1990: German Unity and German Identity in Literary Perspective*, ed. by Arthur Williams, Stuart Parkes and Roland Smith (Bern, Frankfurt am Main, Paris, New York: Peter Lang, 1991), pp. 97–116 (p. 101).

The protagonist Rosalind Polkowski, a historian at a research institute in East Berlin, retreats from society and defects into her imagination. While her predecessor Josefa Nadler had retreated to her bedroom in the second section of *Flugasche*, withdrawal takes the extreme form of physical paralysis in Maron's second novel. The opening sequence, in which the reader encounters a paralysed protagonist confined to her bedroom, has Kafkaesque overtones.[8] Shunning the physical topography of East Berlin and of her strictly regulated professional life, Rosalind embarks upon a phantasmagoric voyage that becomes a journey into the subconscious realm, where she encounters suppressed aspects of her self.

I will first consider how the GDR is depicted in Maron's second novel before examining the deadening discourse from which Rosalind seeks respite. The principal section 'Mit dem Kopf durch die Wand gehen' will explore the powerful topography of the imagination that Maron creates in *Die Überläuferin* and that serves as counter-text to a stultifying external reality.

'Die todlangweiligen Banalitäten ihres bisherigen Alltags': Life in the GDR

Maron evokes in *Die Überläuferin* a tangible sense of place. In the opening sequence of the text, we are provided with a very precise description of Rosalind's route to work. The street names – Becherstraße, Schiffbauerdamm, Albrechtstraße – situate her external reality firmly in East Berlin. The free flight of the seagulls is in stark contrast to the 'verbarrikadierte Spree' (ÜB, p. 11), the barricaded river itself symbolic of a divided city.

This sense of physical confinement extends to the description of Rosalind's workplace. Until her retreat she had spent fifteen years working as a historian at a renowned research institute in East Berlin and was considered to be a talented academic: 'eine talentierte und förderungswürdige Wissenschaftlerin' (ÜB, p. 44). Her working milieu had been an extremely regulated one, under the watchful eye of the institute's director, the aptly named Siegfried Barabas. Rosalind delights in her sudden release from the deadening monotony of her daily routine, from the 'todlangweiligen Banalitäten ihres bisherigen Alltags' (ÜB, p. 12).

---

8   In an interview conducted by Gerhard Richter, Maron revealed that the working title of her second novel had been *Die Lähmung*. 'Verschüttete Kultur', *GDR Bulletin*, 18 (1992), p. 4.

Despite the protagonist's uncharacteristic and protracted absence from her workplace, not a single colleague has telephoned – a fact that underscores her utter dispensability. She has been deleted from her boss's memory, 'wie ein Programm aus einem Computer' (ÜB, p. 12). Martha, one of the figures who populate Rosalind's inner landscape, is scathing in her criticism of this utilitarian approach and of a society dominated by statistics: 'Denn schon ehe du geboren wurdest, hat man dich statistisch aufbereitet und deinen möglichen Nutzen errechnet', she tells the protagonist, concluding: 'kurz: deine Rentabilität ist veranschlagt und wird erwartet' (ÜB, pp. 50–51). It is Martha who highlights the strictly hierarchical nature of the social structures. She notes that Rosalind's boss Barabas is merely one superior in an entire hierarchy 'vom Vorgesetzten bis hin zum Staatsoberhaupt' and warns her: 'Deinem Sklavendasein fehlt nur das Parasitäre' (ÜB, p. 99).

Before her withdrawal the protagonist was frequently overcome by a feeling that she was playing out her life 'in einem Versuchslabor für Menschen' (ÜB, p. 203).[9] The reduction of human life to a laboratory experiment is a particularly chilling image that underscores once again the state's complete control over its citizens. 'Wer zuviel wußte, wurde getilgt' (ÜB, p. 203) is the terrifying conclusion.

Depicting the intellectual and emotional stultification of life in the socialist state, *Die Überläuferin* followed the fate of its predecessors and was published only in West Germany.

'Die Sprache ist keine bunte Wiese': Deadening Language in the GDR

'Die Sprache ist keine bunte Wiese, Madame, auf der man verliebt spazieren geht' (ÜB, p. 156), the representative of the association of male poets warns Martha in an intimidating exchange during which he seeks to reinforce the supremacy of patriarchal discourse. He dismisses her attempts at writing as

---

9   This image recalls Karl Kraus's view of Austria–Hungary, which, by starting the Great War, set in motion a process of technologically empowered dehumanising; as early as July 1914, just before the outbreak of war, he wrote of what was happening 'in der österreichischen Versuchsstation des Weltuntergangs' ('Franz Ferdinand und die Talente', *Die Fackel*, 400–03 (10 July 1914), 1–4 (p. 2)). Maron's use of the image prompts the question of much she consciously adopts and adapts motifs from the past. I will explore this issue of intertextuality in Chapter Four.

presumptuous and in very bad taste and he is disdainful of the lyricism, pathos, self-pity and what he terms 'modisches Feministengeplapper' (ÜB, p. 156) of her texts. He underscores the importance of rationality: 'die Vernunft ist neben der Sprache das höchste Gut des Menschen' (ÜB, p. 160), Martha's interrogator insists.

Rosalind's defection is interrupted by dramatic interludes, or 'Zwischenspiele', during which a host of bizarre figures, caricatures of the socialist state, discuss such topics as the merits of an ordered society and the dangers of an unchecked imagination. Littered with statistics, mathematical formulae, quotations from Marx and Lenin, and describing endless categories and sub-categories of citizen, these dialogues provide examples of the empty phraseology and clichés that pervade the protagonist's external reality. The man in the red uniform, for example, speaks in formulaic language when he accuses Rosalind of 'Unerlaubte Phantasie in Tateinheit mit Benutzung derselben im Wiederholungsfall' (ÜB, p. 170). These figures articulate the doctrines of a rigid society, the 'Lehrsätze, Verhaltensregeln und Vorsichtsmaßnahmen zum Schutz der Ordnung' (ÜB, p. 116) of the governing discourse from which the protagonist seeks to escape. Towards the end of her increasingly nightmarish journey, Rosalind encounters a clone. His speech, littered with the repetition of phrases such as 'es geht mir sehr gut, es geht mir sehr gut, sehr gut geht es mir' (ÜB, p. 200), is an example of meaningless language taken to extremes.[10]

Significantly, the imaginary realm offers a damning satirical commentary on the socialist state and its forms of communication; even as she rejects the deadening jargon of the political state, Rosalind cannot escape it completely.

---

10 With his repetition of 'ich bin heute etwas dekompensiert' (ÜB, p. 200), the clone k329 reminds the reader of Jauer, one of Josefa Nadler's colleagues in *Flugasche*, who describes himself in precisely these terms after a period spent in therapy. The exact nature of this treatment is never specified, but the scar on his forehead bears physical testimony to state control.

'Mit dem Kopf durch die Wand gehen': Withdrawal and Transgression in Die Überläuferin

Looking at the walls that confine her paralysed body, the protagonist decides to defect: 'Und jetzt, sagt Rosalind, werde ich mit dem Kopf durch die Wand gehen' (ÜB, p. 130). In so doing, she rediscovers repressed aspects of her self. Her fantastical journey, interrupted by satirical interludes, or 'Zwischenspiele', becomes increasingly nightmarish as the novel moves towards its conclusion. Rosalind puts her head through the wall in her imagination and thus sets in motion a series of stylistic transgressions that form a turbulent counter-text to an oppressive external reality, even if complete liberation from that reality is ultimately impossible.

Rosalind's bedroom serves as the setting that frames this disjointed narrative: it is the sphere to which she withdraws and the point of departure for her phantasmagoric journey. Significantly, this intimate sphere is also the space to which she returns in the concluding sequence. Referencing Mikhail Bakhtin's concept of the chronotope, Elizabeth Boa notes that the domestic space of the protagonist's room frequently figures as a chronotope in women's writing – she cites as examples Virginia Woolf, Ingeborg Bachmann and Monika Maron. In the Bakhtinian sense, the term 'chronotope', literally 'time space', denotes 'the intrinsic connectedness of temporal and spatial relationships that are artistically expressed in literature.'[11] Describing the private space of the bedroom as a metaphor for the core of the self into which the female subject withdraws, Boa highlights the ambiguity of such a withdrawal: 'Solches Zurückziehen, das aber zur völligen Isolation führen kann, bleibt mehrdeutig: ist es eine Überlebensart, eine Todesart oder gar die letzte Möglichkeit des Widerstands in extremis?'[12] This ambiguity is applicable to Rosalind's withdrawal: her retreat can be read as a form of survival and as the only oppositional gesture possible within – and against – a repressive regime of state control.

---

11   Mikhail Bakhtin, 'Forms of Time and of the Chronotope in the Novel: Notes Towards a Historical Poetics', in *The Dialogic Imagination: Four Essays*, ed. by Michael Holquist (Austin: Texas University Press, 1981), pp. 84–258 (p. 84). *The Dialogic Imagination* was first published in Moscow in 1975.

12   Elizabeth Boa, 'Schwierigkeit mit der ersten Person: Ingeborg Bachmanns *Malina* und Monika Marons *Flugasche, Die Überläuferin* und *Stille Zeile Sechs*', in *Kritische Landnahme: Ingeborg Bachmann im Blickfeld der neunziger Jahre*, ed. by Robert Pichl and Alexander Stillmark (Vienna: Hora Verlag, 1994), pp. 125–45 (p. 133).

It is Rosalind's body that first reacts against such control; her mind follows suit and defects. In an interview Maron articulated the problematic body-mind relationship, which she explores in *Die Überläuferin*, as follows:

> Zum Körper: ja, das muß offenbar ein Problem für mich sein. Das kommt oft vor. [...] Ich nehme meinen Körper wahr als jemand anders, mit dem ich irgendwie gut auskommen muß, sonst gibt's Schwierigkeiten. Es kommt mir also nicht vor wie ich, wir mir mein Kopf vorkommt wie ich. Diese Schizophrenie empfinde ich jedenfalls.[13]

This schizophrenic existence finds expression in *Die Überläuferin*. Long before her complete withdrawal from society, Rosalind's body had frequently rebelled against societal constraints: 'Der Körper rebellierte gegen die aufgezwungene Unfreiheit durch Krankheit' (ÜB, p. 118). She underwent a series of operations. It seemed impossible to reconcile the demands of her mind and of a body 'mit dem sie nicht eins werden konnte' (ÜB, p. 45): 'Rosalind [glaubte] oft [...] sie müsse sich in zwei Personen teilen, wollte sie an dem ihr innewohnenden Zwiespalt nicht irre werden' (ÜB, p. 118). It is only when her body renounces participation in external reality that her mind finally acts in harmony with the body and defects into the realm of dreams and fantasy.

Reading the protagonist's paralysed body as a metaphor for her physical confinement within a stultifying society, Brigitte Rossbacher notes that 'while this condition prevents Rosalind from physically crossing the threshold to the outside world, she delights in the recognition that it frees her mind to traverse topographical and chronological barriers.'[14] Revelling in the incomprehensible amount of time suddenly at her disposal, the protagonist introduces a topographical metaphor: 'Sinnvoller wäre es, dachte sie, die Zeit als einen Raum zu betrachten, in dem sie die Erlebnisse sammeln wollte wie Bücher in einer Bibliothek, ihr jederzeit zugängliche und abrufbare Erinnerungen' (ÜB, p. 13). Memories that Rosalind accesses in the aftermath of retreat include her birth in the midst of war. Memories of her aunt Ida also resurface throughout the increasingly fragmented narrative. Chronology is wilfully abandoned:

---

13   Richter, p. 4.
14   Brigitte Rossbacher, 'The Status of State and Subject: Reading Monika Maron from *Flugasche* to *Animal triste*', in *Wendezeiten, Zeitenwenden: Positionsbestimmungen zur deutschsprachigen Literatur 1945–1995*, ed. by Robert Weninger and Brigitte Rossbacher (Tübingen: Stauffenberg, 1997), pp. 193–214 (p. 202).

past, present and future merge to form a 'wunderbares Chaos ohne Ziel und Zweck' (ÜB, p. 13). Rosalind rejects the 'zielstrebiges, wissenschaftliches Denken' (ÜB, p. 98) of her professional milieu; it is the figure of Martha who best captures the associative and unrestrained mode of thinking to which the protagonist aspires.

As was the case in *Das Mißverständnis*, Rosalind's journey towards an authentic form of expression is intimately connected with a desire to express her most authentic self. She embraces previously repressed facets of her self, symbolised in the sensual excess of Clairchen and in the anarchic individualism of Martha. The former's insatiable desire to be loved leads to 'verzweifelte Exzesse' (ÜB, p. 68), which contrast with the protagonist's strictly regulated existence. Alluding to her enormous size, Clairchen describes herself as a 'Haufen Fleisch' (ÜB, p. 120); the mind has succumbed to the demands of her body: 'dem Kopp blieb nischt weiter übrich, als sich sehenden und tränenden Auges von dem wildjewordenen Fleisch mitschleppen zu lassen' (ÜB, p. 120). In a surreal scene she removes her head to reveal a smaller head resembling Greta Garbo. Susan Anderson interprets this scene as 'reflecting in an exaggerated manner Rosalind's own split between the rational and the sensual.'[15] The protagonist admires Clairchen's ability to embrace her sexuality: 'In Clairchen muß ein anderes, wilderes Blut gelebt haben [...] eins, das sich auflehnen mußte gegen die Dressur' (ÜB, p. 116).

If Clairchen symbolises the freedom to express sensual desires, it is Martha who deliberately flouts societal conventions, with complete disregard for the consequences. She lies, steals and invents stories about her past. Rosalind is envious of this free spirit: 'Eigentlich wollte ich lieber lügen und stehlen können wie Martha' (ÜB, p. 115). She disappears to Spain in search of her father, for whom she invents an adventurous biography. She loves railway stations – a space of emotional turmoil, of passionate arrivals and leave-takings. Cherishing the enigmatic and the mysterious, Martha represents 'die Welt der Geheimnisse' (ÜB, p. 102), which is in stark contrast to the emphasis on the rational, to the 'Vernunft' (ÜB, p. 160) that prevails in the protagonist's external reality.

---

15 Susan C. Anderson, 'Creativity and Nonconformity in Monika Maron's *Die Überläuferin*', *Women in German Yearbook: Feminist Studies in German Literature & Culture*, 10 (1995), 143–60 (p. 151).

Rosalind experiences initial difficulty in embracing a new form of thinking: 'Wie sollte sie so schnell auch ein anderes Denken lernen, dachte sie. Denkwege sind wie Straßen [...] unversehens ging man sie wie gewohnt' (ÜB, p. 26). Realising the necessity of rejecting the regimented thought patterns that she has internalised, she actively seeks the 'Geheimpfade, Schleichwege, unterirdische Gänge und Gebirgsgrate' (ÜB, p. 26). She envies Martha's ability to exploit the imaginative potential within: 'Martha kannte Wege durch die Luft, die hatte Rosalind nie gefunden' (ÜB, p. 26). The protagonist is attracted to her disjointed, dream-like way of thinking: 'Martha dachte, was sie wollte und wie sie wollte, sprunghaft, verträumt [...] geradezu kindlich' (ÜB, p. 98).

It is Martha who impresses upon Rosalind the importance of individual creativity in a relentlessly utilitarian society. Recalling a conversation with a pirate chief, a figure who symbolises the adventurous life that can be played out only in one's imagination, she instructs the protagonist to cultivate those parts of the self that are of no use to the state: 'das Besondere, das Unberechenbare, Seele, Poesie, Musik, ich weiß keinen passenden Namen dafür' (ÜB, p. 51). She urges Rosalind to rediscover these suppressed aspects: 'Dieses scheinbar nutzloseste Stück von dir mußt du finden und bewahren, das ist der Anfang deiner Biografie' (ÜB, p. 51). Significantly, it is Martha who, like Ada before her, seeks to reclaim the concepts of hope and desire. Heinrich, the representative of the association of male poets, dismisses the presence of such concepts in her writing: 'Worte wie Hoffnung, Sehnsucht, Schmerz, Leid einschließlich der dazugehörigen Adjektive sind durchaus überrepräsentiert' (ÜB, p. 156) is his damning verdict.

Encounters with Martha and Clairchen feature prominently within the topography of Rosalind's imagination. The increasingly fragmented narrative is also interrupted by the protagonist's recollection of sojourns in the pub. The pub is frequented by those same characters, including Rosalind's former boyfriend Bruno and the eccentric Karl-Heinz Baron, known to his friends as the Count, who later appear in *Stille Zeile Sechs*; the role of this important space will be considered at length in Chapter Three. With its dazzling linguistic variety – Bruno speaks Latin, while the Graf is a polyglot and Rosalind tries her hand at Eskimo – and its emphasis on the idiosyncratic, the pub forms part of the novel's counter-text. However, its clientele bear the indelible emotional and psychological imprints of the society from which they, too, have retreated. Complete withdrawal appears to be unattainable.

The impossibility of complete escape is also reinforced by the four 'Zwischenspiele' that interrupt Rosalind's fantastical wanderings. These interludes, with their emphasis on uniformity and the supremacy of the collective, function as a satirical commentary on the socialist state. Each member of the bizarre cast is defined by a pronounced trait or physical feature: the man with the sad childhood, the woman with the high-pitched voice, the woman with her own opinion, and the man whose nose bleeds, 'wenn ich bestimmte Sätze nicht sage' (ÜB, p. 38), as he explains to an astonished protagonist. The man in the red uniform is clearly the most important figure, setting the agenda and controlling proceedings. In the first interlude he reiterates the importance of 'Sicherheit und Ordnung' (ÜB, p. 35) and of leading a productive life: 'Der Mensch Wiestolzdasklingt wird […] geboren […] um ein sinnvolles Leben zu führen' (ÜB, p. 37). The family unit is the topic for discussion in the second interlude. The man in the red uniform assumes a more threatening role in the third interlude, introducing himself as 'Beauftragter der Staatlichen Behörde für Psychokontrolle' (ÜB, p. 122) and articulating the dangers that the non-conformist individual poses for society: 'Der unidentische Mensch denkt aufrührerisch und strebt Veränderungen an, was ihn zu einem gesellschaftsgefährdenden Subjekt, in Einzelfällen sogar zum Kriminellen macht' (ÜB, p. 125). During the final interlude Rosalind is accused of succumbing to forbidden imaginative impulses, of 'unerlaubte Phantasie' (ÜB, p. 170). Her interlocutor, the man in the red uniform, extols the virtues of 'eine konstruktive, positive, saubere Phantasie' (ÜB, p. 171). Echoing his earlier refrain 'Es geht um Ordnung und Sicherheit. Um die Sicherheit der Ordnung des Kopfes' (ÜB, p. 174), he now applies this obsession with order to thought patterns. The political state even determines how and what its citizens think, thereby thwarting forbidden, potentially subversive impulses.

Even as she defects, embracing the imaginative possibilities within, Rosalind is confronted with the conformity and functionality of the society from which she has withdrawn. Brigitte Rossbacher describes these interludes as 'dramatic intermezzos that variously stage the mechanisms of social control she has internalized.'[16] After the second interlude the protagonist, addressing the man in the red uniform, concedes: 'da Sie in meiner Erinnerung vorhanden sind, müssen Sie mir in meinem leibhaftigen Leben begegnet sein, daran kann

---

16   Rossbacher, p. 202.

ich nicht zweifeln' (ÜB, p. 94). She gradually renounces any illusion of control over these figures that appear unannounced in her bedroom. The grotesque characters, described explicitly as 'Ebenbilder aus Rosalinds früherem Leben' (ÜB, p. 188), cannot be forgotten: 'Sie würde in der Zukunft mit ihnen leben müssen und sie demzufolge auch nicht vergessen können, solange sie in diesem Zimmer bliebʼ (ÜB, p. 180). These caricatures have become lasting reminders of the society from which the protagonist has sought to escape.

While subverting the prevailing discourse in their sarcastic portrayal of a regimented society, these interludes also highlight the continued influence of state control. Rosalind is disturbed by the extent to which this control extends even into the imaginative realm, as the images of death and decay, which resurface during her phantasmagoric journey, indicate. Beginning with the vivid memory of her birth in the midst of war, with bombs exploding all around, she also remembers wandering with her mother and her beloved aunt Ida through a war-torn landscape of rubble and corpses. She recalls the final moments of her aunt's life and the materiality of decay: 'Ida röchelte in der Agonie […] Idas Gesicht mit der verkrusteten Höhlung, die der Mund war' (ÜB, p. 24). Her father's corpse reminds her of a slaughtered animal (ÜB, p. 21). Rosalind interprets Clairchen's suicide, 'dieses schockierende, ekelerregende und brutale Zeichen der Hilflosigkeit' (ÜB, p. 68), as an expression of the 'Maßlosigkeit ihres Lebens' (ÜB, p. 68).

Even as the protagonist breaks out in her imagination, the sense of confinement remains. As she journeys to the railway station – itself a symbol of endless possibilities – she registers an oppressive cityscape: 'diese fremden Häuserwände, die sie immer enger umschlossen' (ÜB, p. 163). She witnesses the frenetic building of a wall; what she registers as an amputated street (ÜB, p. 193) is a potent symbol of division. Rosalind encounters scenes of destruction and suffering and witnesses bloodstained bodies, fleeing figures, corpses: 'Blutende, Halbtote taumelten schweigend […] überall Blut, Stöhnen, keine Worte' (ÜB, p. 148). The repulsive stench of war and decay hangs in the air. Such is the unrelenting violence of these images that she must ask herself: 'Woher die Leichen, woher das viele Blut in meinem Kopf?' (ÜB, pp. 177–78). The nightmarish scenes culminate in her encounter with a clone, the chilling outcome of a utilitarian world order. Such macabre images reflect Rosalind's inner turmoil as she struggles to liberate herself from the insidious and lasting influence of a controlling society.

The protagonist's increasingly desperate journey to the railway station leads her to the Bowery, a run-down part of Manhattan, where she finds Martha. The novel's penultimate scene provides a visceral description of this New York cityscape and is played out in a space of vomit, sweat, urine and filth. Brigitte Rossbacher interprets Rosalind's 'border crossings' as 'encounters with the abject.'[17] In succumbing to her most base instincts – 'Ich [...] räkle mich wollustig im stinkenden Staub der Straße' (ÜB, p. 218), 'ich finde mich ekelhaft, so gefalle ich mir' (ÜB, p. 219), 'wir paaren uns wie das Vieh' (ÜB, p. 219) – she is liberated from the constraints of a repressive external reality.

Significantly, the defector finds herself back in her bedroom in the novel's closing sequence: 'Das ist mein Zimmer, sage ich, und niemand antwortet mir, denn Martha ist längst verschwunden, und Rosalind saß, die lahmen Beine zum Schneidersitz gekreuzt, allein in ihrem Sessel' (ÜB, p. 220). Bemused that her imaginative excursion has led her back to the physical space, if not yet to the external reality, from which she had defected, she refrains from pursuing the question as to whether this is a sign of strength or weakness. The physical confines of the room remain unaltered; Rosalind's perspective, however, has changed: 'das Zimmer kam ihr verändert vor, enger, niedriger [...] Als würde sie vom falschen Ende durch ein Fernglas sehen' (ÜB, p. 221).

From her armchair the protagonist can merely observe the natural world outside; the rain that has just begun to fall contrasts with the dry air of the room. There are strong overtones in this closing scene of Maron's debut novel *Flugasche*, which also concludes with its protagonist observing the outside world, in particular a bird in flight, from the confines of her bedroom. In the final sentence Rosalind longs to be part of the natural world: 'Den Mund weit öffnen und das Wasser in mich hineinlaufen lassen, naß werden, dachte sie, vom Regen naß werden, das wäre schon' (ÜB, p. 221). The use of the subjunctive captures the inherent ambivalence of this closing sequence and is a fitting conclusion to a text that has resisted categorisation and transgressed stylistic conventions in the creation of a sustained, disconcerting counter-text.

---

17   Rossbacher, p. 203.

Conclusion

The search for an authentic form of expression became a defining feature of Maron's writing in the final decade of the GDR. *Das Mißverständnis* and *Die Überläuferin* demonstrate their author's increasing willingness to experiment with form. Laden with oblique, disconcerting images and peopled by a host of bizarre figures, these are undoubtedly radical texts. The female protagonists enact various stages of withdrawal from a stultifying external reality and from a prevailing discourse that no longer communicates in any meaningful fashion. Transcending physical and ideological constraints, they embark upon journeys of self-discovery, creating vivid imaginary topographies that at once fascinate and disconcert the reader. Highlighting the dangers of an unchecked imagination, the man in the red uniform warns: 'Der Tatträumer von heute ist der Täter von morgen' (ÜB, p. 172). Maron's next novel charts just such a movement; no longer content to merely dream about action, Rosalind becomes a perpetrator in *Stille Zeile Sechs*.

The counter-texts that are created in *Das Mißverständnis* and *Die Überläuferin* are examples of 'Mobilisierung von Phantasie', that privileging of imaginative impulses advocated by Emmerich. The imaginative realm is revealed to be a potentially subversive space, even if complete escape from the physical and ideological confines of the GDR appears to be as unattainable as the land of Nordsüden itself. Eschewing linear narrative, abandoning chronology, and creating potent, explosive and challenging counter-texts, the author of *Das Mißverständnis* and *Die Überläuferin* does, indeed, transgress in style.

CHAPTER THREE

Writing and Rewriting: The Problem of History in *Stille Zeile Sechs*

Monika Maron's third novel *Stille Zeile Sechs* occupies an important position within her literary development because it establishes history, more specifically the writing of history, as a central theme in her oeuvre. The text was published in 1991 to widespread critical acclaim; indeed its author was awarded the prestigious Kleist Prize the following year, thus firmly securing her status as one of the leading female writers from Eastern Germany. Although the novel was not published until 1991, Maron had, in fact, begun work on her manuscript before the tumultuous political events culminating in the collapse of the socialist state. 'Ich hatte das neue Buch schon vor den revolutionären Geschehnissen begonnen', she noted in an interview conducted in November 1991, 'auch weil ich über die Bindung durch Haß, die ich gegenüber der DDR fühlte, reflektieren wollte.'[1] This unequivocal assertion identifies Maron's impetus for writing *Stille Zeile Sechs* in terms of a deep-seated need to reflect on her hatred of the political state in which she had spent some forty-seven years. However, it seems that this reflection was only possible at a physical remove. In a 1992 interview the author established a direct causal relationship between her move to Hamburg in 1988 and the literary portrayal of that state which she had left behind. She explained that geographical distance afforded her the emotional distance she needed to write:

> Komischerweise ist mir der Ton hier in Hamburg viel leichter gefallen. Ich war zwischendurch mal ein paar Wochen in Ostberlin und habe da geschrieben oder versucht zu schreiben und merkte, daß ich sofort in so 'ne alte Aufregung zurückgekommen bin. Es ging nicht, und als ich wieder in Hamburg war, ging es leicht.[2]

---

1   Gerhard Richter, 'Verschüttete Kultur', *GDR Bulletin*, 18 (1992), p. 5.
2   Michael Hametner, 'Von Opfern, die Täter wurden', *Börsenblatt für den Deutschen Buchhandel*, 26 June 1992, p. 44.

This chapter will chart the protagonist's increasing involvement in the history that she is employed to transcribe. The reader first encounters Rosalind Polkowski after she has resigned from her position as historian at a research institute in East Berlin. A chance meeting with the ageing communist Herbert Beerenbaum proves to be a life-changing one for both parties: Rosalind agrees to transcribe his memoirs and soon becomes embroiled in a bitter struggle to record the past. The functionary, for his part, is actively seeking an amanuensis, a substitute, as he puts it, 'für seine tremorgeschüttelte rechte Hand' (SZS, p. 29). As demonstrated in Chapter One, *Flugasche* chronicled the disillusioning experience of writing in a restrictive political state; in *Stille Zeile Sechs* Rosalind writes against this state by challenging the triumphalist version of GDR history that Beerenbaum wishes to consign to print.

I will begin my analysis of Maron's third novel by exploring the interplay between recording and recalling the past, a relationship that is expressed in Rosalind's emotional response to Beerenbaum's interpretation of GDR history. The task of transcription soon becomes a painful confrontation with her own childhood, overshadowed by her father's allegiance to communism at the expense of paternal affection. The novel is set in the East Berlin district of Pankow in the mid-1980s and Beerenbaum embodies the stagnant political order. I will explore how the imminent collapse of this system is reflected in the images of decay that form a distinct topography in Maron's text. The section entitled 'Writing History' will consider how the former state historian is soon re-implicated in the transcription of the socialist success story, as propagated by Beerenbaum. Not only does she defiantly question Beerenbaum's version of GDR history; she also inscribes into her story those figures that have been rigorously excluded from official historiography. The section will focus, in particular, on the manner in which Rosalind problematises the discourse of the victor, even to the point of rewriting seminal passages of her employer's memoirs.

Beerenbaum's atrophy is symbolised most potently in the motif of his withered right hand. The ageing functionary hands his text over to Rosalind in a literal, but, more importantly still, in a symbolic sense. The consequences of this transaction are far-reaching: Rosalind's challenge to the master narrative culminates in a highly-charged final confrontation. So relentless is her interrogation of the old man that he suffers a heart attack. Under the rubric 'Die Fähigkeit zur Täterschaft: Subverting the Victim-Perpetrator Dichotomy', I will demonstrate how Rosalind, in her determination to eschew victim status, becomes a perpetrator in her turn, thus underscoring the essential ambivalence of her position and of Maron's text.

In this novel, which is located on the threshold between pre- and post-Wende literature, Maron explores the lasting influence of the GDR experience on her protagonist. Rereading this text in a post-Wende light, I will demonstrate how Rosalind remains trapped within the socialist metanarrative that she sought to leave behind.

Remembering *Vater Staat*

The task of transcribing Beerenbaum's memoirs becomes for his amanuensis a painful process of recollection. Rosalind first meets the functionary while she sits on a café terrace, observing passers-by. She reads Beerenbaum's facial expression as an ambiguous combination of arrogance, tiredness and disgust and this physiognomy represents for her 'das letzte Gesicht meines Vaters' (SZS, p. 26). As the narrative unfolds, it becomes clear that the functionary is a representative figure onto which Rosalind projects childhood associations. The physical environment in which the transcription sessions take place abounds with childhood memories: Beerenbaum's living room closely resembles that of her parents, even to the extent that the Russian doll on display in the wall cabinet is reminiscent of her father's smaller model. When preparing for the visit of the writer Victor Sensmann to the functionary's home, Rosalind registers something 'obszön Familiäres', 'eine verbotene Normalität' (SZS, p. 104) in her interaction with Beerenbaum. However, the similarity between Beerenbaum and her father Fritz Polkowski extends beyond the personal – it is also generational. Both were self-taught. Rosalind describes her employer as an 'Autodidakt, Professor ohne Abitur' (SZS, p. 168). Her father, for his part, was one of the many teachers who qualified shortly after World War II, frantically memorising the contents of lexica in order to conceal his lack of knowledge: 'aus Furcht zu bleiben, was er war, ein gelernter Dreher mit Volksschulabschluß' (SZS, p. 168), his daughter observes.

Rosalind's recollection of pivotal scenes with her father is interwoven with memories of exchanges with Beerenbaum and with descriptions of his funeral service, which she is attending in the present of the novel. The emotional rift between father and daughter was reflected in the complete absence of any meaningful communication; as the adult Rosalind remembers: 'mein Vater [beschränkte] seine verbalen Kontakte mit mir auf Begrüßungs- und Abschiedsformeln. Außerdem gratulierte er mir einmal jährlich zum Geburtstag und wünschte mir alles Gute zum Neuen Jahr' (SZS, p. 62). Years later, in the course of her exchanges with Beerenbaum, she seeks to make good this communication deficit. As school principal and ardent communist, Fritz Polkowski's conversations with his daughter were limited to educational issues, her political instruction being of particular significance. The adult Rosalind recalls and articulates the debilitating effect of her father's inability to separate public and private life: 'Das Schlimmste ist, wenn draußen die gleiche Macht herrscht und das gleiche Gesetz wie im eigenen Haus. Mein Vater herrschte über meine Schule, und er herrschte zu Hause' (SZS, p. 135). Frauke Lenckos emphasises the significance of this tautology: 'for Rosalind, *Vater Staat* comes to mean a tautology which rules the entirety of her existence'.[3]

Rosalind craves the love of an emotionally distant father. Deprived of paternal affection, she had deliberately formulated provocative questions in a desperate attempt to gain his attention. As she reflects on these episodes, she comes to the devastating conclusion that she occasionally longed for his death: 'Ich war dreizehn. Ich hatte erreicht, daß mein Vater sich nun für mich interessierte. Vor dem Einschlafen wünschte ich mir manchmal, daß er stirbt' (SZS, p. 114).[4] A particularly vivid and traumatic childhood memory is her careful preparation of his favourite dessert in an effort to win his affection, but Fritz Polkowski remained completely indifferent to his daughter's endeavour. This ingratitude had lasting repercussions, as is clear from her response to Beerenbaum's question about her father's political affiliation: 'Ich sagte, ein Kommunist sei jemand, der sich bei einem Kind, das ihm eine große Schüssel Zitronencreme schenkt, nicht bedankt, weil er gerade mit der Weltrevolution

---

3   Frauke E. Lenckos, 'Monika Maron: *Stille Zeile Sechs*', *New German Review: A Journal of Germanic Studies*, 8 (1992), 106–16 (p. 108).
4   Rosalind's fictional predecessor in *Die Überläuferin* had also wished for her father's death: '[ich] wünschte [...] den Tod meines Vaters. Ich habe den Gedanken nie in diesen Worten gedacht, ich wünschte nur seine Abwesenheit' (ÜB, p. 21).

beschäftigt ist' (SZS, pp. 159–60). Significantly, the protagonist rejects her interlocutor's abstract political theorising and instead locates her definition of communism solely in the realm of familial experience and of personal disappointment. This episode illustrates the infringement of the political upon the private sphere and the devastating consequences of such an intrusion.

The adult Rosalind projects her painful childhood memories onto Beerenbaum as embodiment of the political system that had such a stultifying impact upon her childhood. She envisages explaining to Beerenbaum why she must wish for his death: 'weil Sie jedes Haus, jedes Stück Papier, jede Straße, jeden Gedanken, weil Sie alles, was ich zum Leben brauche, gestohlen haben und nicht wieder rausrücken' (SZS, p. 156). She recognises that her relationship with him is condemned to repeat the patterns of her relationship with her own father. In retrospect, she realises that she wanted to defeat Beerenbaum and thus finally emerge victorious in a battle that had been lost so many years earlier: 'Gegen Beerenbaum wollte ich einen verlorenen Kampf nachträglich gewinnen' (SZS, p. 182).

Transcribing Beerenbaum's memoirs evokes in Rosalind such an emotional response that it is no longer possible for her to differentiate between recording the past of another and remembering her own. What she terms her struggle against Beerenbaum is, she realises, an intensely painful, yet essential confrontation with the legacy of a failed father–daughter relationship and with an entire political system that has appropriated her own childhood. The tautology of *Vater Staat* reinforces the lasting impact of GDR political structures on the protagonist's emotional and personal development.

The Decaying State

More overtly than in any of Maron's previous texts, *Stille Zeile Sechs* charts the inexorable decline of a crumbling political order. The novel is strewn with powerful images of decay.[5] During the increasingly fraught exchanges

---

[5] This section of the chapter has as its point of departure my article 'Der Körper als Symptom, die Gefühle als Metaphern: Monika Marons Roman *Stille Zeile Sechs*', in

between Rosalind and Beerenbaum, the latter's frail body is described in detail, thus following a well-established metonymic practice. In *Illness as Metaphor* Susan Sontag noted that an infection in the 'body politic' had long functioned as a standard form of allegory: 'Illnesses have always been used as metaphors to enliven charges that a society was corrupt or unjust.'[6] This had been a topos in GDR literature ever since the publication in 1968 of Christa Wolf's ground-breaking text *Nachdenken über Christa T.* The eponymous Christa T.'s deterioration and eventual death from leukaemia functioned as a metaphor for the insidious, relentless effect of a stultifying state apparatus on the individual.

For Maron, too, the physical health of her characters can be read as reflecting the viability of the political state. In an earlier text 'Herr Aurich', which appeared in the 1982 collection *Das Mißverständnis*, she had already evoked the atmosphere of stagnation and decay that she was to develop in *Stille Zeile Sechs*. The short story charts the physical and mental decline of the communist Erich Aurich. The description of a visibly deteriorating Aurich in his hospital bed anticipates Rosalind's graphic description of the dying Beerenbaum.

While Beerenbaum's allegorical function is central to any analysis of a moribund political state, it is also important to consider other images of decay and sites of desolation that form a very distinct topography in *Stille Zeile Sechs*. A stifling sense of stagnation is evoked in the very opening description of the 'Pankower Villenviertel, vom Volk "Städtchen" genannt, was liebevoller klang, als es gemeint war' (SZS, p. 7), the exclusive but lifeless residential area inhabited by the widows of former government members and once powerful officials such as Beerenbaum. This is an environment of sterile uniformity where people speak in hushed tones during rare exchanges. The atmosphere is one of desolation: 'öde wie eine Goldgräberstadt, deren Schätze nun erschöpft waren' (SZS, p. 9–10). Wall plaques display the names of deceased residents. The past maintains a firm hold on the present: 'Wie von Geisterhand wurde Ordnung gehalten, als wären die, die fort waren, noch da' (SZS, p. 10). An eerie atmosphere pervades in the 'Geisterwelt der Stillen Zeile' (SZS, p. 64).

Sentimente, Gefühle, Empfindungen: Zur Geschichte und Literatur des Affektiven von 1770 bis heute, ed. by Anne Fuchs and Sabine Strümper-Krobb (Würzburg: Königshausen & Neumann, 2003), pp. 221–26.

6   Susan Sontag, *Illness as Metaphor* (New York: Farrar, Straus & Giroux, 1978), p. 72.

Images of decay are present throughout the text. The skeleton motif features prominently in Rosalind's morbid imagination. The protagonist is reminded of skeletons when she sees the barren trees lining the pathway to the chapel in which Rosalind's former lover Bruno presides over the unconventional union of the piano teacher Thekla Fleischer and Herr Solow. A nocturnal tram ride with Bruno through deserted streets becomes in her imagination a journey across a landscape of destruction and desolation: 'Hinter den Häuserwänden lagen die Skelette in verfaulten Betten, oder sie saßen an Tischen und vor Fernsehapparaten wie in der Sekunde ihres Todes' (SZS, p. 184). The tram driver, too, reminds Rosalind of a skeleton, hurtling at a murderous speed through the deserted streets of Pankow. Beerenbaum's milieu is peopled with shadowy figures. On the occasion of her first encounter with his son Michael, Rosalind is struck by his demeanour, the pallor of his skin and, in particular, his grey, motionless eyes. The name of the writer Victor Sensmann carries obvious allegorical overtones; his exceedingly thin body – 'ein dürrer Körper ohne Fleisch und Muskeln, vor dem er die mageren Gliedmaßen quer und kantig verschränkt hielt' (SZS, pp. 105–06) – reinforces his role as harbinger of death.[7]

The graveyard occupies a central role within this morbid topography. As a child, Rosalind's frequent wanderings in graveyards revealed a fascination with death. Secretly she fantasised about burying her parents and teachers, thereby affirming her own vitality: 'Mit dem Triumph derer, die ihr Leben gerade begannen, führte ich es spazieren zwischen den Toten, denen ich, der Sieger, zeigte, daß jetzt ich dran war mit dem Leben' (SZS, p. 163). Beerenbaum's funeral plays an important structural role in Maron's novel. *Stille Zeile Sechs* opens with the protagonist preparing to attend the funeral ceremony, while the closing scene portrays her leaving the graveyard, having buried Beerenbaum and, with him, her own past, ostensibly at least. As witness to the symbolic burial of an entire political generation, Rosalind follows the

---

[7] In his essay 'Vom gefürchteten und gewünschten Tod und von den Freuden des Überlebens: Darstellungen des Todes bei Monika Maron und Dieter Wellershoff', Hans-Gerd Winter describes Sensmann as a 'Todesbote, als ein psychisch erstarrter, lebendig toter Mensch, von dem Rosalind zunächst nicht erkennt, daß er sie in die Gemeinschaft der lebendig Toten hineinziehen will.' *Neue Generationen – Neues Erzählen: Deutsche Prosa-Literatur der achtziger Jahre*, ed. by Walter Delabar, Werner Jung and Ingrid Pergande (Opladen: Westdeutscher Verlag, 1993), pp. 127–38 (p. 135).

mourners from the chapel to the graveside. With what seems like an almost voyeuristic compulsion she accompanies the procession to its final stop: 'Ich hatte noch nicht genug gesehen' (SZS, p. 144), she admits.

Deserted residential areas, hospitals and graveyards form a very distinct topography in *Stille Zeile Sechs*. Moving now to consider Beerenbaum's allegorical function, it quickly becomes apparent that he is the embodiment of a crumbling political state, populated by once powerful Stalinists who in the mid-1980s are nothing more than feeble old men. His physical frailty is emphasised from the outset. Observing Beerenbaum in the café, Rosalind is very much aware of his literal and symbolic atrophy: 'seine Rhetorik [war] ähnlich wie die Schleimhaut seiner Kehle inzwischen vertrocknet und seine Unnachgiebigkeit mit der Verkalkung des Rückgrats brüchig geworden, so, wie seine Macht mit dem Tod seiner Generation langsam ins Vergessen sank' (SZS, p. 30).

Trembling limbs, ageing body parts, even decomposing bodies are described in graphic detail. In the course of the very first transcription session, Rosalind registers her employer's hunched back and stooped shoulders, 'wie die Knochen unter dem Fell eines alten Tieres' (SZS, p. 46). The most striking image of Beerenbaum's physical infirmity is his incessantly shaking right hand. Once a symbol of his authority and political influence, the trembling limb – 'die zu ewigem Zittern verurteilte Hand' (SZS, p. 208) – is now testimony to the inexorable erosion of power that accompanies the onset of old age. It also has a sinister aspect. Before her first transcription session Rosalind registers its unnerving presence: 'Seine rechte Hand lag zitternd auf seinem Oberschenkel und war anwesend wie eine dritte Person' (SZS, p. 47). Most disturbing of all is Beerenbaum's physical reaction when Rosalind visits him in hospital shortly before his death. The scene is played out in her mind on three separate occasions in the text. She realises that she would have sought forgiveness for the relentless interrogation resulting in his heart attack, had it not been for his furtive, yet invasive gesture: 'wie eine weißhäutige Echse schoß sie [Beerenbaums Hand] hervor unter der Decke und sprang mir mit aufgerissenem Maul an die Brust' (SZS, p. 164). Rosalind feels exposed and violated at the hands of an oppressive patriarchal state: 'Es war, als hätte er mein nacktes Herz berührt' (SZS, p. 164), she recalls.

The intense focus on the decrepit body in *Stille Zeile Sechs* may be read in terms of Bakhtin's reflections on the grotesque. The chapter entitled 'The

Grotesque Image of the Body and its Sources' in *Rabelais and his World* contains valuable clues to our understanding of Maron's use of such imagery in her text. Beerenbaum's trembling right hand is depicted as a grotesque creature: 'das helle, wie in fortwährendem Abscheu sich schüttelnde Stück Fleisch' (SZS, p. 47). Grotesque motifs occur throughout the text. Envisaging Beerenbaum lying in his coffin, Rosalind recalls what she had been told about her grandmother's burial in the very hot summer of 1945. The corpse was already in a very advanced state of decay: 'Unablässig fielen aus dem Sarg fette, satte, weiße Würmer' (SZS, p. 56). This repugnant image functions as a motif, recurring as Rosalind observes the corpulent speaker who delivers the funeral oration. She focuses on his enormous double chin, described in grotesque detail, culminating in the repellent speculation:

> Wenn er nun platzt, dachte ich, wie ein aufgeblasener Frosch [...] Und dann passierte es: Durch ein Gemisch von Fettgewebe, Blut und Hautfetzen wühlten sich die Würmer aus dem Sarg meiner Großmutter väterlicherseits. Ich schloß die Augen, riß sie auf, hoffend, ihr Gleichmut könnte das ekelhafte Bild verjagen, [...] nichts half, aus dem aufgerissenen Doppelkinn fielen fette, satte, weiße Leichenwürmer. (SZS, p. 93)

In the context of the grotesque body, Rosalind's final memory of the dying Beerenbaum is of particular significance. She is repulsed by his gaping, toothless mouth: 'darin die dreckige, wie von Schimmel überzogene Zunge' (SZS, p. 164). For Bakhtin, the mouth is the most important grotesque organ: 'It dominates all else. The grotesque face is actually reduced to the gaping mouth; the other features are only a frame encasing this wide-open bodily abyss.'[8] Rosalind's recollection of her hospital visit to the dying Beerenbaum amounts to a grotesque inventory of decaying body parts:

> Darin, wie in einem Kinderbett, lag der geschrumpfte Beerenbaum; der Mensch erkennbar als sein verschlissenes Material: die gallertartige Substanz der Augen, deren Rundung die Höhlen freigaben, die Haut als Pergament, schon losgelöst vom Fleisch, das blaue Geäder hinter den transparenten Schläfen, die Schädelknochen, die sich durch die schlaffe Haut drängten und als das Gesicht des Todes schon sichtbar waren. (SZS, pp. 32–33)

---

8   Mikhail Bakhtin, *Rabelais and his World*, trans. by Hélène Iswolsky (Cambridge, MA: Massachusetts Institute of Technology Press, 1968), p. 317.

In this intense description of wasting body matter, Beerenbaum is a reduced, child-like figure. Georg Leisten points to the inherently grotesque aspect of this scene: 'Hier überkreuzen sich exakt die beiden von Bachtin genannten Lebensstufen des grotesken Körpers: Kindheit und Alter.'[9]

Rosalind's reaction to the degenerating body of the state is an emotional rejection of the political order. She makes no attempt to conceal her inherent aversion towards old men, a repugnance that is activated, she announces at the very outset, by characteristic optical and acoustic signals: a particular walk and a grating, rasping voice. Her fear, hatred and innate disgust at the sight of Beerenbaum's decrepit body serve as political metaphors. There is repeated reference to 'Ekel'. Leisten notes that Winfried Menninghaus has described 'Ekel' as an epiphenomenon of the grotesque.[10] In *Stille Zeile Sechs* the grotesque, ailing body of the state evokes revulsion.

In the introductory chapter I traced the uncomfortable shifts in critical discourse following the collapse of the GDR. The literary critic Wolfgang Emmerich called for a rereading, a re-contextualisation of those texts emerging from a suddenly defunct state. *Stille Zeile Sechs* presents a critical dilemma in this respect. Bakhtin's reflections on the grotesque do not provide any real alternative to the sociopolitical interpretations that have dominated the novel's reception.[11] The grotesque remains associated with the ailing body of the state.

---

9 Georg Leisten, '"Leib wart ihr euch selbst genug ...": Schrift und Körper in Monika Marons Roman *Stille Zeile Sechs*', in *Monika Maron in Perspective: 'Dialogische' Einblicke in zeitgeschichtliche, intertextuelle und rezeptionsbezogene Aspekte ihres Werkes*, ed. by Elke Gilson, German Monitor, 55 (Amsterdam and New York: Rodopi, 2002), pp. 139–56 (p. 144). Leisten's article explores the relationship between writing and the body in *Stille Zeile Sechs*. He devotes a section of his essay to what he terms grotesque corporeality.

10 Winfried Menninghaus, *Ekel: Theorie und Geschichte einer starken Empfindung* (Frankfurt am Main: Suhrkamp, 1999), p. 82 ff. Quoted in Leisten, p. 146.

11 The novel's reception displays continuations of those politicised readings problematised by Emmerich. Hans-Gerd Winter, for example, in an article published in 1993, foregrounds the symbolic function of Beerenbaum's death within the collapse of the state: 'der Tod Beerenbaums [wird] zum Symbol für den erwünschten Zusammenbruch eines verhaßten repressiven Systems, des DDR-Sozialismus' (Winter, p. 130). In an article published almost a decade later, Georg Leisten has recourse to a diverse range of references, including Ernst Kantoworicz's *Die zwei Körper des Königs: Eine Studie zur politischen Theologie des Mittelalters*, Richard Sennett's *Fleisch und Stein: Der Körper und die Stadt in der westlichen Zivilisation*, Bakhtin's *Rabelais und seine Welt*, Winfried Menninghaus's *Ekel: Theorie und Geschichte einer starken Empfindung* and Kittler's *Aufschreibesysteme 1800.1900*. Despite his interest in Beerenbaum's allegorical body and its transformation

Rereading *Stille Zeile Sechs* in a post-Wende light illustrates the complexity of the dilemma facing writers and critics alike after 1989. It seems impossible to separate the novel from its political context. New perspectives on *Stille Zeile Sechs* must recognise the continued validity of politicised readings, even in a post-GDR age. The problem of history remains.

Writing History

This section will explore how Rosalind writes against the moribund body of the state. Coming to terms as a historian with this state from which she has retreated, she challenges the memories to be transcribed, thereby subverting Beerenbaum's model communist biography and undermining the master narrative. She also inscribes into her story those marginal figures who find no place in official GDR historiography.

Writing for the State

Rosalind's first encounter with Beerenbaum occurs some six months after her resignation from a research institute in East Berlin, where she had worked as a professional historian. Her fictional predecessor in *Die Überläuferin* also withdrew from GDR society, although the retreat enacted in the 1986 text assumed the far more extreme form of complete physical paralysis. In *Stille Zeile Sechs* Rosalind's decision not to think for money anymore – 'Ich werde nicht mehr für Geld denken' (SZS, p. 24), as she puts it – had been motivated by the sudden realisation 'daß ich mein einziges Leben tagtäglich in die Barabassche Forschungsstätte trug wie den Küchenabfall zur Mülltonne' (SZS, p. 19).[12] This epiphany had been precipitated somewhat mundanely by the

---

from regal to grotesque, it is significant that the functionary's role as 'Personifikation eines abgelebten Regimes' (p. 145) retains central importance in Leisten's analysis.

12   Rosalind's decision 'nicht mehr für Geld [zu] denken' (SZS, p. 24) echoes Martha's comment in *Die Überläuferin*: 'Es ist pervers, für Geld zu denken [...] wahrscheinlich sogar verboten' (ÜB, p. 44).

sight of a cat following her home from work, prompting Rosalind to reflect upon the discrepancy between the animal's carefree existence and her own monotonous routine. Her working milieu was an extremely regulated one, under the watchful eye of the institute's director: 'unter der Bewachung von Barabas und seinen Knechten' (SZS, p. 21). Rosalind sees Barabas's advancement to the position of director as the result of his pronounced lack of oppositional thinking, coupled with what she terms a despotic pedantry. Her sense of physical confinement is evoked in the analogy of a prison cell: 'Jeden Tag sperrte ich mich freiwillig in einen Raum, der seiner Größe nach eher eine Gefängniszelle war und den man mir ebenso zugeteilt hatte wie das Sachgebiet, dem ich acht Stunden am Tag meine Hirntätigkeit widmen mußte' (SZS, p. 22). She describes the intellectual stultification characteristic of her professional environment: 'Nicht mir wurde das Sachgebiet zugeteilt, sondern ich dem Sachgebiet und auch dem Zimmer' (SZS, p. 22).

Throughout her fifteen-year career at the research institute, Rosalind, in her role as GDR historian, had been required to provide accounts of provincial social and labour history. The first research topic assigned her by Barabas was the development of the proletarian movement in Saxony and Thuringia. Following the sudden recognition that she is wasting her life, she is no longer prepared to serve as paid amanuensis of a state in which history is reduced to a teleological narrative culminating in the triumph of socialism. This realisation renders surprising her decision to transcribe the memoirs of a representative of that very political system which she has ostensibly left behind. The crux of the whole story – Rosalind's agreeing to transcribe Beerenbaum's memoirs – remains strangely under-motivated. By consenting to act as his amanuensis, her complicity with the socialist state never evaporates completely.

Writing his success story appears to be the ultimate contribution made to society by the dedicated socialist pioneer. During the very first transcription session Beerenbaum emphasises that his sense of duty to future generations provides the impetus for dictating his testimony: 'die Pflicht, künftigen Generationen ein Zeugnis zu hinterlassen' (SZS, p. 47). Despite her conviction 'daß es eine Schande ist, für Geld zu denken' (SZS, p. 19), Rosalind agrees to assist him with this task. He assures her from the outset that her intellectual involvement will not be required: 'garantiert keine Kopfarbeit' (SZS, p. 29). The task of transcription seems deceptively uncomplicated, initially at least: 'mit meiner Hand seine Erinnerungen niederschreiben' (SZS, p. 30). However, this separation of the writing process itself from the memories to be recorded becomes increasingly difficult for Rosalind to maintain. Repulsed by the clichéd nature of the socialist success story and projecting onto Beerenbaum the legacy of a troubled father–daughter relationship, she finds it impossible to maintain a disinterested stance vis-à-vis the memories she transcribes and soon transgresses her role as amanuensis. Although she refrains in the first weeks from commenting upon the material dictated to her, she is nevertheless troubled by an increasing sense of complicity: 'Während ich widerspruchslos hinschrieb, was Beerenbaum diktierte, fragte ich mich immer öfter, ob ich mich nicht zum Mittäter machte, ob ich nicht sein Komplize wurde, indem ich ihm half, das eigene Denkmal in Lettern zu gießen' (SZS, p. 77).[13] Unsuccessfully she tries to assuage her feelings of guilt by understating the political nature of Beerenbaum's enterprise. In conversation with Bruno, for example, she describes her role in the most innocuous terms as that of transcribing the family story of a senior citizen for his grandchildren. Although Rosalind attempts to stem the inevitable movement from transcription to complicity, she recognises that Beerenbaum has come to occupy her thoughts: 'Ich muß an ihn denken, obwohl ich nicht an ihn denken will. Ich träume von ihm' (SZS, p. 134). The functionary is a powerful presence, even in her subconscious. He has infiltrated her entire existence.

In *Stille Zeile Sechs* writing GDR history is an inherently subjective process in which both Beerenbaum and his amanuensis are implicated. Against the backdrop of painful childhood memories, the task of transcribing Beerenbaum's version of GDR history becomes a process of intellectual and, more significantly still, emotional investment on Rosalind's part. She concedes: 'Meinem Vorsatz, Beerenbaums Memoirenwerk mit nichts anderem als meinen Händen zu dienen, wurde ich selbst zum größten Hindernis' (SZS, p. 59).

---

13   In an article that explores the issue of collaboration in *Stille Zeile Sechs*, Annie Ring elucidates the significance of the word 'amanuensis' when applied to the relationship between Rosalind and Beerenbaum: 'Stemming from the Latin *servus a manu* (slave-at-hand), her copy-writing task reveals an uncomfortable *ensis* (belonging) to her political enemy.' '"Eine Bindung durch Hass": Double-Agency, Mimesis and the Role of Hands in Monika Maron's *Stille Zeile Sechs*', *German Life and Letters*, 63.3 (July 2010), 250–64 (p. 256).

A Typical Biography

Herbert Beerenbaum's biography is intended to serve State and Party on the basis of its exemplary content: he has lived through – and responded correctly to – the defining moments in GDR history. His is thus a model life that can speak for an entire historical generation and even for an entire country. As such, and quite distinct from the parallels it affords with her own familial experience, it challenges Rosalind in her central beliefs about the society in which she lives.

Simultaneously, the embedding of Beerenbaum's memoirs within the very fabric of Maron's text not only confirms her determination to thematise – even in opposition to the regime – typical and collective experiences, a tendency to which I made reference in the introductory chapter; it also invites reflection on the closeness of those concerns to the literary-historical debates of the GDR. One of the central tenets of socialist realism was the portrayal of positive and, most importantly, typical figures of the historical period. In his studies of nineteenth-century realism, particularly the writing of Balzac and Tolstoy, Georg Lukács insisted upon the typicality of character and attached importance to the historical and ideological perspective in setting the stories of individuals against the historical background of their time. Such elements invariably come to mind when contemplating the representative nature of Beerenbaum and his biography. For Lukács, successful writing was a dialectical play between the individual and the typical, between singular events and the contexts in which they were embedded: 'die Verknüpfung der Tatsachen und ihrer Zusammenhänge [...] des Individuellen und des Typischen'.[14] Lukács's demands for fiction also included that perspective on the better socialist future which Beerenbaum's biography demonstrates, despite the unreflected manner in which he portrays his personal development and situates his story within the larger project of history.[15]

---

14 Georg Lukács, 'Reportage oder Gestaltung?', in *Essays über Realismus* (Neuwied and Berlin: Luchterhand, 1971), pp. 35–55 (p. 40).

15 In his book *The East German Novel: Identity, Community, Continuity* (New York: St Martin's Press, 1984), Dennis Tate outlines Lukács's expectations for literature: '"das große proletarische Kunstwerk" – a novel achieving a Tolstoyan blend of insight into personality growth and totality of social portrayal, written from a perspective which shows the underlying "Entwicklungstendenzen" to be those of revolutionary socialism' (p. 4).

The functionary is a composite figure in which model Stalinist biographies fuse with Rosalind's, and, of course, Maron's familial experience. Maron herself concedes that he is 'eine Art Silhouette',[16] a description that is also true in its most literal sense because the presence of an enormous copper beech in front of the single window casts his study into a state of permanent darkness. While dictating his memoirs, Beerenbaum is positioned in shadows. Reduced to his 'Konturen', he resembles 'Pappfiguren auf Schießplätzen' (SZS, p. 48). Figuratively, too, he remains a 'Silhouette' (SZS, p. 58) whom Rosalind invests with personal significance and childhood memories.

Beerenbaum's biography, more specifically that version of his life which he consigns to print, bears all the hallmarks of the communist success story. During their first meeting and before she agrees to work for him, Rosalind asks if she may hazard a guess as to his biography: working-class origins, early party membership, emigration to Russia in the 1930s, return to Germany in 1945, followed by rapid rise through the party ranks. The accuracy of the résumé she provides convinces her listener that she has already heard of Professor Herbert Beerenbaum, but Rosalind is adamant: 'Ich beteuerte, nicht mehr über ihn zu wissen, als er selbst durch seine Erscheinung mitteilte' (SZS, p. 27), an observation underscoring once again his representative function as the embodiment of an entire political generation.

Rosalind is repulsed by the self-assured tone of the socialist success biography and grows increasingly irritated by what she terms the 'Scheußlichkeit' (SZS, p. 59) of the sentences her employer dictates. While transcribing the sentence 'Schon als kleiner Knirps, wußte ich, daß das Herz links saß und der Feind rechts stand' (SZS, pp. 59–60), for example, she is overcome by a prolonged bout of hiccups, an involuntary physical reaction to a language she so obviously abhors, from long acquaintance in family and school circles. Provoked by her exposure to a discourse in which she is emotionally implicated, Rosalind recalls childhood scenes characterised by that same clichéd language which has had such a lasting impact: 'Mit dieser Sprache war ich aufgewachsen' (SZS, p. 61). For her own father, the boundary between private and public life had become increasingly difficult to maintain: 'Die Grenze zwischen der privaten und der anderen Sprache verlief nicht exakt' (SZS, p. 61), his daughter observes, illustrating once again the encroachment of the political upon the private sphere. When the ardent communist embarked, for

---

16 Interview with Deirdre Byrnes, Zürich, 22 April 1996.

example, upon his daughter's political education, he did so in highly emotive, ideological terms: '[er] sprach vom Bollwerk des Sozialismus, das den imperialistischen Kriegstreibern trotze, vom ruhmreichen Kampf der Kommunisten für die endgültige Befreiung der Menschheit, von letzten Blutstropfen und heiligen Toten, denen auch er geschworen habe' (SZS, pp. 109–10). Rosalind's fantasy of strangling Beerenbaum expresses her hatred of such formulaic, empty language; this imaginary gesture symbolises the irreversible silencing of a discourse that repulses her.

Rosalind's disappointment with Beerenbaum is at once a political and a narratological event. She is disillusioned not only with socialism as it has manifested itself in her professional and personal life, but also with the manner in which the functionary presents his experiences in terms of token achievements. Desiring to bestow meaning upon his life, Beerenbaum locates his experiences within an entirely unreflected and banal, but authoritative teleological narrative of progress and liberation: 'Ich hatte nichts zu verteidigen als mich', Rosalind realises, 'während Beerenbaum einen ganzen Radschwung der Geschichte als sein Werk ansah, das er zu beschützen hatte, wenn nötig, mit der Waffe in der Hand, wie mein Vater oft gesagt hat und vermutlich auch Beerenbaum sagen würde' (SZS, p. 154). He situates his experience within the context of the ultimate socialist triumph. It is precisely this transference of personal experience into the overarching structure of the socialist metanarrative and thus into the discourse of the victors that leads to Rosalind's final and violent alienation from the project.

Writing the Marginalised into History

The typical nature of Beerenbaum's biography represents an absolutising of individual experience to be subsumed into the collective master text of socialism that leaves no place for the individual. Rosalind resents the fact that Beerenbaum and his fellow-officials enjoy an undisputed right to representation in the governing discourse: 'Sie haben immer recht, dachte ich, was ich auch sage, alles Unglück gehört schon ihnen, den glücklichen Besitzern von Biografien' (SZS, p. 141). Historical documentation is the prerogative of those who possess an official communist biography. Not only is Rosalind determined to question the apparent infallibility of such a discourse and its exclusive focus on a master narrative of the victor; she also seeks to inscribe into her story those individuals who do not possess an officially acceptable biography, those who have been rigorously excluded from the governing discourse. In an essay exploring the themes of memory and historiography in *Stille Zeile Sechs*, Brigitte Rossbacher interprets the protagonist's position as follows: 'Rosalind [...] writes into history those "ex-centrics" of the subculture excluded from History.'[17]

Maron creates a very distinct counterculture in *Stille Zeile Sechs*. The lonely, middle-aged piano teacher Thekla Fleischer, Rosalind's former lover Bruno and the eminent sinologist Karl-Heinz Baron, or the Graf, as he is respectfully known to his friends, all belong to this group. Commenting on their insignificance within the political state, Lenckos observes: 'They do not write, nor do they dictate. They leave no trace. They therefore do not exist within documented socialist reality.'[18] However, this eclectic host of characters features prominently in Rosalind's narrative. We are reminded again of the importance Emmerich attaches to the imaginative potential of writing: 'die Mobilisierung von Phantasie' ('Für eine andere Wahrnehmung', p. 17) can be seen in Maron's characterisation of these eccentric figures. The reader is entertained by the comic escapades of the lovesick Thekla Fleischer, including her drastic sartorial and physical transformation as a result of falling in love. With her childlike, reverential refrain of 'Mami war [...] so ein starker Mensch' (SZS, p. 128), she strikes a ridiculous, yet endearing pose. Gentle teasing is also directed at the Graf, such as when Maron describes his unsuccessful attempts to conceal his very obvious hair loss. Her humorous and gently ironic characterisation of these individuals contrasts sharply with her scathing portrayal of communist officialdom.

Intent upon realising her childhood dream of learning to play the piano, Rosalind approaches Thekla Fleischer, the music teacher who lives two floors above her. Thekla seems to be completely unaffected by the political system. Until Rosalind's revelations she had never heard of Beerenbaum: 'Von Politik verstehe sie nichts, sagte sie' (SZS, p. 134). However, the winter wedding ceremony between Thekla and the already married and thus ironically named

---

17 Brigitte Rossbacher, '(Re)visions of the Past: Memory and Historiography in Monika Maron's *Stille Zeile Sechs*', *Colloquia Germanica*, 27.1 (1994), 13–24 (p. 20).
18 Lenckos, p. 111.

Herr Solow, orchestrated by Bruno and Rosalind in the bizarre setting of a graveyard chapel, is a touching scene, far removed from the bitter political exchanges that define the protagonist's relationship with her employer: 'Es war ein Tag wie aus einem anderen Leben. Ich dachte nicht eine Minute an Beerenbaum' (SZS, p. 191). For Rosalind, piano-playing fulfils a similar function to her walks in the unspoilt oasis of the Pankow park, affording escape from society, in particular from the increasingly emotional confrontations with Beerenbaum: 'Man merkte es dabei nicht so' (SZS, p. 198).

Above all, it is the pub that functions as a self-contained emotional and psychological sanctuary: 'eine Gegenwelt, ein Orkus, wo andere Gesetze galten' (SZS, p. 172). Descent into this underworld is simultaneously liberation from the strictures of a highly politicised society, or so it seems: 'Wer das Kneipenreich betrat, entzog sich der Schwerkraft der Oberwelt und fügte sich einer anderen Ordnung' (SZS, p. 172). Frequented by an array of bohemian characters, the pub is a highly individualistic sphere.[19] Hailed by Bruno as the last haven of male freedom, the pub appears to be far beyond Beerenbaum's sphere of influence: 'In der Kneipe endete Beerenbaums Macht' (SZS, p. 173), the protagonist is relieved to observe. However, the outside world has left an indelible mark upon its eccentric clientele. In response to Bruno's inquiry about her transcription task, Rosalind asks if he knows of Herbert Beerenbaum. The discussion has suddenly become serious; there does not seems to be any respite from the political state. Bruno does not attempt to conceal his outrage and condemns Rosalind's position as 'Schreibhilfe bei einem Folterknecht' (SZS, p. 178), while the Graf is visibly distressed at her admission. Twenty-three years previously he had forwarded a doctoral thesis to a colleague who had defected. The disturbing story of Beerenbaum's role in his denunciation and subsequent imprisonment unfolds. It is in this marginal space that Rosalind learns of the Graf's betrayal. She comes to the painful realisation that, in her capacity as amanuensis, she, too has betrayed him, albeit inadvertently.

---

19   Rossbacher sees in the subculture of the pub a fictional counterpart to the rebellious, marginal Prenzlauer Berg literary scene of the mid-1980s: 'both are subversive realms which nonetheless reveal many parallels to the dominant culture, as disclosures on the Stasi infiltration of the Prenzlauer Berg *Szene* have made evident' (pp. 23–24).

There are further indications that the political state has impacted upon the pub's clientele. Alcoholism is rife in this milieu. Although the pub provides refuge from the world outside, Bruno needs alcohol in order to descend into this 'lärmenden und stinkenden Asyl' (SZS, p. 73). It is Bruno's mood that sets the tone and determines whether the gathering will disintegrate into a drinking session or foster instead a lively intellectual debate. On the evening of the revelations about the Graf's past, but before the conversation assumes a decidedly sinister tenor, he sings the same phrase first in Latin, then in German: 'und ich möchte nicht mehr dienen' (SZS, p. 176), following which he reaches for his drink. Despite escapist forays into the pub, clearly essential for their emotional and spiritual survival, this song implies that Bruno and the Graf must serve the political state in the world outside, however debilitating this has proven to be.

Martin Hielscher points out that the pub is ultimately a sphere of inactivity: 'Gleichzeitig symbolisiert sie das Totenreich der Untätigen, die sich nur noch in der Utopie des Kneipengesprächs verwirklichen können'.[20] Bruno openly mocks what he terms Rosalind's 'aktionistische Sehnsüchte [...], als handelte es sich dabei um ein drittes Auge oder einen Klumpfuß, auf jeden Fall um eine angeborene Abnormalität' (SZS, p. 43). The pub is an environment in which integrity and learning are of paramount importance, but changing the world is not.

The hierarchical structure of the socialist state is also reflected in the microcosm of the pub. This bohemian milieu stratifies too, although differently: the hierarchy firmly in place is determined by knowledge of Latin. In the Graf's eyes, Bruno is clearly the most prominent of the 'Kneipenpersönlichkeiten' (SZS, p. 73). The clientele are classified into two very distinct categories: those who can converse in Latin and those who cannot. 'In Brunos Kneipe herrschten die Lateiner über die Nichtlateiner' (SZS, p. 75), the reader learns. Education is of paramount importance to the Graf, his genuine thirst for knowledge in itself far removed from the desire for self-advancement motivating the frantic communist pursuit of knowledge in the post-war years. Bruno has bestowed upon him the respectful title of Graf as a tribute to the extent of his learning. The Graf is a polyglot: as well as German, he speaks French, Chinese

---

20 Martin Hielscher, 'Die Täter werden die Opfer sein', *Deutsches Allgemeines Sonntagsblatt*, 15 November 1991, p. 29.

and, of course, Latin. His idiosyncratic, entertaining and individualistic use of language contrasts with the clichéd, meaningless formulae of communist officialdom. Before the final confrontation with Beerenbaum the protagonist envisages addressing her adversary as 'Professor mit Volksschulabschluß' (SZS, p. 193) and, more damningly still, as 'Nichtlateiner mit Klasseninstinkt' (SZS, p. 193). Ignorance of Latin has come to symbolise the communist lack of education. Alluding directly to the unjust treatment of the Graf, Rosalind is unwavering in her accusation: 'Sie können kein Latein, und darum haben Sie verboten, daß andere Latein lernen. Wer es schon konnte, mußte ins Gefängnis, damit alle vergessen, daß es das gibt: Latein. Alles mußte vergessen werden, damit nicht herauskam, was ihr alles nicht wußtet' (SZS, pp. 206–07). Beerenbaum struggles to defend his past actions and exculpate himself, maintaining, in clichéd terms, that the communist university was the class struggle, 'Unser Latein Marx und Lenin' (SZS, p. 207).

By interrogating Beerenbaum about his treatment of the Graf, Rosalind inscribes into GDR history an individual who has been effectively silenced by the governing discourse, 'zum Schweigen verurteilt' (SZS, p. 204). She is determined to speak in his name, as an oppositional voice. In so doing, she thwarts the expectation that history speak with one voice only, in this instance the master narrative of socialism, and counters the typical biography of communist officials. Thekla Fleischer, Bruno and the Graf feature prominently in Rosalind's construction of her own story, for which Beerenbaum is the foil.

Significantly, it is the eccentric characters marginalised by the dominant discourse that provide an alternative to the environment of politically conventionalised emotions vis-à-vis the ailing body of the state. Rereading these scenes in a post-GDR light, we have considered the pub as a marginal space in which Rosalind and her creator can express imaginative impulses and inscribe into history those eccentric characters that have been written out. However, even in this milieu where emotional authenticity is fostered, the political state has left its indelible mark.

Contested Histories

This section considers Rosalind's sustained challenge to the triumphant discourse adopted by Beerenbaum in his recollection of the past. When dictating his memoirs, he situates himself, as observed earlier in the chapter, unequivocally on the side of the historical victor. Through Rosalind's determination to articulate marginalised, nonconformist voices, *Stille Zeile Sechs* thematises opposition to this historical narrative and to the texts embodying it. In examining a novel that explores the alternatives to a determinist view of history, particularly one complacently written, or at least dictated, by those who imagine that they are going to be victors, only to discover in the next historical catastrophe that their role is that of losers, Walter Benjamin's reflections on history emerge as a crucial point of reference.[21] The whole thrust of his historical treatise is precisely to expose the false optimism of a socialist theodicy, the failure of which was evident in the defeat of socialism in 1940 and again, irrevocably, in 1989. Beerenbaum situates his biography within a teleological master narrative, as Benjamin shows all the hagiographic orthodoxy of socialist historians has done. Rosalind, for her part, inscribes into her story those voices excluded from the governing discourse and thus represents an alternative to the triumphant historicism of official socialist historiography castigated by Benjamin.

In his determination to write his experiences into the metanarrative of a triumphant socialism, Beerenbaum revises the details of his youth. His amanuensis observes 'daß er jedes Detail aus seinem jungen Leben nur im Hinblick auf seine spätere Bestimmung erzählte' (SZS, p. 58). The functionary 'revels' in his childhood (SZS, p. 58) and irritates the protagonist by celebrating his impoverished beginnings, as if to compensate somehow for the acquisition of wealth that accompanied his subsequent rise to power: 'Er zelebrierte die Armut seiner Familie, als wollte er sich entschuldigen für seinen späteren Wohlstand' (SZS, p. 58). So complete is this exercise in revisionism that he has come to believe in the 'Legende seines Lebens' (SZS, p. 148).

Beerenbaum recalls his return to Berlin in 1945. The task facing communists was to undertake the physical reconstruction and the ideological liberation of a city in ruins: 'Und wir, eine Handvoll halbverhungerter und zerschlagener Kommunisten und Antifaschisten, hatten den Karren aus dem Dreck zu ziehen' (SZS, p. 152). Rosalind cannot escape the feeling that she

---

21 In her article '(Re)visions of the Past: Memory and Historiography in Monika Maron's *Stille Zeile Sechs*', Rossbacher applies Benjamin's distinction between historicism and historical materialism to the two modes of historiography juxtaposed in the novel. Historicism promotes a 'master narrative of the victor' (p. 14), while historical materialism focuses on those 'silenced by the relentless flow of history' (p. 14).

has heard it all before. Beerenbaum refers to the opening lines of the GDR national hymn as he continues: 'Auferstanden aus Ruinen und der Zukunft zugewandt, ja, so war es' (SZS, p. 152). Such was Rosalind's exposure as a child to this language of clichés and platitudes that she can, routinely and ad nauseam, finish her employer's sentences: 'Es war eine schöne, aber schwere Zeit, sagte ich, weil ich wußte, daß dieser Satz jetzt gesagt werden mußte' (SZS, p. 153). Beerenbaum is immensely proud of what was accomplished in those early years and is determined to defend the communist achievement against any attempts to reverse the course of history, the 'Rad der Geschichte' (SZS, p. 153), as he puts it. At the beginning of the final, ultimately fatal exchange, he recalls 'ein erfreuliches Kapitel [...] Rückkehr nach Deutschland' (SZS, p. 200) and dictates an emotionally charged account of return to a liberated Germany in 1945: 'Weinend lagen alle Genossen im Zug sich in den Armen. In dieser Stunde wußten wir: Es würde unser Deutschland werden, auf ewig befreit von kriegslüsternen Imperialisten und mordgierigen Faschisten' (SZS, p. 200).

Rosalind, for her part, counters Beerenbaum's glorified rendition of past events by exposing the inaccuracy of and the blatant omissions from the political master discourse. She is determined to address such problematic aspects as the insatiable appetite for power, the 'Machtrausch' (SZS, p. 34) exhibited by working-class comrades, their deep-seated suspicion of anything they did not understand, what she terms 'das Gemetzel im Hotel Lux' (SZS, p. 34).[22] The worker-turned-teacher Fritz Polkowski remained unnerved by the potential of questions to reveal his unsuitability for his post-war career. When Rosalind hears the functionary expound upon his beloved concept of 'Klasseninstinkt, der einem Arbeiter aus dem Ruhrgebiet, wie Beerenbaum sagte, in die Wiege gelegt worden war' (SZS, p. 58), she unsentimentally exposes the hypocrisy of this discourse: 'Mit dem Wort Instinkt beanspruchte mein Vater Unfehlbarkeit' (SZS, p. 59). In the course of their increasingly abrasive exchanges, Rosalind's relentless interrogation of Beerenbaum, interspersed with recollection of deliberately contentious questions that she asked her father, reveal her disillusionment with and rebellion against such spurious claims of infallibility.

22   Throughout the 1920s, 1930s and into the 1940s, the Hotel Lux in Moscow housed communists from other countries. An apparent haven for communists, it quickly acquired notoriety as a site of mass betrayal, denunciation, subsequent deportation and even death.

Not only does the protagonist contest the political master narrative in the form of provocative questions; her increasingly critical response to Beerenbaum's memoirs results in her altering certain significant passages. In so doing, she transcends the role of amanuensis and becomes an active participant in the process of historical representation. The visit of the writer Victor Sensmann is a crucial scene, the first occasion on which Rosalind blatantly amends and then openly denounces her employer's version of events. Although Beerenbaum reiterates that her intellectual involvement will not be required, 'keine Kopfarbeit' (SZS, p. 102), and that her role is merely to record the exchange, he nevertheless introduces Rosalind in unequivocal terms: 'Beerenbaum stelle mich als seine rechte Hand vor und legte zum Beweis das zitternde Stück Fleisch, das ich zu ersetzen hatte, auf den Tisch' (SZS, p. 104). Rosalind is disturbed by the possibility that the visitor may consider her 'Beerenbaums ergebene Kreatur' (SZS, p. 106). Flattered that Sensmann cites the functionary's 'faszinierende Biografie' (SZS, p. 105) as the impetus for his visit, Beerenbaum embarks upon a romanticised version of the sense of expectancy that characterised East Berlin in the 1960s: 'Das war eine aufregende Zeit, wie Sie sich denken können, so kurz nach dem Bau unseres Antifaschistischen Schutzwalls' (SZS, p. 107). Rosalind is outraged at Beerenbaum's choice of language, in particular at his description of the Berlin Wall as a necessary defensive structure protecting against nefarious western influences. She is appalled at the nonchalant manner of his delivery: 'Allein die Zumutung, das Wort hinzuschreiben, als wäre es ein Wort wie Blume, Hund und Mauer, empörte mich' (SZS, p. 107). She deliberately abbreviates his formulation: 'Ich notierte: B: Zeit nach Bau des Antifaschuwa war aufregend' (SZS, p. 107). Beerenbaum's account becomes increasingly sentimental: before August 1961 he was frequently overcome by the vision of the pulsating lifeblood of the young republic, 'Ströme des Lebensaftes der jungen Republik' (SZS, p. 107), escaping to the West. He endorsed the building of the Wall, a necessary measure to stem the flow 'in den gierigen Körper des Feindes' (SZS, p. 108). Providing a further variation on the body as metaphor in *Stille Zeile Sechs*, capitalism is depicted here as an avaricious enemy body. Beerenbaum's highly emotive account appals Rosalind who, misinterpreting the situation and seeing an ally in Sensmann, launches into a scathing verbal assault that carries the body metaphor to its devastating conclusion: 'Da haben Sie das Blut lieber selbst zum Fließen gebracht und eine Mauer gebaut, an der Sie den Leuten die nötigen Öffnungen in den Körper schießen konnten' (SZS, p. 108).

There is a flashback to a childhood memory. Her surprisingly uncontrolled outburst as she screams at both men reminds Rosalind of a confrontation with her parents when she was a teenager. The same sense of confinement is again evoked. Even her position in the room as she hurls abuse is described in very precise terms: 'zwischen der spiegelblanken Schrankwand und der samtbezogenen Polstergarnitur' (SZS, p. 106). Her final gesture before leaving the room is highly symbolic: 'Ich schmiß meinen Bleistift zwischen das Meißener Geschirr mit dem Weinlaubdekor und schrie' (SZS, p. 109). Rosalind attempts to distance herself, both from what has just transpired and from what she has written, by discarding the very instrument with which she has documented the exchange. The repercussions of Sensmann's visit are considerable. Rosalind is overwhelmed by a feeling of powerlessness: 'Alles gehört ihnen, dachte ich [...] Alles gehört Beerenbaum und diesem Mann mit den toten Augen, wahrscheinlich gehört es auch Sensmann' (SZS, p. 118). Despite her efforts to alter the master discourse, she remains implicated, inevitably and inescapably, within it: 'Auch ich gehörte ihnen, sobald ich dieses Haus betrat, das verfluchte Haus Nummer sechs in der Stillen Zeile' (SZS, p. 118).

A further instance of Rosalind's determination to contest Beerenbaum's glorified rendition of the GDR past occurred when she questioned him about the notorious Hotel Lux. During the funeral service she reflects upon the appropriateness of the nine red wreaths adorning the functionary's coffin: 'Wer wagte es, Beerenbaum zum Abschied die Farbe Rot vorzuenthalten; links, wo das Herz sitzt, rot wie das Blut' (SZS, p. 137). This is followed by the startling admission 'Ich habe Beerenbaums Blut gesehen' (SZS, p. 137) and a vivid flashback to the exchange about the hotel that gained notoriety as a site of deportation and murder. Insisting that he had been unaware of any wrongdoing, Beerenbaum continued to assert the discourse of the victor, with reference to the fact that he and his fellow-communists had fought against Hitler and founded a new political state. However, Rosalind's allusion to the denunciations in the Hotel Lux and to the deportations and spate of purges in the Communist Party from the mid- to late-1930s distressed Beerenbaum to such an extent that he suffered a nose bleed, this psychosomatic response itself an admission of guilt. His blood dripped suggestively onto the blank sheet of paper in front of him: 'das unbeschriebene Papier' (SZS, p. 138), laden with potential, is thus symbolically tarnished by a representative of the state. Leisten reads the functionary's reaction to Rosalind's provocative question

Writing and Rewriting: The Problem of History in Stille Zeile Sechs

in terms of the relationship between text and body: 'Schließlich öffnet sich Beerenbaums gesamter Körper explizit zur Schrift, als er auf die Frage nach dem Moskauer Hotel Lux auf das Papier blutet.'[23] On this occasion Rosalind's verbal onslaught was completely unprovoked. In retrospect she wonders: 'Warum hatte ich kein Mitleid' (SZS, p. 139). Only when the tissue was soaked through with blood did she finally relent: 'Erst als das Taschentuch vollgesogen war mit Beerenbaums Blut, ließ ich von ihm ab wie ein satter Blutegel' (SZS, p. 140). This powerful and repulsive image emphasises the relentless nature of the exchange.

As a direct retaliation, Beerenbaum began the subsequent transcription session by dictating three emotionally charged sentences: 'Meine Frau Grete wurde im Herbst 39 verhaftet', continuing: 'Sie kam in das Konzentrationslager Ravensbrück.' He screamed the final sentence: 'Und das liegt nicht in Sibirien' (SZS, p. 141), before leaving the room. Overcome with shame, the protagonist remained speechless and physically unable to transcribe. That Beerenbaum's narrative has been built upon personal suffering is a truth even Rosalind must recognise: 'Kaum mach ich das Maul auf, um meine [Biografie] einzuklagen, stoßen sie mir einen Brocken wie Ravensbrück oder Buchenwald zwischen die Zähne' (SZS, p. 141). However, when Rosalind documented the exchange, the final sentence differed from the original formulation: 'Sibirien liegt bei Ravensbrück' (SZS, p. 142). Several commentators have pointed to the significance of this alteration, the replacing of Beerenbaum's 'nicht in' with 'bei'. Rossbacher notes that Rosalind 'aligns the insidiousness of Stalinism and fascism and, through her revision, writes this alignment into his story and into history',[24] while Lenckos offers a similar interpretation: 'this small change is enough to upset the political meta-narrative; placing Siberia next to Ravensbrück establishes a correlation between the two locations of political deportation and murder.'[25]

It is striking that Maron locates her reflections on the language of victory only against the backdrop of the imminent death of the system. As we conclude this section, we return once again to Benjamin, more specifically to his understanding of history as a combination of the messianic and the

---

23   Leisten, p. 149.
24   Rossbacher, p. 20.
25   Lenckos, p. 112.

catastrophic. In his essay 'Über den Begriff der Geschichte', written in 1940 and published posthumously in 1942, Benjamin's angel of history, although turned towards the past, is nevertheless propelled towards the future by the storm of progress.[26] The continuum of history is 'eine einzige Katastrophe'.[27] This progression through catastrophe is evident in Beerenbaum's personal trauma. It is the double function of stories such as his to articulate a triumphant historical process and to be a memorial to the dead. The functionary's narrative is a disconcerting coexistence of lies and searing truths that even Rosalind has to accept. Although she condemns the manner in which Beerenbaum bestows meaning upon the events of his life by situating them within a master narrative of the historical victor, the Ravensbrück episode highlights once again the inherent ambiguity of Maron's text and the recognition of the undeniable personal suffering endured by the opponents of fascism, even if the sufferers later persecuted in their turn. Despite her sustained challenge to the master discourse, Rosalind is forced to recognise the profundity of Beerenbaum's personal suffering, even if this trauma is being integrated into the language of the historical victor. This differentiated portrayal of Beerenbaum's past enhances Maron's complex reflection on the writing of history.

The Final Confrontation

The final exchange between Rosalind and Beerenbaum is a culmination of the novel's central themes: the body as a potent symptom, the functionary's glorified version of past victories, the transcription process itself, Rosalind's sustained challenge to the master discourse with ultimately fatal consequences. From the outset Beerenbaum is presented as a frail figure with his hunched

---

26   'Der Engel der Geschichte [...] hat das Antlitz der Vergangenheit zugewendet [...] Aber ein Sturm weht vom Paradiese her [...] Dieser Sturm treibt ihn unaufhaltsam in die Zukunft, der er den Rücken kehrt, während der Trümmerhaufen vor ihm zum Himmel wächst. Das, was wir den Fortschritt nennen, ist *dieser* Sturm.' 'Über den Begriff der Geschichte', in *Illuminationen: Ausgewählte Schriften 1* (Frankfurt am Main: Suhrkamp Taschenbuch, 1977), pp. 251–61 (p. 255).
27   Benjamin, p. 255.

back and ashen pallor. Even his right hand trembles more than usual 'als hätte sie den letzten Widerstand aufgegeben' (SZS, p. 200). He suggests dictation of that particularly happy chapter of his life and memoirs which he entitles 'Rückkehr nach Deutschland' (SZS, p. 200). Emphasising the challenging task facing communists in the immediate post-war period, he recites an appropriately rousing poem by Johannes R. Becher, to be inserted in his memoirs. This patriotic poem is delivered with suitable pathos. There is repeated reference to the difficult but rewarding path ahead. The functionary struggles for breath, unable to articulate the final syllables of each line. Even Rosalind is forced to recognise that he is too weak to be questioned about the Graf, but she persists. Dictation has become a physically painful process, and yet Beerenbaum remains determined to integrate his personal experience into a teleological narrative of liberation. He compensates for his physical frailty by recounting, in decidedly forthright terms, the task facing his fellow-comrades in the aftermath of World War II: 'Bis tief in die Arbeiterklasse hinein hatte die antisowjetische Hetze ihr Werk getan. Diese Menschen zu erziehen war eine gigantische Aufgabe' (SZS, p. 202). Once again he casts communists in a redemptive role as they strove to re-educate the population in the spirit of antifascism. Liberating Germany from those he describes as imperialists and bloodthirsty fascists, he situates himself firmly on the side of the historical victor.

Rosalind grows increasingly irritated as she scrutinises 'seine Siege genüßlich repetierenden Beerenbaum' (SZS, p. 203). It is at this point that she questions him about his last meeting with Karl-Heinz Baron. Unwilling to entertain discussion of such contentious issues, Beerenbaum desperately attempts to change the subject and struggles in vain to regain control of his narrative. The ensuing moments remain etched in Rosalind's memory: 'Ich weiß es so genau, als hätte ich diese Minuten zweifach erlebt, als Zuschauerin und Akteurin. Und eigentlich war ich sogar dreifach dabei, denn auch als Akteurin war ich geteilt, in eine, die etwas tat, und eine andere, die etwas zu tun wünschte' (SZS, pp. 204–05) Brigitte Rossbacher notes the significance of the narrative voice fragmenting into three at this point: 'a narrative device which distances her [the narrator] from Rosalind's actions – and Rosalind's imagined actions.'[28]

28 Rossbacher, p. 21.

The physical positioning of the adversaries within the confines of Beerenbaum's study – itself a microcosm of the claustrophobic setting of the GDR in the 1980s – is also significant. Sitting at his desk, he is bathed enigmatically in the light of the table lamp. 'Gefangen im gelben Licht der Tischlampe' (SZS, p. 205), he seems powerless to escape the ensuing interrogation. Rosalind, for her part, is entrenched behind the typewriter. During the transcription sessions the typewriter separated Beerenbaum from his amanuensis. Particularly in this final scene Rosalind sits enthroned 'wie eine Rachegöttin hinter der Schreibmaschine' (SZS, p. 205). On the occasion of her first visit to the Stille Zeile, the typewriter was described as 'ein monströses, Geschichte verströmendes Fossil der Marke "Rheinmetall"' (SZS, p. 48). Exuding history, it becomes, in the course of the exchanges between Beerenbaum and his amanuensis, the instrument through which more recent GDR history is recorded and amended. Commentators have foregrounded Rosalind's subversion through writing of the patriarchal power structure. Lenckos, for example, underscores the importance of the typewriter in the protagonist's 'process of disappropriation and dispersion' through which she subverts the 'power hierarchy established by the writing of the master discourse.'[29] Rosalind uses the ancient typewriter to rebel against the propagation of the socialist metanarrative. The typewriter thus plays a central role in this struggle for the dominance of discourse.

Rosalind interrogates Beerenbaum – 'Rosalind verhörte ihn' (SZS, p. 205) – to the point where he succumbs. Situating *Stille Zeile Sechs* in the corpus of what she terms 'Geständnisliteratur', Hyunseon Lee sees in Rosalind's harsh accusations a grotesque reversal of the Stalinist show trials of the mid- to late-1930s: 'In grotesker Weise steht dieser para-juristische Vorgang in Analogie zu den stalinistischen (Schau-) Prozessen. Doch sitzen die Ankläger nun auf der Anklagebank. Es handelt sich also um ein umgekehrtes Verhör, eine symbolische Umdrehung der stalinistischen Prozesse.'[30] In the name of those

---

29   Lenckos, p. 114. Drawing extensively upon Friedrich A. Kittler's text *Grammophon Film Typewriter*, Lenckos emphasises the typewriter's role in 'dispersing the phallogocentrism of handwriting' (p. 113).
30   Hyunseon Lee, 'Die Dialektik des Geständnisses: Monika Marons *Stille Zeile Sechs* und die autobiografischen Diskurse nach 1989', in *Monika Maron in Perspective*, pp. 57–73 (p. 63). Using Foucault's confessional discourse as her theoretical framework, Lee argues

who have been excluded from the master discourse, Rosalind castigates the ageing functionary and all that he represents. In his defence Beerenbaum again cites the communist struggle: 'Wir haben bezahlt, daß andere studieren durften, immer, zuerst als Proleten mit unserem Schweiß, dann mit dem Geld unseres Staates. Arbeitergroschen. Diese Bildung war unser Eigentum, wer damit weglief, ein Räuber' (SZS, p. 206). He rationalises the imprisonment of the Graf in these terms: 'Ihr Sinologe ein Dieb, jawohl. Ein Dieb gehört ins Gefängnis' (SZS, p. 206). Viewed as a dangerous reactionary and consequently dismissed from his academic post, the real threat posed by the Graf was clearly an intellectual one. The protagonist's tirade continues unabated as she accuses him of 'Hirneigenschaft statt Leibeigenschaft' (SZS, p. 206), followed by the ironic address 'ihr Menschheitsbefreier' (SZS, p. 206). The supposed liberators of humanity are revealed to be fundamentally suspicious of knowledge, confiscating intellectual wealth, such as the Graf's, instead of celebrating it.

As the confrontation nears its inevitable and ultimately fatal conclusion, there is an intense focus on the body: Beerenbaum struggling for breath, 'gestützt auf seine rechte Hand' (SZS, p. 207); Rosalind's distorted face as she screams at him, her diatribe accompanied by a violent banging of her fists on the typewriter. Her invective culminates in the bitter denunciation: 'Menschenfresser seid ihr, Sklavenhalter mit einem Heer von Folterknechten' (SZS, p. 207). The graphic detail in which the brutal attack on Beerenbaum is envisaged indicates the intensity of her loathing for him and for the political system that he embodies: Rosalind's fist raised to attack; Beerenbaum's exposed thigh and genitals; his dentures falling from his mouth, a gesture further reinforcing the extent to which the figure of Beerenbaum fuses with that of her father.[31] The protagonist imagines kicking the old man in the ribs and about the head, relenting only when blood flows from his ear.

---

that the enforced confessions of the Stalinist period have been replaced by voluntary revelations in the post-Wende age. Her essay examines both literary and non-literary examples of spontaneous autobiographical confession.

31 In an earlier flashback Rosalind recalled her father's sudden death at home, sitting on his bed and smoking a cigarette. When his wife finds him the following morning, she tries to wake him. The corpse falls backwards onto the bed: 'Dabei fiel ihm das Gebiß aus dem Mund' (SZS, p. 165). We are reminded again of Bakhtin's reflections on the grotesque body.

Significantly, Rosalind fantasises once again about strangling him: 'die andere Hand an Beerenbaums Hals zwischen Kinn und Kehlkopf' (SZS, p. 208). In terms of challenging the master discourse, this gesture symbolises the desire to suppress Beerenbaum's memoirs at the very source of their articulation. The final images focus on his hands. A spent Beerenbaum lies exhausted in his armchair, 'einzig lebendig an ihm die zu ewigem Zittern verurteilte Hand' (SZS, p. 208). Rosalind studiously ignores his outstretched hand: 'Rosalind sah die ihr entgegengestreckte Hand, sah den sterbenden Beerenbaum und wartete auf seinen Tod' (SZS, pp. 208–09). No longer prepared to act as his right hand, she quite literally rejects his outstretched arm and thus figuratively renounces participation in the governing discourse. Although she appears to have silenced the master narrative, her victory, if the outcome can be described as such, remains a highly ambivalent one. The narrative 'I' intervenes: 'Als ich endlich verstand, daß sie nichts tun würde, um ihn zu retten, fand ich meine Stimme wieder' (SZS, p. 209). Rosalind recovers her voice, but only by the irreversible silencing of Beerenbaum and of the discourse that he represents.

'Die Fähigkeit zur Täterschaft': Subverting the Victim–Perpetrator Dichotomy

During an interview conducted in November 1991, Maron expressed her dissatisfaction with the manner in which her text had been received: 'Das Buch wird schlicht gelesen als ein Buch über Vergangenheitsbewältigung, es wird in seiner Ambivalenz nicht wahrgenommen.'[32] Rosalind's sustained challenge to the master discourse culminates in a relentless and ultimately fatal final confrontation. Hers is a very ambivalent victory in the struggle to record the past. *Stille Zeile Sechs* thus deconstructs the dichotomy between victim and perpetrator. As the author herself explained: 'Mir geht es um die Nichtaussöhnung mit sich selbst, denn jeder sollte wissen, daß er die Fähigkeit zur Täterschaft jederzeit in sich trägt.'[33]

---

32   Richter, p. 5.
33   Hametner, p. 43.

From the outset Rosalind longs for action: 'Die Sehnsucht nach einer Tat existierte in mir gegen meinen Willen und unstillbar' (SZS, p. 51), this desire setting her apart from the pub's clientele who diagnose it as weakness of character. *Stille Zeile Sechs* reflects on the issue of the function of activism and its relationship to the victim-perpetrator dichotomy. It is in this context that the writer and political activist Ernst Toller assumes significance within the character's experience. Rosalind first encounters the life and work of Toller while in employment at the historical institute and researching an article on the 1919 Soviet Republic, the *Räterepublik*, in Munich. Toller's question 'Muß der Handelnde schuldig werden, immer und immer? Oder, wenn er nicht schuldig werden will, untergehen?' (SZS, p. 41) preoccupies the protagonist and serves as a refrain throughout. Rosalind takes over her interest in this influential figure from her creator. In her essay on Toller, published in 1988, Maron interprets his reflections on the relationship between the taking of action and occasionally unforeseen consequences within the context of his own tragic biography.[34] The dilemma continued to haunt him, even after its initial formulation in the trauma of the failed *Räterepublik*. A committed pacifist, he had encouraged the American and European governments to support his Spanish Relief Plan and provide financial aid for the starving population during the Civil War. Horrified to discover that a considerable portion of the money had found its way into the hands of Franco, he committed suicide in 1939. In the concluding paragraph of her essay, Maron explains the significance of this figure who always felt compelled to take action: 'Die Ahnung von der Vergeblichkeit allen Tuns und dem lebenslangen Versuch, diese Ahnung zu widerlegen, waren es, die Tollers Leben mir zum ermutigenden, wenn auch tragischen Gleichnis werden ließen' (*Begreifungskraft*, p. 62).

Rosalind is troubled by feelings of complicity. Early in her working arrangement with Beerenbaum she realises that she has become a 'Mittäter' (SZS, p. 77), recording the memoirs of an official who identifies himself completely with the political system that his amanuensis abhors. In an attempt to justify what she terms her 'Handlangerdienst' (SZS, p. 77), Rosalind imagines herself as a spy, as 'jemand, der einen perfekten Mord plante und vorher sein Opfer akribisch studierte' (SZS, p. 77), a simile acquiring particular

---

[34] Maron's essay 'Ernst Toller' was first published in her column for the magazine *Du* in June 1989 and later appeared in the collection *Nach Maßgabe meiner Begreifungskraft* (pp. 60–62).

significance in the context of the ultimately fatal final confrontation between amanuensis and employer. Her attempts at self-exculpation ring hollow: 'Wer würde eine Schreibmaschine für schuldig halten, nur weil ein Mörder sein Geständnis auf ihr geschrieben hatte?' (SZS, p. 121), she reflects, before demolishing this comparison in the very next sentence. Instead she struggles with increasingly physical manifestations of guilt: 'Derweil [...] breitete sich etwas in mir aus, ein gestaltloses Gewächs, [...] das um mein Herz wucherte und den Magen einschnürte, so daß ich manchmal fürchtete, es fehle meinem Brustkorb der Raum zum Atmen' (SZS, p. 122). The full extent of her complicity becomes clear to Rosalind when she learns about the more disturbing aspects of Beerenbaum's biography: 'Plötzlich, ohne wirklich schuldig zu sein, war ich in das Unglück des Grafen verstrickt' (SZS, p. 181).

Immediately consumed with remorse in the aftermath of the final confrontation, Rosalind prays for Beerenbaum's recovery and realises: 'Ich hätte ihn nicht so hassen dürfen' (SZS, p. 212). In spite of Thekla's reassurance to the contrary, Rosalind insists upon her guilt. Looking back on her novel, Maron herself is unequivocal in this regard: 'Sie ist schuldig an ihm', she asserted in a 1996 interview, 'Sie ist ähnlich brutal wie er.'[35] Lenckos interprets the protagonist's affirmation of guilt positively: 'It is the only way she can escape both hypocrisy and victimization, and leave her assigned state of paralysis to claim agency.'[36] In her determination to assume an active role, Rosalind realises that she has something in common with her adversary: 'Alles, nur nicht Opfer sein. Das wußte auch Herbert Beerenbaum, der Arbeiter aus dem Ruhrgebiet: Alles, nur nicht noch einmal Opfer sein' (SZS, p. 210).[37] Beerenbaum, once a victim of fascism, persecutes in his turn. He denounces comrades during the spate of purges in the Hotel Lux and incarcerates potentially dangerous intellectuals. Determined to eschew victim status, Rosalind also becomes a perpetrator. Her relentless verbal assault precipitates the functionary's heart attack and hastens his death. She is forced to answer Toller's question in the affirmative, assuming, albeit all too late, responsibility for her actions.

35   Deirdre Byrnes, Interview with Monika Maron, Zürich, 22 April 1996.
36   Lenckos, p. 108.
37   This determination to eschew victim status is also thematised in Maron's essay on the writer Leonora Carrington: 'Sie kämpft um die Täterschaft [...] nicht Opfer sein wollen'. 'Wo war Leonora Carrington?' (1988/89), in *Nach Maßgabe meiner Begreifungskraft*, pp. 63–65 (p. 65).

The hope articulated in her refrain 'Übermorgen war der Tag nach Beerenbaums Tod' (SZS, p. 155), a hope that has sustained her throughout the increasingly fraught exchanges, fails to materialise. There is no sense of relief or liberation: 'Beerenbaum ist tot, begraben. Und alles ist wie vorher. Übermorgen ist der Tag nach Beerenbaums Tod. Wann ist übermorgen? Morgen, vorgestern, übermorgen? Ist übermorgen schon gewesen, und ich habe es nicht bemerkt?' (SZS, p. 216) In the closing frame Michael Beerenbaum fulfils his father's wish and hands Rosalind the package containing the memoirs, which, despite her innate unwillingness, she feels compelled to accept. In the final line she appears determined to liberate herself from the psychological and emotional weight of this 'Vermächtnis und fesselndes Band zugleich.'[38] She reiterates, as if to convince herself: 'Ich werde es in die nächste Mülltonne werfen. Ich werde es zwischen den Papierbergen im unteren Fach meines Bücherregals begraben. Ich werde es auf keinen Fall öffnen' (SZS, p. 219). The inherent ambivalence of this closing sequence overrides the protagonist's attempts to convince herself that Beerenbaum is finally a closed chapter of her life. Although she succeeds in challenging the official version of GDR history promulgated by Beerenbaum, she remains implicated in the very political system that she wishes to leave behind.

Conclusion

With her third novel Monika Maron created a powerful and complex memory narrative in which competing versions of GDR history vie for expression. A retired historian-turned-amanuensis challenges the authenticity of the memories to be recorded, thereby subverting the communist success story typified in Beerenbaum's account of his past. By appointing Rosalind to transcribe his memoirs, the ageing functionary hands his text over to her, a transaction affecting the entire process of historical representation. Beerenbaum renounces control of his memoirs; Rosalind, for her part, questions, denounces, even

---

[38] Klaus Siebenhaar, 'Ach Pankow!: Ein Endspiel in einem unwirtlichen System', *Der Tagesspiegel*, 9 October 1991, *Literatur*, p. v.

blatantly amends his romanticised version of the GDR. She inscribes into history those individualistic, potentially subversive figures excluded from participation in the governing discourse. By confronting her employer with the case of Karl-Heinz Baron, she exposes the omissions from Beerenbaum's memoirs. Maron thus anticipates a significant aspect of her 1999 text *Pawels Briefe*, the family story in which she is determined to probe her mother's 'Erinnerungslücken' (PB, p. 17). Maron's mother Hella is selective in her recollection of the GDR; Beerenbaum, too, omits from his memoirs such contentious aspects as the denunciations in the Hotel Lux and the imprisonment of intellectuals.

Rosalind delivers a damning indictment of a political system that has had such lasting repercussions for her own life. She locates her experience of GDR history in the context of a troubled father–daughter relationship. The protagonist succeeds in challenging the master narrative, presenting an interpretation of GDR history that is deeply rooted in her personal experience and that contradicts on so many levels the official version propagated by communist officialdom. While Beerenbaum clings to the myth of the antifascist state upon which he has carefully constructed his past, Rosalind's writing and rewriting of history are motivated by deeply personal concerns.

Rosalind writes against the decaying political body that evokes such revulsion. However, she remains unable to write herself out of this political system completely. Even the pub – the milieu in which imaginative impulses and authentic expression are fostered and which acts as a counter-text of sorts – does not provide respite from the state that has impacted so profoundly upon its eccentric clientele. Despite her success in presenting a very different version of GDR history, the protagonist's denunciation of Beerenbaum and, through him, of her own distant and unaffectionate father, culminates in a very ambivalent victory. Rosalind retains the memoirs that she has transcribed, questioned and amended. The problem of history remains.

Stille Zeile Sechs interweaves two apparently contradictory narratives. Through recollection of the transcription sessions, Rosalind writes, albeit unwittingly, the story of Beerenbaum's life – including his personal suffering as well as his hagiographic rendition of a triumphant socialist past – into her text. The protagonist's position may serve as a metaphor for Maron's entire oeuvre, which reflects continuously on the complex and lasting influence of the GDR experience. The rereading of *Stille Zeile Sechs* advanced in this chapter demonstrates that Rosalind remains implicated in the very metanarrative which she has struggled to transcend.

CHAPTER FOUR

Love and Loss after the Wall: *Animal triste*

The 1990s marked a pronounced inward turn in Maron's writing.[1] Her fourth novel *Animal triste*, published in 1996, is a story of erotic love, of a clandestine, all-consuming and ultimately fatal affair. In a laudatory review for the *Spiegel*, the literary critic Marcel Reich-Ranicki situates Maron's text within the context of the collapse of the GDR and observes that her criticism of that state and her relentless confrontation with communism had repressed all other motifs from her writing until 1989: 'Für die Liebe war da kaum Platz.'[2] Reich-Ranicki describes *Animal triste* as a study of sexual obsession. He concludes that Maron, unlike many of her contemporaries who experienced a sudden loss of purpose following the collapse of the GDR, had, in fact, found her theme: 'sie hat mit "Animal triste", dem Roman über der Liebe Fluch und Segen, ihr Thema gefunden.'[3]

Two years previously, in an interview for the *Spiegel*, Maron had articulated her sense of liberation following the Wende and had welcomed the attendant thematic and stylistic freedom: 'in der Gegenwart fehlt dieser Würgegriff des Systems, diese Bedrohung beim Schreiben. Mir hilft das sehr, eine andere Sprache mit mehr Distanz entsteht. Ich hab' ein freies Herz.'[4] When asked about those themes which interested her in a post-GDR age, she cited the

---

[1] Commenting on the professions of Maron's protagonists, Brigitte Rossbacher notes 'a compelling progression or, more accurately, a regression: a movement back in time from journalist to historian to paleontologist'; she writes of their 'inward turn'. 'The Status of State and Subject: Reading Monika Maron from *Flugasche* to *Animal triste*', in *Wendezeiten, Zeitenwenden: Positionsbestimmungen zur deutschsprachigen Literatur 1945–1995*, ed. by Robert Weninger and Brigitte Rossbacher (Tübingen: Stauffenberg, 1997), p. 211.
[2] Marcel Reich-Ranicki, 'Der Liebe Fluch', *Der Spiegel*, 12 February 1996, pp. 185–89 (p. 186).
[3] Reich-Ranicki, p. 189.
[4] Martin Doerry and Volker Hage, 'Ich hab' ein freies Herz: Monika Maron über Autoren in der Politik und die Zukunft des VS', *Der Spiegel*, 25 April 1994, pp. 185–92 (p. 188).

sensuous elements of life: 'Die Kehrseite der permanenten Auseinandersetzung mit dem System, die sinnlichen Spuren des Lebens, die immer verschattet waren von der alles überwuchernden Politik'.[5] The death of the political system resulted in a turn towards more intimate themes. However, the sociopolitical dimension of Maron's writing did not diminish completely; the love story recalled in *Animal triste* unfolds against the turbulent backdrop of Berlin in the immediate post-Wende period. It is this interplay of the sensual and the political which I will foreground in my analysis of Maron's fourth novel.

Animal triste is a passionate story of love and loss, but it is also a text about the ageing body, about writing history, about repressed memories. Like the protagonist of Maron's earlier novel *Die Überläuferin*, the anonymous first-person narrator, an East German palaeontologist, has withdrawn from society. Having decided to live out the remainder of her life as 'eine nicht endende, ununterbrochene Liebesgeschichte',[6] she is sustained by memories of her great love story. Her lover Franz was part of a West German delegation that was assigned the task of inspecting the Natural History Museum in East Berlin, where the protagonist worked, and determining its future. From decidedly mundane beginnings – Franz's innocuous remark 'Ein schönes Tier' (AT, p. 24), as he contemplates the enormous brachiosaurus that she guards so protectively in the Natural History Museum – the relationship comes to obsess the narrator, even if or perhaps because her lover leaves her bed at precisely half past twelve each night and returns home to his wife. She reinterprets her entire life in light of this chance meeting with Franz: 'ein einziges, langes Warten auf Franz' (AT, p. 51). The narrator's all-consuming passion, captured in Penthesilea's defiant refrain 'dich zu gewinnen oder umzukommen' (AT, p. 132), culminates in her lover's death under the wheels of a bus.

In the first section of this chapter, I will consider the nature and function of the intertextual references strewn throughout *Animal triste* – Kleist's anarchical and bloody drama *Penthesilea* emerges as a significant intertext. The section entitled 'The Discourse of the Body' encompasses the ageing body, the body as metaphor, and the body as the site of erotic memories. The

---

5   Doerry, p. 192.
6   Monika Maron, *Animal triste: Roman* (Frankfurt am Main: S. Fischer, 1996), p. 13. Quotations from the novel will be followed in parentheses by the abbreviation AT and the relevant page number.

'Embodying History' section will examine the interplay of individual event – a tempestuous love affair – and historical context, the political chaos of the Wende and its aftermath mirroring the narrator's emotional turmoil. I will also consider the relativising presence of the past in the imposing figure of the brachiosaurus. *Animal triste* prefigures Maron's interest in the workings of memory, explored in her family story *Pawels Briefe*. The 1996 novel is a powerful, if somewhat eccentric depiction of memory and its repression, as the final section of this chapter 'Remembering the Repressed' will illustrate.

'Dich zu gewinnen oder umzukommen': *Penthesilea* and Other Intertexts

Throughout the 1970s and 1980s writers in the GDR turned increasingly to intertexual references in order to challenge the socialist master text. The whole series of works engaging with the outsiders of the Romantic era, such as Wolf's *Kein Ort. Nirgends*, and with mythological figures, including Kassandra, are examples of such subversive intertextuality. Intertextuality, however, was not always equated with subversive intent. Canonical texts, such as passages from Marx and Lenin and their interpretations by the GDR authorities, were deliberately worked into the fabric of texts, particularly during the early years of the state. In this context literary critics found themselves under pressure to legitimate GDR writers by demonstrating the presence of the historical master discourse in their work.

The intertextuality of Maron's work is thus symptomatic of the situation of all writers of her generation in the GDR. As I demonstrated in Chapter One, the journalist Maron was very much aware of the importance of including the set pieces, the formulations approved and demanded by the governing discourse, within her own contributions to the *Wochenpost*. Far from subversive, such intertextuality was a gesture of conformity, a compromise manoeuvre and the prerequisite for publication. In *Flugasche* such formulations read in a deliberately artificial manner – Josefa's mental 'Porträt über den Arbeiter Soundso' (FA, p. 13) comes to mind – and, as such, subvert their apparent message. Maron also includes in her debut novel extracts from such non-approved sources as the Old Testament *Song of Songs*. In *Stille Zeile Sechs* Beerenbaum's propagation of the socialist master discourse is challenged by his amanuensis. As discussed in Chapter Three, Rosalind denounces the language of clichés and platitudes that the functionary has internalised. Far from the slavish copying of the master text, the protagonist problematises, reformulates and even rewrites Beerenbaum's glorified version of the past.

Animal triste exemplifies the impressive breadth of Maron's cross-referencing and is strewn with literary allusions and intertextual echoes, from Kleist's Amazonian anti-heroine Penthesilea to Wilhelm Raabe's nineteenth-century novel *Stopfkuchen*. However, Maron's 1996 text is puzzling in its use of intertextuality. Unlike *Flugasche* or *Stille Zeile Sechs*, the primary function of the intertextual references does not seem to be a subversive one. This is not merely a result of the collapse of the GDR and the subsequent end of that system of control and censorship which gave such subversiveness a function in Maron's earlier works. The effect of the intertextuality here is more complex. The narrator is certainly not coy in the importance she attaches to her affair, seeing her relationship with Franz within a long list of passionate, ultimately tragic love stories from the world of literature: 'Mit der Liebe ist es wie mit den Sauriern, alle Welt ergötzt sich an ihrem Tod: Tristan und Isolde, Romeo und Julia, Anna Karenina, Penthesilea, immer nur der Tod, immer diese Wollust am Unmöglichen' (AT, p. 59). In an essay tracing the Romantic longing for escape from the rational world as a motif in Maron's writing, Henk Harbers reveals the destructive impulses inherent in the striving of these literary figures towards the ideal of absolute love: 'Dabei geht es um die alte Verbindung von Liebe und Tod, um das Ideal einer absoluten Liebe, das in dieser Absolutheit nicht erreichbar ist und deswegen den Tod sucht.'[7]

The narrator compares her school friends and childhood sweethearts Karin and Klaus to Romeo and Juliet and to Schiller's Ferdinand and Luise. However, the exaggerated character of such unbroken evocation contributes

---

[7] Henk Harbers, 'Gefährliche Freiheit: Zu einem Motivkomplex im Werk von Monika Maron', in *Monika Maron in Perspective: 'Dialogische' Einblicke in zeitgeschichtliche, intertextuelle und rezeptionsbezogene Aspekte ihres Werkes*, ed. by Elke Gilson, German Monitor, 55 (Amsterdam and New York: Rodopi, 2002), pp. 123–37 (p. 132).

to the grotesque aspect of the text.[8] These examples of everlasting love cede to the sobering realisation: 'Karin and Klaus [...] waren kein Liebespaar auf Leben und Tod, sie waren ein Ehepaar fürs Leben' (AT, p. 93). Klaus leaves his wife for a younger woman. The husband of the narrator's friend Sieglinde moves in with his first love, while another friend, Rainer, leaves his wife after fifteen years of marriage. Against this backdrop of marital disappointment, the vision of all-consuming, enduring love, 'eine Liebe auf Leben und Tod' (AT, p. 146), comes to obsess the narrator.

When Franz and his wife leave on a trip to Hadrian's Wall, the protagonist returns to the Natural History Museum. Sitting before the calming presence of her beloved brachiosaurus, she is reminded of Penthesilea's defiant refrain: '"Doch von zwei Dingen schnell beschloß ich eines/dich zu gewinnen oder umzukommen"' (AT, p. 132). Determined to eschew victim status, she is inspired by the avenger's 'Aufruhr des Allesodernichts, des Dasodersterbens' (AT, p. 142). Her continuous identification with Kleist's brutal avenger signals the extent of the passions that, once aroused, are impossible to control. Marcel Reich-Ranicki describes her passionate excesses:

> Sie tobt, sie rast, aber sie kann nichts ändern. Ihre Begierde hat keine Grenzen. Ihr Fühlen und Verlangen kennt ein Ziel – und überhaupt kein Maß [...] Was Kleists Penthesilea, die grausame Königin der Amazonen, dem König der Griechen herausfordernd gesteht, bildet, hier mehrfach zitiert, das Zentrum des Romans.[9]

In her essay 'Nach Maßgabe meiner Begreifungskraft', which was first delivered as her acceptance speech on being awarded the Kleist literary prize for *Stille Zeile Sechs* in 1992, Maron interprets the tragedy of his violent Amazonian warrior:

> Die Tragödie der Penthesilea beginnt mit dem Sturz ihres Volkes aus der Natur in die Gesetze des Amazonenstaates, die sie akzeptiert als natürliche Verpflichtung. Und sie vollendet sich, wenn Penthesilea, als einzelne, zum zweiten Mal den Sturz wagt, aus der Kultur, der sie entstammt, in ihre individuelle natürliche Bestimmung. (*Begreifungskraft*, p. 111)

---

8   Mikhail Bakhtin isolates exaggeration, hyperbolism and excessiveness as 'fundamental attributes of the grotesque style.' *Rabelais and his World* (Cambridge, MA: Massachusetts Institute of Technology Press, 1968), p. 303.
9   Reich-Ranicki, pp. 188–89.

Penthesilea is a figure consumed by her own passions: 'die androgyne Gestalt des vor leidenschaftlichem Wollen rasenden, letztlich das unmäßig Gewollte und damit sich selbst verzehrenden Menschen' (*Begreifungskraft*, p. 111). Maron describes the fatal consequences of Penthesilea's succumbing to the brutal excesses of her desire: 'Die Maßlosigkeit, die der Ausbruch braucht, um vollzogen zu werden, zerstört zugleich seinen Sinn, die Ausbrecherin und was sie gewinnen wollte' (*Begreifungskraft*, p. 111). In *Animal triste*, too, the extremes of passion, captured in the narrator's evocation of Penthesilea's refrain 'dich zu gewinnen oder umzukommen', results in the death of her lover and her subsequent withdrawal from the world.

Penthesilea is a subversive, radical text. Its anti-heroine succumbs to her most animalistic impulses:

> Sie liegt, den grimmigen Hunden beigesellt,
> Sie, die ein Menschenschoß gebar, und reißt, –
> Die Glieder des Achills reißt sie in Stücken![10]

The drama culminates in a bloody end, 'im kannibalischen Liebesakt' (*Begreifungskraft*, p. 111), as Maron herself describes the barbaric outcome. In *Animal triste* the clandestine affair ends in blood, but not before the text has descended into the banal. Accompanying her lover to the bus stop, where he is to get the bus home to his wife – itself a grotesque, blackly humorous scenario – the narrator fears that Franz is about to return to his wife for good. The text assumes an increasingly ambivalent aspect: 'Halte ich ihn, stoße ich ihn, reißt er sich los. Ein nie gehörtes Geräusch, als würde nasse Pappe auf Eisen klatschen [...] Im Rinnstein sammelt sich eine Lache. Ein zerquetschter Männerarm unter dem Vorderrad' (AT, p. 238). The precise circumstances surrounding Franz's death remain shrouded in uncertainty. He may have been deliberately pushed under the wheels of the oncoming bus; alternatively, his fatal fall may have been a tragic accident. In any case, the narrator assumes responsibility: 'So oder so, ich habe Franz getötet' (AT, p. 238). We are reminded of her earlier remark, which, in retrospect, reads as a warning: '"... dich zu gewinnen oder umzukommen", so ein Satz gehört zu einem Anfang oder zum Ende' (AT, p. 142).

---

10   Heinrich von Kleist, *Penthesilea: Ein Trauerspiel* (Stuttgart: Reclam, 1999), pp. 87–88. Kleist's drama was first published in 1808.

While critics read the repeated reference to Penthesilea as an indication of the passions evoked, the ironic distance within such intertextuality remains overlooked to a large extent.[11] There is a sense that Maron is mocking her narrator, revealing her comparison with Penthesilea to be nothing more than a pretentious delusion. On the evening of the momentous Kleist revelation, the protagonist visits her actress friend Ate. The latter, upon learning of the narrator's decision to adopt Penthesilea's defiant refrain as her motto, delivers an impromptu rendition of a scene from the drama:

> Otrere war die große Mutter mir
> Und mich begrüßt das Volk: Penthesilea. (AT, p. 146)

The banal context is glaringly at odds with the heady passions of Greek tragedy and the scene descends into the realm of farce.

The intertextual echo of Kleist's anarchical drama resonates throughout *Animal triste*. We are reminded again of a desire, both in Maron's work and in her self-understanding as a writer, to move beyond a stultifying reality into the imaginative realm. We are reminded, too, of Wolfgang Emmerich's proposal to focus on the imaginative dimension of writing, 'die Mobilisierung von Phantasie' ('Für eine andere Wahrnehmung', p. 17). However, the flights of fantasy in *Animal triste* are brought abruptly to earth. The narrator appears to be blissfully unaware of the disparity between her secret affair and the brutal excesses of Penthesilea's desire. The Amazonian queen's all-consuming passion reads as grotesque, even ridiculous, when transported to the reality of an illicit affair between a lonely, middle-aged palaeontologist and a bland natural scientist from Ulm. Significantly, in Maron's first post-Wende novel the imaginative flights, expressed in the narrator's unbroken identification with the anti-heroine of Greek tragedy, are constantly undermined by the author herself. The enigmatic use of the intertextual in *Animal triste* thus complicates Emmerich's expectations for post-Wende writing and criticism.

---

11 The comic effect of this intertextuality is recognised by Andrea Geier: 'Die Identifikation mit literarischen Figuren wird zwar von der Erzählerin ernst genommen, erzeugt aber gerade in den Differenzen – dass sich die Erzählerin z.B. in der Königin Penthesilea wiederfindet und der "graue" Franz folgerichtig Achill sein müsste – für die LeserInnen natürlich vor allem Komik.' 'Paradoxien des Erinnerns: Biografisches Erzählen in *Animal triste*', in *Monika Maron in Perspective*, pp. 93–122 (p. 119).

The Discourse of the Body

Although the withdrawal enacted in *Animal triste* is far less radical than Rosalind's in *Die Überläuferin*, it is no less absolute. The first-person narrator has retreated into carefully chosen memories of snatched moments with Franz. Her self-imposed isolation is interrupted only by essential ventures into society, such as grocery shopping and trips to the bank. The text opens with her admission that, as a young woman, she envisaged a dramatic death in her prime because she did not wish to contemplate the inevitability of ageing and physical decay: 'für den allmählichen Verfall war ich nicht bestimmt, das wußte ich genau' (AT, p. 9). This is followed by the startling announcement: 'Jetzt bin ich hundert und lebe immer noch' (AT, p. 9). Details of her life after Franz remain conspicuously absent. Following her lover's departure she smashed all the mirrors in her apartment: 'als ich beschloß, den Episoden meines Lebens keine mehr hinzuzufügen' (AT, p. 10). In *Die Überläuferin* and in *Animal triste*, the body thus offers an extreme form of retreat from society, even if differing motivation propels this withdrawal. Particularly in the later novel, the body has become a repository for personal, non-historical memories.

The narrator describes the ageing process in the most corporeal of terms: 'Das langsame Ertauben, Erblinden, Erstarren, Verblöden' (AT, p. 144). She categorically rejects any attempts to interpret this process positively. She views her imperfect, failing body with a detached irony: 'In meinem Alter gilt es schon als Schönheit, wenn man seinen Mitmenschen keinen Ekel verursacht' (AT, p. 14). The reader is reminded of the revulsion that the protagonist of *Stille Zeile Sechs* felt at the sight of Beerenbaum's decrepit body. However, it is the female body that evokes similar disgust here. Even as a child, the narrator was repulsed by what she terms her mother's alarmingly female body and by her own pubescent transformation: 'Mein nackter Körper in seiner eindeutigen Bestimmung war mir widerwärtig' (AT, p. 74). Later, as the mother of an only child, the mere thought of becoming pregnant again filled her with disgust. Offering a psychoanalytical interpretation, Alison Lewis notes that this revulsion towards the female body is 'indicative of a much deeper ambivalence towards femininity and corporeality.'[12] During a conversation

---

[12] Alison Lewis, 'Re-Membering the Barbarian: Memory and Repression in Monika Maron's *Animal triste*', *The German Quarterly*, 71.1 (1998), 30–46 (p. 36). In her analysis Lewis draws on Freudian and Lacanian theories and on Julia Kristeva's concept of abjection.

with her friend Ate in which they bemoan the passage of time, the narrator reveals that she never liked her body. Her jealousy of Franz's petite, perfectly proportioned wife is tempered somewhat by the comforting thought that even her rival cannot escape the onset of old age.

In *Die Überläuferin* sickness and eventual paralysis were the body's response to societal constraints; in *Stille Zeile Sechs* the imminent collapse of that societal order was embodied in the figure of the decrepit communist functionary Herbert Beerenbaum. In *Animal triste* the female body, in its grotesque and exaggerated characteristics, symbolises various states of emotional distress. The story is told of Sieglinde, whose husband leaves her for a much younger woman after twenty-four years of marriage. The scorned wife promptly sheds thirty pounds. However, the eczema from which she suffered throughout her married life also mysteriously disappears, a powerful outward sign of inner liberation. Lewis notes that 'the hieroglyphics of the allergies and rashes' marking Sieglinde's body tell a 'tale of deformation and domination'.[13] The narrator, another abandoned woman, goes to the most drastic lengths, even at the expense of her sight, to maintain some sort of emotional bond with Franz. The scorned lover begins wearing the glasses that he left behind: 'und verschmolz meine gesunden Augen mit seinem Sehfehler zu einer symbiotischen Unschärfe als einer letzten Möglichkeit, ihm nahe zu sein' (AT, pp. 10–11). Just before she remembers to the gruesome end, to that fateful autumn night when Franz was killed, the narrator describes her body as a site of endless discomfort: 'Mein Körper ist eine einzige Plage. Er kneift und beißt mich, er zerrt an mir, meine Füße sterben ab, und mein Rücken schmerzt' (AT, p. 232). Her body bears powerful physical testimony to her sense of abandonment and complicity. Gabriele Eckart offers a Lacanian interpretation when she notes that, in the aftermath of Franz's death, the symbolic order inscribes itself onto the female body in the most brutal fashion: 'Kaum ist der Geliebte fort, zeigt sich die Einschreibung der symbolischen Struktur in den Leib brutal.'[14]

The pronounced physicality of the novel is also reflected in the lovers' professions. Before her withdrawal from society the narrator worked as a palaeontologist in the Natural History Museum, the scene of her first encounter with the natural scientist Franz. The constant presence of the brachiosaurus

---

[13] Lewis, p. 39.
[14] Gabriele Eckart, 'Ost-Frau liebt West-Mann: Zwei neue Romane von Irina Liebmann und Monika Maron', *Colloquia Germanica*, 30.4 (1997), 315–21 (p. 320).

was a source of comfort to her. The space beneath the imposing figure had become her sanctuary: 'dieser Quadratmeter unter dem kleinen Kopf des Brachiosaurus gehörte mir, mir allein' (AT, p. 204). She is distressed to discover that Franz's wife has, in fact, encroached upon her sacred spot. It is only when her lover embarks upon a trip to Scotland with his wife that she can reclaim this territory as her own. For the narrator, her beloved brachiosaurus is also 'der Inbegriff des Maßlosen' (AT, p. 219), epitomising extremes of passion, of enduring desire:

> Daß das Unbezähmbare meiner Gefühle für Franz in ihrer Saurierhaftigkeit bestand, erkannte ich aber erst später, oder anders: Ich begriff, daß es das Saurierhafte an mir war, das so liebte, etwas Uraltes, atavistisch Gewaltsames, jede zivilisatorische Norm mißachtend, und nichts, was Sprache brauchte, konnte recht haben gegen meine Liebe zu Franz. (AT, p. 131)

If 'ausgestorbene Einzelgänger' (AT, p. 210) were a source of inspiration for the narrator, Franz's professional focus was on the tiniest of creatures, the ant kingdom. The narrator refused identification with their perfectly ordered, collective existence that leaves no place for emotions, choosing instead the passionate excesses of her lone brachiosaurus.

As I indicated earlier in the chapter, the body in *Animal triste* is a site of intimate memories. It is only through the recollection of her sexual relationship with Franz that the narrator celebrates her body: 'Das eigentliche Wunder waren unsere Körper' (AT, p. 108), she recalls. During their lovemaking their bodies rejoice in their depoliticised autonomy, becoming 'eigenmächtige Akteure' (AT, p. 109).[15] The narrator celebrates her own 'Tierhaftigkeit' (AT, p. 165), at once an expression of liberation from societal constraints and of sexual longing. She frequently recalls Franz lying on her bed like a pale-skinned animal. Succumbing to her sexual desires, she compares herself to an ape: 'Wie eine Äffin umklammerte ich Franz mit Armen und Beinen, und für eine Weile hatte ich das schöne Gefühl, mir sei ein Fell gewachsen, ein dichtes kurzes Tierfell bedeckte meinen Körper und mein Gesicht' (AT, p. 207).

Significantly, the disconcerting and surreal final scene sees the narrator become animal-like. Lying between the flesh-eating plants that pattern her

---

15   In *Flugasche*, too, Josefa and Christian lose themselves in the act of lovemaking, becoming 'fliegende Tintenfische' (FA, p. 154).

Love and Loss after the Wall: Animal triste

sheets, she feels the protective gaze of animals surrounding her. The concluding sentences read: 'Ich bin eins von ihnen, eine braunhaarige Äffin mit einer stumpfen Nase und langen Armen, die ich um meinen Tierleib schlinge. So bleibe ich liegen' (AT, p. 239). On one level, this enigmatic scene underscores the narrator's absolute identification with her animal self. A further possible reading foregrounds the link between the closing scene and the novel's title. Mourning the loss of her beloved, the narrator has become, quite literally, an animal triste. The ambivalence of the novel's title is also recognised by Elke Gilson who situates the text in its post-Wende context: 'Das Zitat aus dem manchmal Aristoteles und manchmal dem Kirchenvater Augustinus zugeschriebenen Spruch (in der lateinischen Fassung), "omne animal post coitum triste", könnte natürlich auf die kurz nach 1990 in den beiden Teilen Deutschlands aus verschiedenen Gründen entstandenen "postkoitalen Tristesse" anspielen.'[16]

Animal triste portrays the inexorability of physical decline. The female body reads as a potent symptom of psychological and emotional states. The narrator embraces her sexual desires and succumbs to the animalistic impulses within. Her body becomes a repository of intimate, non-political memories. However, the political context does not disappear completely: in the post-Wende period the female body has become for Maron an extended metaphor for the whole of Berlin. In *Animal triste* history is written onto the body, as I will demonstrate in the following section.

Embodying History

In *Animal triste* the interplay of the personal and the political finds expression in the mapping of the narrator's body on Berlin, on the historically and fictionally coded images of division and change. 'Dabei hatte ich mich der Stadt nie so ganz und gar zugehörig gefühlt wie in diesen Tagen oder Monaten' (AT, p. 209), she comments about the period immediately after the fall of the Wall. The affair between East German palaeontologist and West German

---

16 Elke Gilson, *Wie Literatur hilft, 'übers Leben nachzudenken': Das Oeuvre Monika Marons*, Studia Germanica Gandensia, 47 (Gent, 1999), p. 31.

natural scientist unfolds against the tumultuous backdrop of the immediate post-Wende period. His arrival in East Berlin and into the narrator's life occurs 'in den Wirrnissen der Um- und Neuordnung' (AT, p. 214). She portrays the insecurity characterising those first months after the explosive events of autumn 1989. The narrator recalls her own 'umstürzlerische Gier' (AT, p. 90), mirroring the physical transformation of a city in flux. Towns and streets were renamed, monuments demolished, new military alliances forged. Her relationship with a city undergoing momentous political change reads as a symbiotic one: 'Ich war ein Stein der stürzenden Gemäuer', she dramatically announces, 'so aufgebrochen wie die Straßen der Stadt war ich' (AT, p. 209).

The narrator describes the collapse of communism in the light of her fateful encounter with Franz: 'Den unverhofften Zeitenwandel verstand damals jeder als das Signal, auf das er insgeheim gewartet hatte […] Ich traf Franz' (AT, pp. 98–99). Her interpretation of a momentous historical process exclusively in terms of her personal experience is taken to exaggerated extremes, particularly her presumptuous conviction 'daß die Mauer in Berlin nur eingerissen worden war, damit Franz mich an diesem Morgen unter dem Brachiosaurus hatte treffen können' (AT, p. 98).

Animal triste is undeniably an example of a private story clinging to public, collective history. The narrator sees herself enacting with Franz the history of her city, her country and their divergent historical pasts. Parallels with Wolf's *Der geteilte Himmel* underscore this point still further. It is the building of the Wall that seals the differences between the lovers. Rita is not willing to follow Manfred upon his defection to the West.[17] What happens in *Animal triste* is ultimately an inversion of that theme: the Wall comes down so that the lovers may be together – at least that is how the narrator perceives the overlapping of private and public histories. Linking the personal and the political, Brigitte Rossbacher notes: 'Her personal salvation through Franz intersects with the political narrative of German unification'.[18]

---

17   Wolf's 1963 text projects onto the fragile love story between Rita and Manfred the heady optimism of the reconstruction years and the building of the Wall. While Manfred willingly embraces the opportunities to further his career that life in West Germany affords, Rita does not share his enthusiasm: 'Man ist auf schreckliche Weise in der Fremde' is her summation of life in the West. *Der geteilte Himmel* (Munich: Deutscher Taschenbuch Verlag, 1997), p. 208.

18   Rossbacher, p. 210.

Love and Loss after the Wall: Animal triste

Even an event in Roman history is interpreted in terms of the narrator's obsession with Franz and offers further variation on the theme of walls and division. Franz and his wife embark on a trip to Scotland; Hadrian's Wall is an important stop on their itinerary. During a tense telephone conversation Franz reacts to his lover's jealous outburst by explaining that Hadrian's biographer described the Wall as the demarcation line between Romans and Barbarians. The narrator is suddenly convinced that he has categorised her as a barbarian: 'Für einen Satz hatte er mich zur Barbarin ernannt, vor der sich zivilisierte Römer wie Franz und seine Frau durch eine Mauer schützen mußten' (AT, p. 156). In an interpretation that focuses on the sociopolitical dimension of the text, Lewis concludes: 'For the narrator there remains little alternative but to become the barbarian Franz implies she is and to embrace the return of the repressed in becoming West Germany's uncivilized other.'[19] Unification is thus depicted in a highly ambiguous light: the civilised West sets out to colonise its barbarian neighbour, the ancient border between Romans and Barbarians symbolising the suspicion and lack of understanding on the West German side.

The protagonists of earlier Maron novels were concerned with recording the events of the present or the past, as journalists or historians. The profession of the anonymous narrator of *Animal triste* is also significant. As a palaeontologist at the Natural History Museum, her task is not the writing of the past, but rather its preservation. Her area of expertise is 'die Erforschung urzeitlicher Tierskelette' (AT, p. 15). Within this temporal framework the forty years of the GDR are viewed as 'eine todgeweihte Mutation [...], deren Überleben weltgeschichtlich nicht einmal die Zeit einnehmen würde, die der Brachiosaurus brauchte, um einen seiner Füße vom Boden zu heben' (AT, pp. 31–32). Despite relativising the brief history of the GDR by retreating into the prehistoric, and even if criticism of the socialist state is far less frequent or indeed scathing than in previous Maron novels, the GDR is still portrayed in consistently negative terms. The narrator makes increasingly sporadic references to her life before Franz, a period repeatedly described as 'die seltsame Zeit' (AT, p. 40). In the aftermath of the Wende she is still baffled as to how the division of Europe could ever have transpired and wonders 'wie es damals einer als internationale Freiheitsbewegung getarnten Gangsterbande

---

[19] Lewis, p. 40.

gelingen konnte, das gesamte osteuropäische Festland [...] von der übrigen Welt hermetisch abzugrenzen und sich als legale Regierungen der jeweiligen Länder auszugeben' (AT, p. 30). The prevailing sense of confinement is evoked in the image of dreaming about distant countries 'wie Häftlinge von ihren Lieblingsspeisen' (AT, p. 86). The narrator recalls the fate of a co-worker who had always dreamt of using the museum's glass roof as the starting point for his balloon flight westwards. Although this escapade never materialised, her colleague did disappear one day, never to return, a postcard from Rome the only allusion to his successful defection. The narrator reflects on the arbitrary nature of the decisions made by the governing apparatus in the GDR and impacting upon millions of lives in the most cruel of fashions: 'Wie jedes Leben in Osteuropa geriet auch meins unter die Willkür des Absurden und wurde grausam zugerichtet' (AT, p. 32). Her disparaging reference to the dim-witted head of state, 'ein gelernter Dachdecker' (AT, p. 41), is a barely concealed allusion to Erich Honecker's early biography. 'Selbst Willkür bedarf auf Dauer einer ausgebildeten Intelligenz' (AT, p. 41) is her caustic comment on his incompetence.

The GDR – 'die vierzig Jahre Bandenherrschaft' (AT, p. 31), as the narrator calls it – insisted on a narrow perspective in its historical vision, imposed arbitrarily by what she terms a band of gangsters. The building of the Wall is described as a gangster's trick, this 'steinerne Anmaßung' (AT, p. 33) so abhorrent to the narrator because it separates her not only from the rest of the world, but, more intolerably still, from the ancient history so precious to her: 'sie raubte mir alles, dem ich mein Leben hatte verschreiben wollen' (AT, p. 34).

As a palaeontologist, the narrator willingly retreats from her contemporary society into the prehistoric era. A potent symbol of this distant past is the imposing brachiosaurus, the largest dinosaur housed in the Natural History Museum. Franz's description of the dinosaur as 'ein schönes Tier' (AT, p. 24) instantly endeared him to the narrator, for whom the brachiosaurus was an infinite source of comfort and hope: 'Während der seltsamen Zeit hatte er als Symbol eines anderen, von mir als höher anerkannten Sinns getaugt, weil die Gewißheit, daß, da er untergegangen war, alles einmal untergehen würde, so banal wie rettend war' (AT, pp. 130–31). This relativisation of the present through the prehistoric must be seen as part of the intertextuality of *Animal triste* for it is also a feature of Wilhelm Raabe's celebrated novel *Stopfkuchen*,

Love and Loss after the Wall: Animal triste

published in 1891. In his conscious withdrawal from a society that he regards dismissively as philistine and dishonest, the protagonist collects fossils, pride of place occupied by the skeleton of a bradypus.[20] For Stopfkuchen, the bradypus has become a 'Symbol erstrebenswerter überzeitlicher Gelassenheit; das verhindert geradezu die Verabsolutierung und Negativierung seiner Isolation.'[21] Similarly, in *Animal triste*, the majestic brachiosaurus symbolises constancy in the midst of chaos, its lasting presence pointing beyond the 'absurdity' (AT, p. 130) of the GDR and bringing to the narrator an 'ordnende Ruhe' (AT, p. 131). This intertext, far from being subversive, is a conscious temporal coexistence; the parallel with Raabe's novel represents a relativising of the present through the device of intertextuality.

The past is very much present in *Animal triste*. The narrator may not be a historian; yet, as Lewis observes, 'the past looms larger than life.'[22] Liberated from the despised 'Herrschaft des Absurden' (AT, p. 79), the former East Germany searches for meaning. The fall of the Berlin Wall initiates momentous historical and political change, which the narrator recalls only in the context of her love affair. The sociopolitical aspect of Maron's writing, although less explicit than in her pre-Wende texts, has not been abandoned completely. Preservation of the past is the focus of the narrator's professional life and, in this respect, the prehistoric brachiosaurus is invested with symbolic significance. On a personal level, too, the narrator is sustained by memories of her past with Franz, even if this obsessive and highly selective recollection is at the wilful exclusion of the present.

---

20 Stopfkuchen describes the bradypus as an essential part of his geological museum: 'Die Pièce de résistance, die Krone, mein Mammut'. Wilhelm Raabe, *Sämtliche Werke: Braunschweiger Ausgabe*, ed. by Karl Hoppe, xviii: *Stopfkuchen* und *Gutmanns Reisen* 2nd edn (Göttingen: Vandenhoeck & Ruprecht, 1969), p. 76.
21 Günther Matschke, *Die Isolation als Mittel der Gesellschaftskritik bei Wilhelm Raabe* (Bonn: Bouvier, 1975), p. 105.
22 Lewis, p. 30.

Remembering the Repressed

The interplay of forgetting and remembering, which was to inform the behaviour of all three generations in Maron's family story *Pawels Briefe*, was already being explored in her 1996 novel. Repression is at work on a grand scale in *Animal triste*; the full extent of the trauma at its source is revealed only on the final pages.

The narrator has retreated from the world in the wake of her lover's death. In this environment of self-imposed isolation, time has lost all significance: 'Für mich ist die Zeit mit Franz eine zeitlose, durch kein Zählwerk geordnete Zeit geblieben, in der ich mich seitdem befinde wie im luftigen Innern einer Kugel' (AT, p. 126). She is unsure even of her precise age. She begins by claiming to be one hundred years old, later conceding that she may be ninety or younger still. The length of time that has elapsed since Franz's departure remains unspecified. This uncertainty is reflected in the use of adverbs such as 'vielleicht' (AT, p. 9) and 'wahrscheinlich' (AT, p. 10) and of concessive remarks such as 'Es ist möglich, daß' (AT, p. 11). She is certain only of the season of her abandonment: Franz left on a rainy evening in autumn.

The narrator vividly remembers her lover's smell and touch. Bizarrely, however, she has forgotten his real name, choosing to call him Franz because it is 'ein schönes dunkles Wort wie Grab oder Sarg' (AT, p. 18). The narrator focuses on the sound of her lover's name: 'Man kann auch den Namen Franz sehr schön aussprechen, indem man das "a" möglichst dehnt, es tief ansetzt und am Ende leicht nach oben zieht, auf keinen Fall zu stark, das klänge albern, nur eine Nuance, damit der einzige Vokal zwischen den vier Konsonanten nicht zerquetscht wird' (AT, p. 18).

The narrator does not understand the urge to retain veritable mountains of irrelevant details in one's memory, as if these were somehow proof of an active life. In fact, her existence before Franz remains shrouded in uncertainty. Only a handful of childhood memories are recalled in detail. The first is her description of playing happy families with her friend Hansi amidst the rubble of the immediate post-war period. This family idyll is quickly shattered when she recalls her father's return from war and the submissive role subsequently assumed by her mother. As in Maron's earlier novels *Die Überläuferin* and *Stille Zeile Sechs*, the narrator's relationship with her father is marked by tension and distrust. A further childhood memory is initiated by Franz's comment about

Love and Loss after the Wall: Animal triste 113

Hadrian's Wall. He reacts to his lover's suspicion and jealousy by explaining that Hadrian's biographer described the Wall as the border between Romans and Barbarians. The narrator's 'Gefühl höllischer Verlorenheit' (AT, p. 158) prompts recollection of a painful memory. As punishment for a childhood misdemeanour, she was locked into the family apartment, while her parents attended a birthday party. A distraught narrator screamed her loss through the keyhole. Many years later a similar sense of abandonment propels her to scream down the telephone line 'daß ich keine Barbarin sei' (AT, p. 158)

Significantly, the narrator employs an archaeological analogy when she describes her memory as 'uraltes Gestein, in dem sich hier und da ein Abdruck findet, so wie die seltsamen vogelartigen Fußspuren in Pliny Moodys Garten' (AT, p. 111).[23] She reflects on the arbitrary nature of recollection, the brachiosaurus providing an appropriate example. Forgotten by humanity for some one hundred and fifty million years, an archaeological discovery initiates a sudden interest in this prehistoric creature. The narrator also notes the paring down of memories accompanying the passage of time: 'Wir haben Zeit, unsere Erinnerungen so zu feilen und zu schleifen, bis die Versatzstücke am Ende zu einer halbwegs plausiblen Biographie verschraubt werden können' (AT, p. 145). This mention of set pieces prefigures Maron's reference in *Pawels Briefe* to the perfectly choreographed packets of memory that her mother Hella has stored away, ready to be recalled upon request (PB, p. 166–67).

Certain motifs recur throughout the narrator's erratic recollection: the greyness of Franz's eyes, his lying between the flesh-eating plants that pattern the sheets and form the bizarre backdrop to their lovemaking.[24] Lewis notes that, in Freudian terms, these are screen memories: 'significant [...] in terms

23 Long before she met Franz, the narrator had dreamt of travelling to Massachusetts because she wished to see 'die seltsamen vogelartigen Fußspuren [...], die Pliny Moody aus South Hadley, Massachusetts, schon am Anfang des neunzehnten Jahrhunderts in seinem eigenen Garten gefunden hat' (AT, p. 33).
24 Lothar Bluhm interprets this motif as another example of intertextuality in the novel: 'Die Bezüge zwischen Marons Paläontologin und der Kleistschen Dramenfigur sind vielfältig und reichen ins Detail: So findet sich etwa die zentrale Szene des Kleist-Dramas, Penthesileas anthropophages Zerreißen des von ihr getöteten Geliebten, bei Maron im Motiv der fleischfressenden Pflanze auf der Decke des Liebes-Bettes bildlich aufgenommen.' '"Irgendwann, denken wir, muß ich das genau wissen": Der Erinnerungsdiskurs bei Monika Maron', in *Mentalitätswandel in der deutschen Literatur zur Einheit (1999–2000)*, ed. by Volker Wehdeking (Berlin: Erich Schmidt, 2000), pp. 141–51 (p. 146).

of what they conceal from the narrator's consciousness and conscience.'[25] By replaying these apparently insignificant details, the narrator represses the trauma that ensued after the comforting bedroom scene.[26] It is only in the final pages of the text that the full extent of this personal trauma is revealed. For the first time she remembers to the end: 'heute will ich mich bis ans Ende erinnern und dann niemals mehr. Heute werde ich aufhören, auf Franz zu warten' (AT, p. 198). His death ends their love story in a brutally irreversible manner: 'Das Ende ist eindeutig und entscheidet alles, das Ende ist nicht korrigierbar. Darum habe ich es vergessen' (AT, p. 232). Repression has its roots in personal trauma that is too painful for the narrator to remember, not only because of her profound sense of loss, but also because of her implication in Franz's death. Andrea Köhler interprets the novel's title in terms of poignant memories: 'Der Mensch ist das traurige Tier, weil er sich erinnert.'[27]

In *Animal triste* Maron examines the post-Wende attitude to remembering and forgetting. Before her retreat from society the narrator was acutely aware that forgetting was considered to be 'sündhaft' (AT, p. 17). In *Pawels Briefe* Maron goes on to criticise the confessional climate and public nature of recollection in a unified Germany, commenting that her mother's inability to remember has become synonymous with repression and lies (PB, p. 11). Despite her observation that forgetting is 'die Ohnmacht der Seele' (AT, p. 17), the narrator of *Animal triste* concedes that she has conditioned herself to forget unpleasant aspects of her past, recovering only chosen comforting memories from the 'Unendlichkeit meines Vergessens' (AT, p. 37). She does not conceal her contempt for the fashionable trend of remembering: 'von den

---

25   Lewis, p. 33.
26   In his essay 'Über Deckerinnerungen', first published in 1899 in the *Monatsschrift für Psychiatrie und Neurologie*, Freud theorises that we construct the past in the service of the present. He describes the unconscious fabrication of childhood memories that enables us to displace disturbing aspects of the past: 'eingehende Untersuchung zeigt [...], daß solche Erinnerungsfälschungen tendenziöse sind, d.h. daß sie den Zwecken der Verdrängung und Ersetzung von anstößigen oder unliebsamen Eindrücken dienen.' 'Über Deckerinnerungen', in *Gesammelte Werke: Chronologisch geordnet*, i: *Werke aus den Jahren 1892–1899* (London: Imago Publishing, 1952), pp. 531–54 (p. 553).
27   Andrea Köhler, 'Der Mensch, das traurige Tier', *Neue Zürcher Zeitung*, 22 February 1994, p. 41. For Köhler, the love story is far less important than the text's reflections on the 'Eigengesetzlichkeit der Erinnerung und "die Ohnmacht der Seele"'.

Menschen zur Kostbarkeit erhoben' (AT, p. 107). Unequivocal in her disdain for the contemporary obsession with memories, 'eigentlich eine Krankheit' (AT, p. 107), she embarks on a deliberate course of forgetting. Franz acts as a catalyst for the drastic extinguishing of her past life. She forgets other lovers, former acts of tenderness and experiences of passion. Lewis underscores the importance of the adverb 'nachträglich': Franz is 'that principle which bestows meaning retrospectively [...] the cause and telos of a rewriting of the narrator's life history'.[28] The narrator reflects: 'Nachträglich scheint es mir, als ergäbe mein ganzes Leben vom Tag meiner Geburt an nur einen Sinn, wenn ich es als ein einziges langes Warten auf Franz verstehe' (AT, p. 51). Later in the text she concedes: 'Wir schreiben unser Leben um, weil es uns nachträglich sein Ziel offenbart hat' (AT, p. 181).

The narrator appears happy to rewrite her life story in light of her momentous encounter with Franz. In so doing, she forgets her previous life. Even her husband and daughter have become nothing more than a distant memory. She has also repressed the rather gruesome ending to her love story. The absurd nature of the repressed in the text – the grotesque type of murder and the mystery in which it remains shrouded – is significant. In *Animal triste* Maron explores and confidently subverts the post-unification pressure to remember.

Conclusion

Animal triste is an intimate exploration of all-consuming love and loss. 'Man kann im Leben nichts versäumen als die Liebe' (AT, p. 23), the narrator announces at the very outset. The contrast between the passions of the Amazonian queen and the banality of the context in which such passions are invoked emphasises the author's ironical treatment of Kleist's tragedy. The intertextuality of the novel is constantly undermined by a relentless pragmatic realism.

---

28 Lewis, p. 32.

Animal triste moves away from certain preoccupations of the previous texts, most obviously the sustained attack on the GDR, and this turning away assumes an exaggerated, grotesque character. However, the novel also belongs within a continuity of Maron's writing, taking up several of the themes addressed in *Stille Zeile Sechs*, while also prefiguring the concerns of *Pawels Briefe*. The pronounced physicality of the text, particularly its preoccupation with the ageing body, recalls *Stille Zeile Sechs* and anticipates a central theme in *Endmoränen*.

The narrator's carefully constructed 'jahrzehntelanges Vergessenswerk' (AT, p. 32) finally collapses when she remembers to the end, confronting the painful reality of her culpability. In *Pawels Briefe* Maron's probing at familial gaps in memory, or 'Erinnerungslücken' (PB, p. 17), also initiates an unearthing of the repressed. Anticipating a seminal concern of Maron's family story, *Animal triste* is a sustained, if unconventional reflection on the interplay of remembering and forgetting.

The narrator's recollection of intimate memories marks an inward turn in Maron's writing. However, the personal and the political coalesce; history is inscribed onto the body, a city in political turmoil forming the explosive backdrop to the love affair. The narrator's obsession with Franz is so intense that a milestone in German history is processed only in terms of her personal biography. The sociopolitical dimension of Maron's writing never evaporates completely, not even in this veritable *tour de force* of erotic and personal memory.

CHAPTER FIVE

Exposing the Gaps in Memory: Forgetting and Remembering in *Pawels Briefe*

Monika Maron's family story *Pawels Briefe*, published in 1999, is a sustained reflection on the workings of memory. As such, it testifies to the thematic continuity of her writing. *Stille Zeile Sechs* had juxtaposed conflicting memories of life in the GDR; Beerenbaum's hagiographic account of defining moments in GDR history contrasted sharply with Rosalind's childhood experience. The narrator of *Animal triste* had retreated into the most intimate of memories; the full extent of the trauma that she attempted to repress only became clear on the final pages of the text. Memory is the central theme in *Pawels Briefe* as Maron attempts to probe her mother's memory gaps and reconstruct a family story brutally ruptured by her grandfather's execution at Nazi hands. The author herself underscores the central importance of memory and its repression in her text: 'Und mich interessierte, wie die Erinnerung auf uns kommt, durch welche Temperamente und Überlebenstechniken sie gefiltert wird und wie viel für immer dem Vergessen anheim gefallen ist.'[1] In this chapter I will explore memory transmission, generational memory gaps, and the interplay of forgetting and remembering that informs Maron's family story.[2]

Pawels Briefe: Eine Familiengeschichte encompasses three generations: the eponymous Pawel, his daughter Hella and his granddaughter Monika. In

---

1   Monika Maron, 'Rollenwechsel: Über einen Text und seine Kritiker', in *Quer über die Gleise: Artikel, Essays, Zwischenrufe* (Frankfurt am Main: S. Fischer, 2000), pp. 95–116 (p. 107). 'Rollenwechsel: Über einen Text und seine Kritiker' was part of the series of lectures on poetics that Maron delivered in Zürich in 1999. Quotations from the text will be followed in parentheses by 'Rollenwechsel' and the relevant page number.
2   This chapter has its genesis in my article 'Exposing the Gaps in Memory: Forgetting and Remembering in Monika Maron's *Pawels Briefe*', which was published in *Cultural Memory: Essays in European Literature and History*, ed. by Edric Caldicott and Anne Fuchs (Oxford: Peter Lang, 2003), pp. 147–59.

a 1992 interview to which I referred in the introductory chapter, Maron had emphasised the exemplary aspects of her family story. 'Das Schicksal unserer Familie ist wie ein Muster in das Schicksal dieses Landes eingezeichnet',[3] she explained, thereby situating her turbulent family biography within the interstices of twentieth-century German history. Historical processes, such as the rise and devastating consequences of fascism, the founding of the GDR and the ultimate collapse of the antifascist state, are described as they shape her family story. From Pawel's arrival in Berlin at the turn of the century to his execution in 1942, from the liberation of Berlin in 1945 to the post-unification period, *Pawels Briefe* articulates the reciprocal relationship between individual experience and overarching historical structure, a relationship in no way diminished by the radical breaks in that structure. In 'Rollenwechsel', Maron's reply to the varied and even contradictory responses that the text had evoked amongst critics, she foregrounds the sustained fracturing of her family biography: 'die fortgesetzten Brüche in den Lebensläufen aller beteiligten Generationen' (p. 107). The rupture in the generational structure – as a result not only of Pawel's execution, but also of polarised political systems and ideologies down through the generations – thus echoes the fragmented experience of twentieth-century German history.

I will begin my analysis of *Pawels Briefe* by considering how Maron finally came to write the story of her maternal grandparents, who were figures of continuity in her writing, having featured even in the opening sequence of her debut novel. The section entitled 'Reconstructing the Past' will examine the role of the documentary material, including rediscovered family photographs and letters, which serve as the point of departure for the imaginary reconstruction of her grandparents' life together. The subsequent section explores the interplay of forgetting and remembering that is present throughout Maron's family story: Pawel's renunciation of his Jewish faith, Hella's repression of traumatic aspects of her past, and, in the third generation, Maron's reluctance to confront her Stasi-involvement some two decades previously. Earlier Maron texts had depicted the protagonists' confrontation with *Vater Staat*; in *Pawels Briefe* she explores for the first time her relationship with her mother, as the final part of this chapter 'Mending a Fractured Family Biography: The

---

[3] Michael Hametner, 'Von Opfern, die Täter wurden', *Börsenblatt für den Deutschen Buchhandel*, 26 June 1992, p. 42.

Mother–Daughter Relationship' will illustrate. Maron's family story can be situated within a contemporary theoretical landscape concerned with the nature and function of memory and its repression.

'Erinnerungen haben ihre Zeit'

In the opening sequence of *Pawels Briefe*, Maron ponders her reasons for finally consigning her grandparents' story to print: 'warum jetzt, warum erst jetzt, warum jetzt noch' (PB, p. 7). Following a reading in Berlin in 1999, she described her maternal grandparents as 'Portale' in her work, having been a source of inspiration from the very beginning of her writing career.[4] She had originally intended that the story of Pawel and Josefa function as a counter-text to Josefa's experiences in *Flugasche*. However, 'alles wurde überwuchert von meinem Hadern mit der DDR', she concedes.[5] Although remembering the past is an important theme in *Flugasche*, the issues and struggles of the GDR were so overwhelming that there was no space for those familial memories extending further into the past.

In the opening paragraph of *Pawels Briefe*, Maron compensates for these deficits by reminding her readers that the first chapter of her debut novel was devoted to Pawel and Josefa. The heroine of *Flugasche* was also called Josefa, her surname 'Nadler' the German translation of Pawel's family name, in Polish 'Iglarz'. She describes her grandfather's execution in the very first lines: 'den Großvater Pawel hatte man [...] in ein polnisches Kornfeld getrieben. Als der Großvater und die anderen Juden in der Mitte des Kornfeldes angekommen waren, hatte man es von allen Seiten angezündet' (FA, p. 7). In the opening sequence of *Flugasche*, Maron had thus already anticipated the profound sense of loss that was to resonate throughout her poignant tribute to her grandfather two decades later.

---

4   'Meine Großeltern stehen wie Portale in meinem Schreiben', Maron commented during the discussion that followed her reading in the Brecht-Haus on 22 April 1999.
5   Literaturforum im Brecht-Haus, 22 April 1999.

This has not been her grandparents' only appearance in Maron's writing: Pawel and Josefa also featured in her autobiographical essay 'Ich war ein antifaschistisches Kind', published in 1989. She writes there of their conversion to the Baptist faith and of their life in Neukölln before Pawel's expulsion in 1938. He and Josefa returned to Poland the following year. Maron relates what a Polish relative told her of Pawel's execution: 'Deutsche waren es [...], die ihn und andere Juden aus dem Ghetto in einen Wald brachten, ihn zwangen, sein eigenes Grab zu graben, und ihn erschossen' (*Begreifungskraft*, p. 14). Maron was to revisit significant stations of Pawel's life and death in her family story published a decade later.

'Erinnerungen haben ihre Zeit' (PB, p. 7), Maron announces in the very opening sequence of *Pawels Briefe*. This observation implies that there is an opportune or, at very least, an enabling time for recalling particular memories. In an interview conducted in February 1999, the author established a direct correlation between the collapse of the GDR and the opportune moment for recording a story that had lain dormant for so many years:

> Es gibt einfach Geschichten, die bleiben einem, die trägt man mit sich herum und denkt: irgendwann, irgendwann mache ich das richtig [...] Ich weiß gar nicht, ob ich dazu gekommen wäre, wenn die DDR fortbestanden hätte [...] Ich glaube, daß ich das gebraucht habe – diese Freiheit zu sagen, es ist vorbei. Da ist nichts mehr [...] Ich habe eine Ruhe. Ich kann mich auch mit den Geschichten danach in Ruhe befassen, mit einer Gerechtigkeit, die so ein Stoff braucht. ('Zwischentöne')

The liberating impulse of the Wende facilitated the reconstruction of her grandparents' story. However, the author's attempts to recover the details of her grandparents' life and death were themselves filtered through the complexities of how mother and daughter remembered a shared GDR past. The demise of the antifascist state thus continued to shape Maron's text on familial remembering.

The arrival of a Dutch television crew in Berlin in the summer of 1994 to film a documentary on the Germans acted as the catalyst for composition of *Pawels Briefe*. Motivated by the question 'Wann werden die Deutschen endlich normal?' (PB, p. 10), they interviewed people from a variety of professional backgrounds and belonging to different generations, Maron's mother included. In the search for relevant photographs, Hella unearthed a bundle of old letters that she had acquired upon the death of her sister eleven years previously. The correspondence dated from the early 1940s, the final months of Pawel's life before his execution: 'Briefe meines Großvaters aus dem Ghetto und Briefe seiner Kinder an ihn' (PB, p. 10). Shortly before this discovery, a newspaper had suggested to the author that she write about a chosen destination. She had decided upon Ostrow-Mazowiecka, the Polish village where Pawel was born. Maron comments: 'Zwei Wege führten zur gleichen Zeit an denselben Ort, nachdem jahrzehntelang alle Wege an ihm vorbeigeführt und ihn höchstens für Minuten am Horizont hatten aufscheinen lassen' (PB, p. 12). The reference to an opportune time for remembering implies a readiness on Maron's part to look beyond the tensions of a strained mother–daughter relationship: 'Ich mußte aufgehört haben, meine Eltern zu bekämpfen, um mich über das Maß der eigenen Legitimation hinaus für meine Großeltern und ihre Geschichte wirklich zu interessieren' (PB, p. 13). The enabling moment is thus intimately connected with Maron's desire to pursue familial bonds: 'Ich mußte bereit sein, den Fortgang der Geschichte, die Verbindung zu mir, das Leben meiner Mutter, einfach nur verstehen zu wollen, als wäre es mein eigenes Leben gewesen' (PB, p. 13). A sequence of events – the collapse of the GDR, the discovery of photographs and letters, and Maron's own willingness to explore familial affiliation – all facilitated recollection and the opportune time for the composition of *Pawels Briefe*.

Reconstructing the Past

At the very beginning of her text, Maron explains that remembering is, in fact, the incorrect term to describe the manner in which she attempts to access her grandparents' past: 'Erinnern ist für das, was ich mit meinen Großeltern vorhatte, eigentlich das falsche Wort, denn in meinem Innern gab es kein versunkenes Wissen über sie, das ich hätte zutage fördern können [...] Das Wesen meiner Großeltern bestand für mich in ihrer Abwesenheit' (PB, p. 8). Maron it thus deprived of communicative memory, a term coined by the historians Jan and Aleida Assmann to describe the memories transmitted via everyday communication between family members.[6] Maron was only one year old when

---

6 In his essay 'Collective Memory and Cultural Identity', Jan Assmann explains that the most important characteristic of communicative memory is its limited temporal horizon,

Pawel was executed: she can at best reconstruct his story from the written and visual traces documenting his past: 'eine imaginäre Wiederherstellung'[7] is how Frank Schirrmacher aptly describes her task. The author emphasises the importance of montage as a literary form of reconstruction, in particular its potential to bring past and present together. She describes her text as 'eine ganz und gar kontrollierte Montage, die es mir ermöglicht hat, Vergangenes und Gegenwärtiges ständig in Bezug zu setzen' ('Rollenwechsel', p. 108). In this section I will explore the interplay between the documentary material and the imaginary act Maron invests in the reconstruction of her family story.

Presence and Absence: The Role of Photographs

Photographs of various family members feature throughout Maron's text. The immediate visual impact of photographs ostensibly promotes recollection and authenticates the past. However, their role in Maron's narrative is complex and occasionally ambiguous. 'All photographs are *memento mori*', Susan Sontag writes in her influential text *On Photography*, first published in 1977, 'A photograph is both a pseudo-presence and a token of absence.'[8] In his text *La chambre claire: Note sur la photographie*, Roland Barthes also articulates this dual function: a photograph is at once 'un certificat de présence,'[9] and 'cette image qui produit la Mort en voulant conserver la vie'.[10] In a book that has come to occupy an important place in discussions on memory, *Family Frames: Photography, Narrative and Postmemory*, Marianne Hirsch develops

---

extending no more than eighty to one hundred years into the past. This generational structure has obvious resonances for Maron's family story. It is this temporal aspect that distinguishes communicative memory from cultural memory, which is characterised by distance from the everyday. *New German Critique*, 65 (1995), 125–33 (p. 127).

7 Frank Schirrmacher, literary editor of the *Frankfurter Allgemeine Zeitung*, in which *Pawels Briefe* had been serialised prior to its publication by the S. Fischer publishing house, introduced Maron before her reading in the Schaubühne, Berlin on 21 February 1999.

8 Susan Sontag, *On Photography* (Harmondsworth: Penguin 1979), pp. 15–16.

9 Roland Barthes, *La chambre claire: Note sur la photographie* (Poitiers: Gallimard Seuil, 1980), p. 135.

10 Ibid., p. 144.

Exposing the Gaps in Memory: Forgetting and Remembering in Pawels Briefe 123

the concept of postmemory in relation to the children of Holocaust survivors, explaining that it is also applicable to other second-generation memories of cultural and collective trauma. It is distinguished from memory by generational distance and from history by deep personal connection. Hirsch explores what she terms the photographic aesthetics of postmemory: 'the photograph's capacity to signal absence and loss and, at the same time, to make present, rebuild, reconnect, bring back to life.'[11] The fluctuation between presence and absence is essential to analysis of the visual images in *Pawels Briefe*. The photographs testify to this dual role: they facilitate reconstruction of a family story, even if any attempts to recall a pre-war past are overshadowed by Pawel's horrific death.

We turn at this point to the photographic images reproduced in Maron's text. A single photograph of Pawel's father is the only evidence of a childhood and youth spent in Ostrow. A detailed description accompanies the image. The enlarged close-up of the old man's hand resting upon an open book prompts Maron to consider the discrepancy between the learned aura that the photograph evokes and the reality of her great-grandfather's illiteracy. Far from authenticating the past, this image misleads its viewer. Interpreting this particular photograph, Sibylle Cramer sees in the open book an important symbolic dimension: 'Mit Hilfe der einzigen erhaltenen Photographie des Urgroßvaters blättert Pawels Enkelin die Geschichte familiären Vergessens zurück'.[12] Structuring her text around the rediscovered photographs, Maron attempts to counter familial forgetting.

In the early 1920s the family decided to emigrate, tempted by the promise of a better life and an uncle already living in America. The only evidence of this daring enterprise, thwarted by the uncle's sudden death, is a family portrait destined for the immigration authorities and accompanied in Maron's text by a lengthy description. One aspect, five-year-old Hella's face, appears on a subsequent page, in a slightly enlarged format. As the youngest child, Hella is sitting, flanked by Pawel and Josefa, while the three older siblings stand behind their parents and sister. Maron is enthralled by what she terms the elegance of the family's pose, proud of their immaculate clothing and

---

11   Marianne Hirsch, *Family Frames: Photography, Narrative and Postmemory* (Cambridge, MA and London: Harvard University Press, 1997), p. 243.
12   Sibylle Cramer, 'Der Sprung durch die Zeit und die gerettete Geschichte', *Süddeutsche Zeitung*, 20/21 February 1999, *Literatur* p. IV.

of their brave, even haughty demeanour. Looking at the photograph, she is overcome by an indeterminate longing, inspired by the 'Glücksverheißung' (PB, p. 46), the promise of happiness that the picture contains.

A number of photographs document her grandparents' life in Berlin before the devastating rupture of their family story caused by Pawel's deportation and execution: Josefa in the kitchen, Pawel surrounded by members of his cycling club. With the imminent outbreak of World War II, the Jewish-born Pawel was sent to a camp on the German-Polish border, returning to Berlin in the summer of 1939. A photograph that Maron assumes was taken during this two-week period depicts an exhausted, despairing Pawel: 'der Mund sehr verschlossen, als hätte er das Sprechen aufgegeben; Augen, in denen sich keine Erwartung mehr spiegelt, nur schreckliche Gewißheit. Ein erschöpfter, ein verzweifelter Mann' (PB, p. 84). Following expulsion from Germany, Pawel and Josefa returned to her native Kurow, where they lived with her sister Jadwiga until Pawel's internment in Belchatow in 1942. A particularly poignant photograph, reproduced first as a complete shot, shows husband and wife sitting together behind Jadwiga's house in July 1939 shortly after their arrival. The subsequent close-up of their hands placed side by side expresses the couple's intimacy and devotion. Josefa is looking into the distance, an inscrutable expression on her face, leading Maron to ponder: 'Weint sie? Oder betet sie? Fragt sie ihren Gott, womit sie diese Strafe verdient hat?' (PB, p. 97) What Aleida Assmann terms the irreducible ambivalence of pictures is evident here, the apparent immediacy of a visual image tempered by its inherent 'Intransparenz'.[13] Despite this fundamental impenetrability, Maron probes further and imagines what Pawel may have said to comfort his wife: 'Juscha, sagt mein Großvater. Was sagt er noch? Was kann er, der sich als Verursacher ihres Unglücks fühlt, ihr sagen?' (PB, p. 97) This series of questions is emblematic of the tension in photographs between, as Hirsch observes, 'the little a photograph can reveal and all that it promises to reveal but cannot.'[14]

---

13   Aleida Assmann, *Erinnerungsräume: Formen und Wandlungen des kulturellen Gedächtnisses* (Munich: Beck, 1999), p. 220. Quotations from the text will be followed in parentheses by the word *Erinnerungsräume* and the relevant page number.
14   Hirsch, p. 119. Sontag formulates this tension as follows: 'the camera's rendering of reality must always hide more than it discloses' (*On Photography*, p. 23).

In the first section of *Pawels Briefe*, Maron seeks to reconstruct her grandparents' past from the surviving documentary evidence. Photographs deepen her understanding of figures who clearly exercised a formative influence. Maron's recollection of her life in the GDR shapes the second, shorter part of the text. Here the photographs document the political context far more explicitly. Hella features in all of the photographs from the post-war period: Hella, her sister Marta and friends celebrating the liberation of Berlin by the Soviet Army in 1945, Hella at the Party School two years later, mother and daughter in 1953. Maron describes in particular detail one small, frayed photograph and estimates that it dates from 1946/47. Reproduced in the text, it depicts a political march and shows Hella and Monika in the midst of the demonstrators. In marked contrast to the private and intimate nature of the photos hitherto, the collective nature of photographs in the GDR emerges here, together with their role as official chronicles. The collective involves natural structures such as the family, but includes them within the obviously ideological structures of class and party. This photograph portrays the importance of political and ideological direction after the defeat of fascism. A close-up of Monika, clutching her mother's hand as they march through a landscape of rubble, appears on a subsequent page. Maron finds it hard to recall either the photograph or its deeper message. Hella, for her part, can no longer remember the precise details of the event: perhaps a May Day demonstration or Remembrance Day for the victims of fascism. In retrospect, her daughter questions the authenticity of the image: 'Ob ich die flüchtigen Bilder, die sich für mich mit dem Foto verbinden, wirklich auf dieser Demonstration gesehen habe [...] oder ob ich sie nur aus einem Film kenne, der mich an das Foto erinnert hat, kann ich nicht sicher sagen' (PB, p. 164). However, this childhood scene evokes a sense of solidarity and belonging: 'Die Gewißheit, daß Genossen bessere und klügere Menschen sind als andere, war Teil meines kindlichen Denkens' (PB, p. 165), Maron reflects. The mother–daughter relationship depicted in this photograph is subsumed into the official GDR narrative. Maron's comment 'Die Menschen waren Genossen, und wir gehörten dazu' (PB, p. 165) underscores the inherently collective nature of life in the socialist state and locates this photograph at the intersection of private and official history.

Photographs are an integral element of *Pawels Briefe*. Dotted throughout the text, they portray an individual family story, but also function as sociohistorical documents. The photographs of Pawel and Josefa are 'media of mourning',[15] testimony to a life overshadowed by its horrific end. Maron introduces visual images in order to counter familial forgetting. Simultaneously, however, they testify to the difficulty of such an ambitious task. Friederike Eigler observes: 'vielmehr werden die Fotos selbst Zeichen für die Schwierigkeit, die Familiengeschichte anhand spärlicher Zeitdokumente zu rekonstruieren.'[16] Indeed, as Barthes argues, photographs may actually hinder recollection: 'Non seulement la Photo n'est jamais, en essence, un souvenir [...] mais encore elle le bloque, devient très vite un contre-souvenir.'[17] Maron seems to show that they remind of things that may not be their apparent subject. Hirsch situates photographs at the junction between forgetting and remembering when she writes: 'Photographs, ghostly revenants, are very particular instruments of remembrance, since they are perched on the edge between memory and postmemory, and also, though differently, between memory and forgetting.'[18] In Maron's text, too, photographs occupy this tentative position as 'the leftovers, the fragmentary sources and building blocks, shot through with holes, of the work of postmemory. They affirm the past's existence and, in their flat two-dimensionality, they signal its unbridgeable distance.'[19]

Written Records

Together with the reproduction of family photographs, Maron also considers written records from the period in which her grandfather lived. In order to recreate the atmosphere of Berlin in the 1930s, she inserts documentary material about Neukölln into her narrative: an extract, for example, from the *Neuköllner Tagesblatt* of November 1930, a medical report from the

---

15   Hirsch, p. 256.
16   Friederike Eigler, 'Nostalgisches und kritisches Erinnern am Beispiel von Martin Walsers *Ein springender Brunnen* und Monika Marons *Pawels Briefe*', in *Monika Maron in Perspective: 'Dialogische' Einblicke in zeitgeschichtliche, intertextuelle und rezeptionsbezogene Aspekte ihres Werkes*, ed. by Elke Gilson, German Monitor, 55 (Amsterdam and New York: Rodopi, 2002), pp. 157–80 (p. 164).
17   Barthes, p. 142.
18   Hirsch, p. 22.
19   Ibid., p. 23.

Neukölln school doctor dated 1931. Official documents are introduced at intervals throughout the text, beginning with a copy of Pawel's birth certificate located among the rediscovered papers: 'Diese Urkunde [...] anmutet wie eine Nachricht, nicht nur aus einem anderen Jahrhundert, sondern aus einer anderen Welt' (PB, p. 15), his granddaughter observes. The copy, in the Russian original and in German translation, dates from February 1939. Intending to marry her German boyfriend Walter, who was Maron's biological father, Hella had acquired the necessary official documentation: 'Geburts- und Heiratsurkunden [...] alle beschafft und übersetzt, um die schützende Ehe mit einem Arier zu schließen, was nicht gelang' (PB, p. 16). She attempted to convince the German authorities that her father, a convert to the Baptist faith, was not Jewish, 'was auch nicht gelang' (PB, p. 16). When confronted with a document for which she herself had applied more than fifty years previously, Hella's 'Erinnerungslücken' (PB, p. 17) open up. Maron speculates that Hella, realising the devastating repercussions of her father's Jewish name, had wished to replace it with another: 'Und weil das nicht möglich war, hat sie ihn in ihrem eigenen Kopf getilgt' (PB, p. 17). The birth certificate is more than mere historical record; Hella has repressed whole sequences of her past, as is evident in her bewildered reaction to the recovered document. These gaps in memory, which appear to characterise an entire generation, will be explored later in the chapter.

The surviving letters from Pawel are the most valuable written records that his granddaughter has at her disposal. Maron structures the first part of her text around the extracts from Pawel's correspondence, providing a framework that facilitates her attempts to understand the grandfather she never knew. A profound sense of loss resonates throughout:

> Seine Briefe klingen nach wie ein endloser weher Gesang [...] Unter meinen Erinnerungen mischt sich [...] die verspätete Sehnsucht nach meinem Großvater. Ich wünschte, es hätte ihn in meinem Leben gegeben. Ich kann mir einfach nicht vorstellen, daß unser Leben mit Pawel ebenso verlaufen wäre, wie es ohne ihn verlaufen ist. (PB, pp. 180–81)

During his period at the border camp Pawel made repeated efforts to save himself. Three letters, which are addressed to him and integrated into Maron's text, document his ultimately futile attempts to secure an entrance permit for England. In the next letter reproduced in the text, a letter written three years later, Pawel reproaches himself for what he perceives as cowardice, for his unability, during his two-week stay in Berlin in the summer of 1939, to carry out his intention of committing suicide in order to spare Josefa the subsequent pain of separation from her children. In letters written during the months prior to his execution, he asks for forgiveness: 'Von ihnen erbittet er Verzeihung für seine Abstammung, für das Unglück der Mutter, für seine Ohnmacht vor ihrem Tod' (PB, p. 138). A postcard addressed to Hella is reproduced in the text. The Belchatow postmark and June 1942 date appear in an enlarged format on a subsequent page, at once historical document and ominous reminder of the ineluctable fate awaiting its sender.

There is frequent reference to Monika in Pawel's correspondence. In his penultimate letter he instructs his children: 'Zeigt niemals dem Kinde, daß es Haß, Neid und Rache giebt. Sie soll ein wertvoller Mensch werden' (PB, p. 112). When Maron reads her name in this context, the temporal distance between past and present is overcome, albeit fleetingly:

> Wenn ich in Pawels Briefen meinen Namen finde, [...] wenn ich mir vorstelle, daß der Mann, der diese Briefe schrieb, an mich dachte, auf mich hoffte, verliert das Wort Vergangenheit für Minuten seinen Sinn. Dann werden die Jahre durchlässig und der 26. Juli oder der 8. August 1942 gehören zu den Tagen meines erinnerbaren Lebens. (PB, p. 141)

Pawel's letters thus occupy a central position within the montage format, enabling Maron to trace the fate of what she terms a submerged generation: 'die Schicksale dieser gerade versunkenen Generation' (PB, p. 7).

The Topography of Memory

In her book *Erinnerungsräume: Formen und Wandlungen des kulturellen Gedächtnisses*, the Konstanz historian Aleida Assmann explores the media in which memories are preserved: writing, visual images, the body, in particular as corporeal expression of traumatic memories, physical spaces. I have examined the role of photographs and of written records in the reconstruction of Maron's family story; the focus now moves to the geographical sites of memory that form a very distinct topography within her text.

In his seminal text *Les Lieux de Mémoire*, published in 1984, the French historian Pierre Nora argues that in the modern era memory has given way to

Exposing the Gaps in Memory: Forgetting and Remembering in Pawels Briefe 129

history as events disappear with increasing rapidity into an irretrievable past: 'un basculement de plus en plus rapide dans un passé définitivement mort.'[20] He postulates that memory has become a process of minute reconstruction. Modern memory is archival: 'Elle s'appuie tout entière sur le plus précis de la trace, le plus matériel du vestige, le plus concret de l'enregistrement, le plus visible de l'image.'[21] Nora coined the term *lieu de mémoire*: 'Les lieux de mémoire, ce sont d'abord des restes. La forme extrême où subsiste une conscience commémorative'.[22] *Pawels Briefe* depicts several such realms of memory and it is to these sites that our attention now turns.

As part of her effort to reconstruct her grandparents' past, Maron, her son Jonas and her mother Hella embark in the mid-1990s upon a journey to Ostrow, the Polish village where Pawel was born. Instead of finding a physical realm of memory, however, the visitors encounter resistance to memories. The hostile response of the Ostrow community derives from a deep-seated reticence to discuss the past, particularly as the past that Maron wishes to reclaim is a Jewish one. In Kurow the house of Josefa's sister Jadwiga is no longer standing. Maron wonders if what she does in fact discover – the church where her maternal grandmother was baptised, Josefa's grave bearing the incorrect date of death (1947 instead of 1942) – hinders rather than advances her attempts to arrive at a better understanding of the past Pawel seemed so determined to leave behind. She is filled with doubt: 'Schon in Kurow hatte ich Zweifel [...] [ich] fragte [...] mich, ob mich all diese Bilder nicht eher störten, ob die

---

20   Pierre Nora, 'Entre Mémoire et Histoire: La problématique des lieux', in *Les Lieux de Mémoire*, sous la direction de Pierre Nora (Paris: Éditions Gallimard, 1997), pp. 23–43 (p. 23). *Les Lieux de Memoire* comprised seven volumes that were first published 1984–92. The English translation by Arthur Goldhammer reads as follows: 'Things tumble with increasing rapidity into an irretrievable past.' *Realms of Memory: The Construction of the French Past*, trans. by Arthur Goldhammer (New York: Columbia University Press, 1996), p. 1.
21   Nora, p. 30. Goldhammer's translation reads: 'It relies entirely on the specificity of the trace, the materiality of the vestige, the concreteness of the recording, the visibility of the image' (p. 8).
22   Nora, p. 28. Goldhammer provides the following English translation: '*Lieux de memoire* are fundamentally vestiges, the ultimate embodiment of a commemorative consciousness' (p. 6). Nora emphasises the inherently symbolic aspect of the *lieux de mémoire*: 'un cercle à l'intérieur duquel tout compte, tout symbolise, tout signifie' (p. 43). Goldhammer translates as follows: 'a circle within which everything counts, everything is symbolic, everything is significant' (p. 20).

Festlegungen mir meinen Weg der Annäherung nicht verstellten' (PB, p. 94). All traces of her grandfather's Jewish origins have been obliterated: 'In Ostrow-Mazowiecka leben keine Juden mehr. Unter dem Wort Jüdisch findet sich im Telefonbuch nichts, keine Gemeinde, kein Museum, kein Büro, nichts. Wir haben keine Inschrift gefunden, keinen Gedenkstein' (PB, p. 100). The absence of visual evidence leads Jonas, himself a professional photographer, to ask 'wie er das Nichts fotographieren solle' (PB, p. 103).

Maron and Jonas visit the former concentration camp at Kulmhof, now the commemorative site of Chelmno. In a nearby wood, photographed by Jonas and presumably the location depicted on the inside of the book's cover, Jews were executed. Maron has no precise details of her grandfather's death. Pawel may have been gassed in a concentration camp or shot in that same wood. A museum houses remaining possessions of the victims – 'die letzte Hinterlassenschaft der Toten' (PB, p. 184) – and displays photographs, bills, official commands, and even a letter to Heinrich Himmler, praising the service shown by the soldiers attached to the special unit in Kulmhof. In his book *The Texture of Memory: Holocaust Memorials and Meanings*, James E. Young describes the role of such memorial spaces in creating 'a topographical matrix that orients the rememberer and creates meaning in both the land and our recollections.'[23] The quest for meaning and a desire to orientate her own life within the context of her family story – and within the larger context of German history – have led Maron to this site. The section concludes with a single statistic: 'In Kulmhof starben 150 000 Juden' (PB, p. 186). This site is a chilling reminder of the devastation wrought by war on a single family and on an entire people.

Aleida Assmann's description of landscapes of memory has particular resonance for Maron's text: 'Traumatische Orte, Erinnerungsorte und Generationenorte überlagern sich in dieser Gedächtnislandschaft wie die Schriftzüge in einem Palimpsest' (*Erinnerungsräume*, p. 339). In *Pawels Briefe* Maron sets out to reconstruct her family story and reverse the familial tendency to forget. However, the visual images, personal letters, and even the geographical sites of memory signify both presence and absence, depicting 'fragments of history' that form a 'narrative of unassimilable loss', reinforcing 'at once incomprehensibility and presence, a past that will neither fade away nor be integrated into the present.'[24] Maron herself attaches particular

---

23 James E. Young, *The Texture of Memory: Holocaust Memorials and Meaning* (New Haven, Connecticut: Yale University Press, 1993), p. 7.
24 Hirsch, p. 40.

significance to the montage form as a stylistic device that enabled her to reflect on this continuous interplay of remembering and forgetting: 'eine ganz und gar kontrollierte Montage [...], die mir Raum für die Reflexionen über Erinnern und Vergessen geboten hat' ('Rollenwechsel', p. 108).

The Interplay of Forgetting and Remembering

Aleida Assmann's reflections on the relationship between remembering and forgetting are particularly applicable to Maron's family story. What the Konstanz historian terms 'Erinnerungsräume' are created by that partial illumination of the past which an individual or group needs in order to bestow meaning, establish identity, orientate their lives, motivate their actions. Such individual or collective remembering is fundamentally a matter of perspective. An extract from the past is illuminated from the perspective of a particular present and this selective recollection is necessarily accompanied by forgetting: 'Was zur Erinnerung ausgewählt wird, ist stets von den Rändern des Vergessens profiliert' (*Erinnerungsräume*, p. 408). Assmann insists throughout upon the symbiotic relationship between remembering and forgetting: 'Vom Erinnern [...] ist das Vergessen nicht abzulösen, es hat notwendig an ihm teil und geht in es ein' (*Erinnerungsräume*, p. 411). This section examines the relationship between memory and its repression in *Pawels Briefe*, exploring how the repression that informs each generation of Maron's family story is caused by political and personal trauma and by a subsequent strategic politics of remembering.

The Case of Pawel Iglarz

From the outset, Maron foregrounds the exemplary aspect of her grandparents' story. The horrors of the Holocaust find devastating expression in the deportation, internment and subsequent execution of the Jewish-born Pawel. The author felt compelled to write about Pawel and Josefa, despite the fact that her grandparents' story had already been consigned to the annals of history: 'nachdem die Schicksale dieser gerade versunkenen Generation der Historie zugeordnet und in ihr vermauert wurden, selbst die ihrer Kinder'

(PB, p. 7). Maron individualises the historical process. Sealed into the history of fascism and its consequences, the story of Pawel and Josefa has nevertheless lived on in their granddaughter's imagination as 'der gute, der geheiligte Teil der furchtbaren Geschichte. Der konvertierte Jude und die konvertierte Katholikin [...] lebten in mir als der kleine, vorstellbare Ausschnitt der unvorstellbar grausamen Geschichte' (PB, p. 8). The individual story of one couple thus comes to represent an entire historical generation.

Pawel Iglarz was born in Ostrow in 1879 to Jewish parents. In 1905 he and Josefa arrived in Berlin, where they lived for thirty-four years. Shortly before the outbreak of World War II, Pawel spent nine months in a border camp, followed by expulsion from Germany in the summer of 1939. Josefa left Berlin with him and they returned to her native Kurow, remaining there until Pawel's internment in Belchatow in 1942. Already terminally ill, Josefa died a number of weeks before her husband's execution. A particularly unusual aspect of Pawel and Josefa's story is their rejection of Judaism and Catholicism respectively. They had converted to the Baptist faith even before leaving Poland and were subsequently disowned by their respective families. Maron reflects on the lasting implications of this rupture with one's geographical, religious and cultural home: 'Einen Glauben oder eine Weltanschauung abzulegen, in denen man erzogen wurde, verlangt mehr als ein gewisses Maß an Mut und Charakterstärke; es erfordert eine andauernde intellektuelle und emotionale Anstrengung' (PB, pp. 30–31). Maron knows nothing about her grandfather's education or formal training. She can merely speculate as to why he seemed determined to dissociate himself so radically from his religious and cultural heritage. In conversation with Hella during their trip to Poland, her grandson Jonas comments that Pawel had sought to forget his origins: 'Eigentlich hat ja dein Vater mit dem Vergessen angefangen' (PB, p. 109). Hella cannot recall her father ever speaking about his family or birthplace. Even in his letters from the ghetto, Pawel seems intent upon renouncing his origins. He mentions his Jewish family only once, in a letter dated May 1942, and on that occasion 'nur als die unfreiwillige Herkunft, die ungewollten Eltern. Sogar im Ghetto, zurückgeworfen in die jüdische Schicksalsgemeinschaft, verwünscht er noch einmal seine Abstammung, indem er sich noch einmal von den Eltern lossagt' (PB, pp. 98–99).

However, Pawel does not succeed in effecting a complete rupture with his past. In his penultimate letter, which Maron terms his 'Vermächtnisbrief' (PB, p. 111), he urges his children to support one another. His granddaughter reflects on the emotional repercussions of Pawel's self-imposed rupture with his Jewish heritage: 'Es ist das einzige Zeugnis für das Leid, das der Bruch mit seiner jüdischen Familie in Pawel hinterlassen haben muß, gegen das er die eigene Familie gegründet und eingeschworen hat: haltet zusammen' (PB, p. 149). Complete denial, bureaucratically, personally or indeed narratively, of one's origins proves to be impossible.

Hella's 'Erinnerungslücken'

In the context of the relationship between memory and its repression, Hella's reaction to the recovered correspondence is particularly significant. She has absolutely no recollection of ever having read her father's letters or indeed of having written to him during his imprisonment. Visibly distressed at her complete inability to remember such deeply traumatic events, she seeks to overcome her sense of powerlessness: 'Meine Mutter nahm die Spur ihres Vergessens auf und suchte weiterhin in den alten Papieren, die offenbar zuverlässiger waren als ihre Erinnerung' (PB, p. 11). Apparently more reliable than her own memories, the rediscovered correspondence documents the efforts of the twenty-four-year-old Helene Iglarz to prevent her threatened deportation to Poland, an entire episode in her life that Hella has apparently denied or forgotten. Faced with this remarkable situation, Maron reflects on the innate human ability to forget: 'Unsere Fähigkeit zu vergessen empfinden wir oft nur als die Unfähigkeit, uns zu erinnern' (PB, p. 11). Presented with a letter dated July 1940, in which she informed Pawel that Walter had been awarded the Iron Cross for bravery, Hella reacts to this information as if hearing it for the first time.

Hella's desperate attempts to remember occur and are contextualised explicitly in a post-Wende Germany where forgetting has become synonymous with repression and lies. 'Als meine Mutter sich an einen Briefwechsel, in dem es um ihr Leben ging, nicht erinnern konnte, war das Vergessen in der öffentlichen Meinung gerade zu einem Synonym für Verdrängung und Lüge geschrumpft' (PB, p. 11), her daughter observes. This repression relates both to the recollection of the GDR years and of the Holocaust. The remark is also significant because it situates individual forgetting at the intersection of private and public domains. Against the backdrop of a questioning and suspicious public arena, Maron insists that her mother's forgetting is 'unschuldig' (PB, p. 12). Hella, however, views her inability to remember as unacceptable.

By articulating themes of this kind, Maron is doing more than merely catching up on the theoretical discourse of the post-Wende world. She has recourse – not for the first time in her oeuvre, as I indicated in the preceding chapter – to the pioneering work of Christa Wolf. What Maron terms her mother's 'Erinnerungslücken' recall *Kindheitsmuster*, a text that had emphasised the importance of remembering within the GDR: 'Im Zeitalter universalen Erinnerungsverlustes [...] haben wir zu realisieren, daß volle Geistesgegenwart nur auf dem Boden einer lebendigen Vergangenheit möglich ist.'[25] It is striking that both authors establish parallels between the Nazi past and the GDR present. As is the case with *Pawels Briefe*, Wolf's text, published in 1976, pointedly explored generational forgetting and traced the influence of one generation's memory failures on the next. There was reference to the 'Gedächtnislücken, welche die frühe Kindheit betreffen' (KM, p. 294) and later to a very deliberate process of forgetting:

> Bestimmte Erinnerungen meiden. Nicht davon reden. Wörter, Wortreihen, ganze Gedankenketten, die sie auslösen konnten, nicht aufkommen lassen. [...] Weil es nämlich unerträglich ist, bei dem Wort 'Auschwitz' das kleine Wort 'ich' mitdenken zu müssen: 'Ich' im Konjunktiv Imperfekt: Ich hätte. Ich könnte. Ich würde. Getan haben. Gehorcht haben.
> Dann schon lieber: keine Gesichter. Aufgabe von Teilen des Erinnerungsvermögens durch Nichtbenutzung. (KM, p. 312)

Maron, for her part, is determined to probe the gaps in Hella's memory that demand an explanation. These omissions, '[die] als ein erklärungverlangendes Warum über den Jahren nach 1939 [stehen]' (PB, p. 17), are an expression of the involuntary tendency to repress deeply traumatic events: her father's deportation, her mother's fatal illness, Pawel's internment and subsequent execution. We recognise in these omissions a process originally discussed by Freud, namely that of repression, the expulsion of painful events from consciousness and memory: 'aus dem Bewußtsein und aus der Erinnerung getrieben'.[26]

---

25   Christa Wolf, *Kindheitsmuster* (Frankfurt am Main: Luchterhand, 1988), p. 209. Quotations from the novel will be followed in parantheses by the abbreviation KM and the relevant page number.
26   Sigmund Freud, 'Über Psychoanalyse, Zweite Vorlesung', in *Gesammelte Werke: Chronologisch geordnet*, viii: *Werke aus den Jahren 1909–1913* (London: Imago Publishing, 1943), pp. 17–26 (p. 25).

In order to imagine her grandparents' life together before the devastation wrought by war, Maron is dependent upon her mother's stories of a carefree, idyllic childhood. However, for Maron too, forgetting the irreversible rupture of her family biography is the prerequisite for envisaging the happiness characteristic of her childhood up to 1939: 'Um mir das alltägliche Leben meiner Großeltern vorstellen zu können, muß ich vergessen, wie sie gestorben sind' (PB, p. 23).

In June 1942 Pawel sends his children Josefa's final letter to her husband, dictated on the day before her death. He instructs them to have the letter translated. Both copy and original are to be kept in a safe place and shown to Monika as soon as she is old enough. In fact, more than fifty years elapse before his granddaughter happens upon the poignant text. Maron reflects at length on possible reasons for such a drastic omission:

> Vor diesem Vergessen stehe ich ratlos, so ratlos wie Hella selbst. Das Jahr 1945 sei für sie wie eine Wiedergeburt gewesen, hat Hella gesagt. Eine Wiedergeburt ohne Eltern, ein Neuanfang ohne die Vergangenheit? Mußten nicht nur die Täter, sondern auch die Opfer ihre Trauer verdrängen, um weiterzuleben? [...] Und später, als das Leben längst weitergegangen war, als die Zeitungen 'Neues Leben', 'Neuer Weg', 'Neue Zeit' und 'Neues Deutschland' hießen, als die Gegenwart der Zukunft weichen mußte und die Vergangenheit endgültig überwunden wurde, wurde da auch die eigene Vergangenheit unwichtig?
>
> Oder waren die Jahrzehnte davor so aufs Überleben gerichtet, daß zum Innehalten und Zurückblicken keine Zeit war? Wir haben immer so nach vorn gelebt, sagt Hella.
> (PB, pp. 113–14)

This quotation implies that rebirth, *tabula rasa* style, is impossible. In the aftermath of World War II, survival and progress were the order of the day. In *Nachdenken über Christa T*, published in 1968, Christa Wolf had criticised the 'Rausch der Neubenennungen'[27] that dominated the early years of the new socialist state; in *Pawels Briefe* Maron criticises the pervasive obsession with renaming that characterised the immediate post-war period. Hella's refrain 'Wir haben immer so nach vorn gelebt' articulates collective orientation towards the future. This collective forgetting supplanted confrontation with the past. Maron also refers explicitly to the repression of grief that appears to have defined her mother's behaviour in the new Germany. Determined to

---

27 Christa Wolf, *Nachdenken über Christa T.* (Munich: Deutscher Taschenbuch Verlag, 1993), p. 38.

embrace the future and imbued with unfaltering political conviction, Hella sought to construct a new, post-war existence 'ohne die Vergangenheit, ohne Pawel und Josefa' ('Rollenwechsel', p. 108).

Conceding that Pawel was the family member who had, in fact, initiated, albeit unwittingly, the entire process of forgetting, Maron realises that certain 'Erinnerungslücken' can never be made good. Hella's siblings are dead: 'Es ist niemand mehr da, der ihr [...] helfen könnte, den Weg des Vergessens zurückzugehen' (PB, p. 18). However, her daughter is determined that Hella confront a deeply traumatic past. Maron composes a text depicting the brutality of a history that her mother has repressed for more than half a century. The horrors of the Holocaust are evoked not only in Pawel's reflections from the ghetto, expressing his utter despair; the reader is also confronted with a series of horrifying statistics and dates:

> Das Ghetto Belchatow wurde im März 1941 gegründet und im August 1942 liquidiert. Eine kleine Gruppe der Insassen wurde in das Ghetto von Lodz überführt [...] Ein anderer Teil der Belchatower Juden wurde in den umliegenden Wäldern von Belchatow erschossen. Der größte Teil kam nach Kulmhof (Chelmno), das erste Vernichtungslager für Juden, wo auch die Tötung von Menschen durch Abgase fahrender Lastwagen erprobt wurde. (PB, pp. 88–89)

Passages such as these challenge Hella's repression of a traumatic past, in particular the devastating repercussions of the Holocaust on her family biography.

Pawels Briefe is not only a probing exploration of forgetting and remembering in the context of World War II. As in her previous texts, the author once again problematises the political state in which she grew up, delivering an intensely personal account on this occasion. Her claim that *Pawels Briefe* was unwritable during the lifetime of the GDR should not be taken to imply that the two themes led independent lives or that some prioritisation dictated the sequence in which issues were handled. In the essay 'Rollenwechsel' Maron emphasises the extent to which both parts of the text, pre- and post-1945, are intertwined: 'Ich hätte den ersten ohne den zweiten Teil nie geschrieben, weil mich vor allem dieser Wandel interessierte, der biographische, der kulturelle, die fortgesetzten Brüche in den Lebensläufen aller beteiligten Generationen' (p. 107).

A bundle of old letters and photographs serves as the starting point for the reconstruction of her grandparents' life together; it is her mother's personal notes from 1945 onwards which frame the second section of the text. Hella experienced the year 1945 as a 'Wiedergeburt' (PB, p. 155). She revelled in her role as 'Sieger der Geschichte' (PB, p. 156) and her memoirs detail 'die wilde Nachkriegszeit' (PB, p. 155). Her notes evoke the sense of limitless opportunity that characterised the immediate post-war period. Many high-ranking communist officials returned from emigration in Moscow; Berlin was to be transformed. In conversation with her daughter, Hella recalls the liberation of Berlin by Soviet officers, her glowing account reminiscent of Herbert Beerenbaum's glorified rendition in *Stille Zeile Sechs*. In May 1945 she became secretary to Karl Maron, Chief of the People's Police. Hella's appointment at the City Hall emerges from her memoirs as the most momentous turning point in her life: 'Kein anderer Tag ragt so gewichtig und deutlich aus Hellas notierten Erinnerungen wie dieser' (PB, p. 153). Maron immediately challenges Hella's interpretation of that fateful day when she began work for the man who was to become her husband and whom her daughter ominously describes as 'mein biographisches Schicksal' (PB, p. 83).

Maron defines her mother's political affiliation in collective terms: 'Hella gehörte zu ihren Genossen und zum Magistrat, wie sie früher zum Fichte-Balalaika-Orchester gehört hatte' (PB, p. 157). Entrusted with the task of orchestrating the rebuilding of a city in ruins, her administrative position quickly assumed heroic dimensions: 'Hella saß also im Vorzimmer des Genossen Maron und allem, was sie tat, haftete auf natürliche Weise etwas Heroisches an. Die Stadt mußte wiederbelebt werden [...] Jede U-Bahn, die wiederfuhr, war auch Hellas Erfolg' (PB, p. 157). This collective emphasis pervades Hella's memoirs. The French sociologist Maurice Halbwachs's theory of collective memory can be applied to Hella's remembering. In his seminal text *On Collective Memory*, published posthumously in 1992, Halbwachs emphasised the extent to which memories are socially constructed and embedded: 'it is in society that people normally acquire their memories. It is also in society that they recall, recognize, and localize their memories.'[28]

---

[28] Maurice Halbwachs, *On Collective Memory*, ed., trans., and with an Introduction by Lewis A. Coser (Chicago and London: University of Chicago Press, 1992), p. 38.

Hella's marriage in 1955 to Karl Maron, who became GDR Interior Minister that same year, sealed the relationship between personal story and official GDR history. Her daughter interprets this year as a caesura, bringing the story of Pawel, Josefa and their children to an abrupt end. If Hella wholeheartedly embraced the spirit of the antifascist state, embodied for her in the person of Karl Maron, her daughter provides a very different perspective: 'ab jetzt bestreite ich ihr die alleinige Interpretationshoheit für ihr Leben' (PB, p. 154).[29] Maron categorically disputes her mother's right to a singular interpretation of events. She immediately counters Hella's idealised and romantic vision of heroic rebuilding in the aftermath of war by launching a scathing attack on what she views as an utterly corrupt political system:

> Nichts in ihrem Leben vor diesem Mai 1945 – weder ihre Herkunft noch ihre Erziehung, weder ihr Sinn für Gerechtigkeit noch ihre Freiheitsliebe – kann mir erklären, warum sie für die nächsten Jahrzehnte zu denen gehörten, die ihre politischen Gegner in Gefängnisse sperrten, Christen drangsalierten, Bücher verboten, die ein ganzes Volk einmauerten und durch einen kolossalen Geheimdienst bespitzeln ließen. (PB, p. 154)

Although Hella is unwilling to remember the blatant failures of the antifascist state, her daughter's outburst catalogues a veritable litany of injustice and oppression: incarceration of political opponents, censorship, religious intolerance, an insidious and highly effective secret police. Maron's indictment of the GDR is rendered even more damning through the implied parallel between communist and fascist régimes.[30]

29 In the introduction to her book *Phantoms of War in Contemporary German Literature, Films and Discourse: The Politics of Memory* (Basingstoke: Palgrave Macmillan, 2008), Anne Fuchs explains the connection between the narratives included in her study: 'they all explore the family as an intersection of the private and the public, a site where official representations of the past are contested by alternative memories from below' (p. 4). It is precisely this contestation that lies at the very heart of the emotive exchange between Rosalind Polkowski and Herbert Beerenbaum; in *Pawels Briefe* Maron provides an alternative to her mother's and, by extension, to the official representation of the GDR.

30 This is a recurring theme in Maron's writing. In her essay 'Ich war ein antifaschistisches Kind', she emphasises this point very forcefully: 'In diesem Jahrhundert wüteten zwei barbarische Regime in Europa. Nicht selten wurden die Opfer des einen zu den Tätern des anderen [...] Auf unbegreifliche Weise ahmten sie [die Kommunisten] ihre Peiniger nach, bis in die Fackelzüge und Uniformen' (*Begreifungskraft*, pp. 17–18). For Maron, this is the ultimate irony: a state founded on what Emmerich has termed the antifascist

Exposing the Gaps in Memory: Forgetting and Remembering in Pawels Briefe 139

Another family member unwilling to accept the failings of communism was Hella's brother Paul. Struck off the list of Party members because of his inactivity, he continued to engage in contentious political debates with his sister and brother-in-law. According to Hella, he provoked her 'mit den Lagern und mit Stalin' (PB, p. 187) to the point where they were no longer on speaking terms.[31] Determined to address the problematic aspects of Stalinism, Paul provided a further challenge to Hella's singular interpretation of life in the socialist state. By her own admission, Hella understands history 'als etwas [...], das zwischen Bauernkrieg und der Oktoberrevolution stattgefunden hat' (PB, p. 156). Her daughter underscores the fact that there is no reference to contemporary political events in Hella's memoirs from the momentous year 1955 onwards: 'Über die vierzig Jahre bis 1995 finde ich, außer Privatem, in Hellas Notizen kaum etwas über die Zeit, in der wir lebten, als hätte sich Hellas Biographie, bis dahin auf fast natürliche Weise verwachsen mit der deutschen Geschichte, vom Zeitgeschehen gelöst' (PB, p. 190). Maron is surprised at what she views as her mother's lack of sensitivity to the suffering and injustices of the period. It appears that Hella had repressed problematic aspects of life in the GDR. Maron exposes the prominent omissions from her mother's portrayal of events: 'In ihren Aufzeichnungen erwähnt Hella weder das Jahr 1953 noch das Jahr 1956, kein Wort über den Mauerbau 1961' (PB, p. 191). There is no mention of the political turmoil in Prague. 1968 is experienced as a significant year only on a personal level as Hella worried about her husband's depression following his retirement from office.

In the context of the interplay between forgetting and remembering, Maron's description of her mother as someone who remembers naively is especially significant. Hella is, her daughter claims, a 'naive Erinnernde' (PB,

---

'Gründungsmythos' (*Kleine Literaturgeschichte der DDR*, p. 29) almost immediately began to exhibit the same desire for power characteristic of the fascist system it claimed to reject.

31 Despite Pawel's request that his children support one another ('haltet zusammen', PB, p. 149), Hella and Marta were not on speaking terms with their brother for over thirty years as a result of Paul's rejection of communism. Reconciliation never came about. In 'Ich war ein antifaschistisches Kind', Maron writes: 'Hella verstand erst durch den Tod der anderen die Tragik ihrer Entscheidung von 1956' (*Begreifungskraft*, p. 20). This severing of familial relationships, as a result of apparently irreconcilable political differences, reads as even more futile and poignant in light of Pawel's plea for tolerance.

p. 166) who, when asked to recall particular events in her life, promptly offers 'ein naturbelassenes Stück Erinnerung voller Düfte, Temperaturen, Geräusche' (PB, pp. 166–67). The kind of memory games that the naive remembering implies appear to be Proustian in their sensual dimension: the associations are with smell and sound. Yet this remembering is far from involuntary; in her mind Hella has carefully filed away particular events 'in einem Regal mit der Jahreszahl 1932 oder 1945 oder 1976' (PB, p. 166) – an ordering, then suspending in time, of episodes that can be recalled upon request. Living in an official household, Hella's omission, consciously or otherwise, of politically significant dates is somewhat strange and certainly unexpected. Her 'naive' memories are diametrically opposed to the politically loaded dates conspicuously absent from her diary. Having repressed the trauma of World War II, overshadowed by her mother's death and her father's execution at Nazi hands, she proceeded to omit problematic aspects of the new life she had embraced with such enthusiasm. She is selective in her recollection of the GDR. Her daughter expresses it succinctly: 'Hella erinnert sich an Glück' (PB, p. 70). Her notes capture the unwavering optimism of the immediate post-war period: 'die wilde Nachkriegszeit, in der alles möglich schien: der richtige Beruf, der richtige Staat, die richtige Liebe' (PB, p. 155). Maron interprets her mother's exclusively positive memories in the context of Hella's innate pragmatism, of her ability, 'dem Leben seine freundlichen Seiten abzugewinnen' (PB, p. 126). Hella displays an almost brutal determination to remember being happy: 'Manchmal kommt es mir fast gewalttätig vor, wie sie den Tatsachen ihres Lebens das Glück abpreßt, als könnte sie einen anderen Befund nicht ertragen' (PB, p. 70).

The strategic politics of remembering practised by Hella resulted in the very deliberate forgetting of highly controversial dates in the history of the GDR. Repression thus characterises Hella's attitude to two periods of her past: the trauma of the Holocaust and contentious political events in the GDR. This double repression indicates Maron's willingness to acknowledge and pursue the complexity of a theme that permeates her text: the interplay of forgetting and remembering.

Monika Maron's Memories

Having categorised her mother in terms of the symbolic opposition between naive remembering and political forgetting, Maron appears to pride herself on the fact that she is most definitely *not* someone who remembers naively. What motivates her from an early stage is her apparent determination not to emulate her mother. The naive remembering of which she is so dismissive is thus linked to the rhetoric of her own self-portraying: 'Jedenfalls bin ich keine naive Erinnernde wie Hella' (PB, p. 166). The interplay of remembering and forgetting also informs Maron's relationship to her own childhood in the GDR. In the absence of specific childhood memories, she has formulated various theories 'für mein Vergessen' (PB, p. 166). She speculates that the constant changes in her life have rendered it impossible to consign all experiences to memory. Significantly, the changes she cites are motivated by almost exclusively political concerns: moving from West to East Berlin in 1951, Hella's marriage to a member of the GDR nomenklatura, the beginning of her writing career, reading Khrushchev's secret speech, and leaving Berlin for Hamburg in the late 1980s. Unlike her mother, Maron appears willing to remember politically, and yet the explosive revelations of her Stasi-involvement, to which I shall return later in this section, seem to contradict this self-proclaimed willingness to recall the political.

She wonders if she has carried forward only important and valuable aspects into each subsequent stage of her life: 'vielleicht habe ich ja, ohne es zu wollen, [...] nur mitgenommen, was mir wichtig und kostbar erschien oder was sich, auch wenn ich gewollt hätte, nicht vergessen ließ' (PB, p. 166). She is frequently unsure whether she is, in fact, remembering the past: 'oder ob ich mich an eine meinem Alter und Verständnis angepaßte Neuinszenierung meiner Erinnerung erinnere' (PB, p. 167). Maron once again problematises the process of remembering: recollection of childhood scenes from an adult perspective invariably leads to a retrospective reworking of comfortingly familiar memories. Aleida Assmann's observation that memories are invariably reordered against the backdrop of a constantly changing present is particularly applicable: 'Das Erinnern verfährt grundsätzlich rekonstruktiv; es geht stets von der Gegenwart aus, und damit kommt es unweigerlich zu einer Verschiebung, Verformung, Entstellung, Umwertung, Erneuerung des Erinnerten zum Zeitpunkt seiner Rückrufung' (*Erinnerungsräume*, p. 29).

Maron does not dispute the authenticity, as she expresses it, of the few 'saved' moments that have remained intact in her memory: mimicking Russian soldiers, standing in the corner of the classroom as punishment for a childhood misdemeanour, concealing from a policeman the fact that she was clandestinely delivering Pioneer newspapers to subscribers. However, for the most part, precise recollection has been dissolved, replaced by rather vague scenes, atmospheric reproductions of childhood memories. Maron concludes: 'Das meiste hat sich aufgelöst in einem allgemeinen zusammenfassenden Wissen, in atmosphärischen Szenen, deren genauer Hergang zu erfinden wäre, vielleicht nicht unwahrer als die wirkliche Erinnerung, aber doch erfunden' (PB, p. 168).

In an interview the author explained her wish to portray the inherently vague, incomplete and ultimately changeable aspect of memory: 'Und ich habe versucht, einen Ton zu finden, in dem sich Erinnerung als ständiger Wechsel von Annäherung und Zurückweisung erzählen ließ. Ich wollte das Erinnern als etwas Vages, Unvollständiges, Veränderbares vorführen.'[32] In those passages of *Pawels Briefe* in which Maron consciously reflects upon her own recollection, she succeeds in capturing the essentially indeterminate nature of memory.

Towards the end of *Pawels Briefe* Maron turns to the contentious issue of her Stasi-involvement in the mid-1970s. She interweaves her recollection of this period with a caustic commentary on the negotiation of memory between private and public domains. Maron consented to supply information on West German journalists and diplomats, with the stipulation that she never be required to inform on friends and acquaintances. In return, she was granted the precious exit visa for West Berlin. She dismisses the incident as 'eine kuriose und komische Episode [...], auf die ich nicht sonderlich stolz war, für die ich mich aber auch nicht schämte', insisting that her involvement could not be classified as a 'Spitzel-Affäre' (PB, p. 199).

Maron foregrounds the political climate in which the *Spiegel* revelations of 1995 occurred:

---

32   Tilman Krause, 'Wir waren ja immer ganz eng: Ein Gespräch mit Monika Maron über ihre Familie, das Erinnern und das Verschwinden der DDR', *Die Welt*, 27 February 1999, <http://www.welt.de/print-welt/article567167/Wir_waren_ja_immer_ganz_eng.html>.

Exposing the Gaps in Memory: Forgetting and Remembering in Pawels Briefe

> Als der 'Spiegel' 1995 diese Geschichte als eine der vielen Spitzel- und Denunzianten-geschichten enthüllte, schuf sich die Öffentlichkeit gerade nachträglich ihr Gedächtnis für die Vergangenheit, für die Schuld, Verdrängung und Lüge der vierzig Jahre DDR. Zum zweiten Mal mußte eine Vergangenheit bewältigt werden. (PB, p. 199)

The author situates her personal story in the context of a post-Wende public arena determined to uncover, albeit retrospectively, the lies and repression of the GDR. Confrontation with the past was suddenly in vogue, even if this trend distorted the authenticity of individual biographies: 'das öffentliche Gedächtnis [...] stellte meine Biographie ab 1976 auf den Kopf, damit sie in eine allgemeine Biographie paßte' (PB, p. 199). Maron resents the fact that no distinction was made between personal and public recollection in this instance. Her individual biography was subsumed into a more general and publicly motivated biography of deceit and repression. Reinterpretation was the order of the day: 'Die Bedeutung des Vorfalls wurde nicht aus ihm selbst abgeleitet, sondern aus dem Bedürfnis nach Umdeutung' (PB, p. 199).

Maron's two reports for the Stasi – the first describing her impressions as a visitor to West Berlin in 1976, the second a brief report on her conversations with West German journalists – appear in the volume of essays *Quer über die Gleise: Artikel, Essays, Zwischenrufe*, published in 2000. She seems determined to avoid any further accusations of repression. In 'Rollenwechsel', a text featuring later in that same anthology, she writes that the decision to include in *Pawels Briefe* details of her Stasi-involvement was a deliberate gesture on her part in order to avoid accusations of forgetting: 'ich habe mich der öffentlichen Meinung gebeugt, weil ich dem Vorwurf des Verschweigens entgehen wollte.' She concludes bitterly: 'Es hat mir nichts genutzt' (p. 115). Maron's very public confrontation with a contentious aspect of her past seems to contradict her repeated claim that there is an opportune moment for recollection. Succumbing to the pressure of public opinion, the author supplies in these pages of *Pawels Briefe* her 'Tribut an die öffentliche Meinung' ('Rollenwechsel', p. 115) and illustrates how memories are negotiated in the public domain.

Mending a Fractured Family Biography: The Mother–Daughter Relationship

Friederike Eigler reads *Pawels Briefe* as 'both a commentary on and a response to the multiple ruptures of communicative memory in a century marked by opposing ideological systems'.[33] Maron sets out to restore those familial links that historical forces had so brutally severed. She seeks to re-establish the ties binding her life to that of her grandparents: 'den Faden [...] suchen, der mein Leben mit dem ihren verbindet' (PB, p. 12). She is motivated by the desire to discover 'warum ich wohl geworden sein könnte, wie ich bin' (PB, p. 166), echoing a central question in *Kindheitsmuster*: 'Wie sind wir so geworden, wie wir heute sind?' (p. 284). Recollection is an attempt to derive meaning and impose order on the chaos of the past; as Maron observes in the opening sequence: 'weil man das Chaos der Vergangenheit nicht erträgt, korrigiert man es ins Sinnhafte, indem man ihm nachträglich ein Ziel schafft' (PB, p. 13). By exposing the generational gaps in memory, *Pawels Briefe* charts Maron's attempts to mend retrospectively her fractured family biography.

The theme of conflicting beliefs informs all three generations of Maron's family story: 'In unserer Familie ist niemand dem Glauben treu geblieben, in dem er erzogen wurde' (PB, p. 192). Pawel and Josefa's rejection of Judaism finds its parallel in the next generation in Hella's renunciation of the Baptist faith of her parents. Her allegiance to communism caused an irrevocable rift between Hella and her brother Paul. In the third generation, Maron denounces communist practice in the GDR. Significantly, the concluding sequence of the text is devoted to Maron's reflection on religious and ideological convictions. She describes her son Jonas as 'unser erster Nicht-Konvertit seit vier Generationen' (PB, p. 205), 'der gar nicht konvertieren kann', she proudly declares to Hella, 'weil er auf keinen Glauben eingeschworen wurde' (PB, p. 205). Although she fleetingly experiences the familiar feeling of powerlessness, 'das alte Gefühl der Ohnmacht' (PB, p. 205), when she hears the triumphant shouts emanating from the PDS party in her apartment building

---

33   Friederike Eigler, 'Engendering Cultural Memory in Selected Post-*Wende* Literary Texts of the 1990s', *The German Quarterly*, 74.4 (2001), 392–406 (p. 403).

following the 1998 elections, she realises: 'Meine Großeltern haben ertragen müssen, daß keines ihrer Kinder sich taufen ließ; Hella hat gelernt zu ertragen, daß ich Antikommunistin wurde; und ich muß ertragen, daß Hella Kommunistin bleibt' (PB, p. 205). This awareness indicates Maron's willingness to transcend the obvious political differences between mother and daughter and reveal the essence of those representative figures, Pawel and Hella, who have shaped her identity.

In the shorter second part of the text, the montage form, in particular Maron's reflections on her mother's memoirs, reinforces the polarised political convictions of mother and daughter. Her subjective experience of childhood and youth in the GDR contrasts with the version of events that her mother has consigned to print. In the novel *Stille Zeile Sechs*, an entire generation of communist functionaries was embodied in the quasi-fictitious figure of Beerenbaum; this individualising of hierarchical power structures is a personal experience in *Pawels Briefe* also. Karl Maron embodies the state so abhorred by his stepdaughter. Maron's personal, familial conflict with him becomes inseparable from her confrontation with the GDR itself. She expresses her contempt in the most unequivocal terms: 'Hellas neuer Mann war [...] mein biographisches Schicksal. Es gab Jahre, in denen ich ihr das Recht bestritt, mir dieses Schicksal zugemutet zu haben' (PB, p. 83).

Interwoven with Maron's reflections on Hella's version of a shared family past are snatches of the conversations between mother and daughter following the discovery of Pawel's letters. These discussions demonstrate diametrically opposed political attitudes. Maron recalls heated debates on 'Klasseninstinkt' (PB, p. 128), a topic particularly favoured by her mother. She criticises Hella's intransigence, her 'Unbelehrbarkeit' (PB, p. 179): 'Später werde ich Hella fragen müssen, wie es sich mit ihrem Klasseninstinkt verhielt, als sie in den Augen der Arbeiter des Arbeiter- und Bauernstaates zu einer Bonzenfrau geworden war und ich zu einem Bonzenkind' (PB, p. 128–29). Imbued with an unwavering belief in the socialist cause, Hella refused to contemplate Stalinist crimes or the shortcomings of socialism, even after the collapse of the GDR. The fall of the Berlin Wall was the only occasion when Hella's conviction faltered. For a fleeting moment she did not belong to any party or political system: 'für eine Sekunde in der Geschichte' (PB, p. 131) she was not defined by the collective. It was her daughter's turn to boast, albeit in ironic fashion, of being the 'Sieger der Geschichte' (PB, p. 130).

Appalled by her mother's unwillingness to contemplate Stalinist crimes and the failures of communism, Maron wonders: 'Was hatten Pawels Töchter Hella und Marta unter solchen Leuten zu suchen?' (PB, p. 154), thus seeking to overcome the ideological rift between the generations by emphasising familial affiliation. There is a genuine desire to understand the motivating forces in her mother's life: 'Ich habe verstehen und erzählen wollen, wie meine Mutter, die allein aufgrund ihrer Herkunft als Kind armer polnischer Einwanderer, später als rassisch Verfolgte, unfähig zur Macht und zur Schuld war, nach dem Bruch der Verhältnisse auf der Seite der Machthaber ankommt' ('Rollenwechsel', p. 106).

Overlooked in earlier Maron texts, which focused on the rebellious daughter's confrontation with a stultifying *Vater Staat*, the relationship between mother and daughter emerges as a central theme in *Pawels Briefe*. In 'Rollenwechsel' Maron explains that she did not seek to conceal their irreconcilable political differences: 'Den unlösbaren Zwiespalt unserer politischen Ansichten habe ich nicht verschwiegen, sie sind Teil unserer Geschichte und Gegenstand unseres Gesprächs und sogar ein Vehikel des gemeinsamen Erinnerns' (p. 106). She reflects on the political and personal choices her mother has made. She describes Hella as a paradoxical figure, embodying the contradictions 'zwischen [...] der Welt der Tradition und der öden Traditionslosigkeit des Arbeiter- und Bauernstaates' ('Rollenwechsel', p. 108). Her daughter realises that Hella has legitimated her life in the GDR by considering it the only possible response to the devastating effect of fascism on her own family. Maron recognises that her biography is inextricably bound to her mother's life story. This familial relationship is shaped by completely different experiences of communism. The GDR experience thus continues to bind. However, *Pawels Briefe* marks a development in Maron's treatment of this metanarrative by presenting a differentiated portrayal of Hella. She is depicted as a complex figure whom her daughter seeks to understand by probing beneath the obvious ideological differences: 'Dass man einen Menschen, dessen politische Überzeugungen man entschieden nicht teilt, verstehen und lieben kann, habe ich schreiben wollen und, wie ich fest glaube, auch geschrieben' ('Rollenwechsel', p. 106).

Conclusion

Deprived of familial continuity, Maron sets out to mend retrospectively her fractured biography: 'mir ist die Dialektik familiärer Kontinuität vorenthalten geblieben. Nachträglich schaffe ich mir nun die Bilder, an die ich mich, wären meine Großeltern nicht ums Leben gekommen, erinnern könnte, statt sie zu erfinden' (PB, p. 51). Inspired by her grandfather's poignant letters and family photographs, she envisages the character of the man she never knew. Hirsch describes postmemory as a powerful and very particular form of memory 'precisely because its connection to its object or source is mediated not through recollection but through an imaginative investment and creation.'[34] The montage form demonstrates that Maron's family story, itself played out against the turbulent backdrop of twentieth-century German history, is not so much mended as reconstructed in her imagination and this is done in a manner that makes the fractures visible.

Pawels Briefe charts Maron's ultimately successful efforts to expose the 'Erinnerungslücken', the gaps in memory that characterise her family story. Pawel seemed intent upon renouncing his Jewish heritage. In her determination to view her life as 'ein harmonisches, kompaktes Werk' (PB, p. 70), his daughter Hella has completely repressed personal trauma. In the third generation, Maron counters this repression by reconstructing, with the aid of photographs and letters, the final years of her grandparents' life together. She also challenges what she terms Hella's 'naive' recollection of the socialist state. Mother and daughter offer two opposing interpretations of a shared past, but Maron probes beyond these differences in an attempt to understand a central figure in her life.

Maron's family story is embedded in an era concerned with the individual, collective and cultural construction of memory. Both specialised accounts, such as Hirsch's analysis of postmemory, and more global studies, including Halbwachs's theory of collective memory, Nora's depiction of realms of memory and, of course, Freud's analysis of repression, can be applied fruitfully to Maron's text. *Pawels Briefe* contributes to memory discussions on many

---

34 Hirsch, p. 22.

levels: the relationship between memories and identity formation, the extent to which memories are socially constructed, the recovery of the repressed, the selective nature of recollection. The text demonstrates how the past is continuously reconstructed under the dictates of the present and how memory is negotiated at the intersection of private and public domains. Present throughout the text is the sustained interplay of forgetting and remembering that informs all three generations of this family story.

A decade after the Wende, the experience of GDR history continued to shape Maron's writing. Her attempts to access the details of her grandparents' final years were themselves refracted through conflicting memories of life in the GDR. Through this complex interplay, *Pawels Briefe* makes a significant and particularly East German contribution to contemporary theoretical debates on memory and its repression.

CHAPTER SIX

Lebensentwürfe, Zeitenbrüche: Biographers and Biographies in *Endmoränen* and *Ach Glück*

As I sought to illustrate in earlier chapters, Maron's post-Wende texts are characterised by an inward turn. Her 1996 novel *Animal triste* was a powerful study of sexual obsession; its protagonist had retreated into memories of a clandestine and ultimately doomed love affair. *Pawels Briefe*, published in 1999, continued this exploration of memory and its repression as Maron probed generational memory gaps in her attempts to reconstruct her family story. Her most recent novels – *Endmoränen*, published in 2002, and its sequel *Ach Glück*, which appeared in 2007 – continue this turn towards more personal themes. Both texts offer a reflection on the ageing process and the often elusive nature of happiness. Most significantly, *Endmoränen* and *Ach Glück* explore identity crises and the quest for meaning in a post-GDR age.

Pawels Briefe captured the fragmented experience of twentieth-century German history. With the help of rediscovered photographs and letters, Maron sought to reconstruct a family biography radically ruptured by the Holocaust. The rupture of individual biographies by historical forces is also a central theme in *Endmoränen*; the caesura caused by the implosion of the GDR leaves the protagonist Johanna grappling with the insignificance of her professional and personal biography in a post-GDR society.

'Lebensentwürfe, Zeitenbrüche', Maron's address at the 2002 *Historikertag* in Halle, is a reflection on the manner in which we construct and bestow meaning upon our biographies. Volker Hage has rightly termed this lecture a commentary on *Endmoränen*.[1] In a central passage Maron articulates the difficulties experienced by former GDR citizens as they struggle to make sense of their biographies in a radically-altered society:

---

1   Volker Hage, 'Deutschland im Herbst', *Der Spiegel*, 21 September 2002, pp. 180–83 (p. 182).

> Wer in einer Diktatur [...] lebt, neigt dazu, was immer ihm geschieht oder nicht geschieht, dem anzulasten, der ungebeten in sein Leben eingreift [...] Verschwindet die Diktatur, bleiben die Menschen mit ihren als unzureichend oder gar als misslungen empfundenen Biografien allein zurück. Ein Teil von ihnen wird die Chance nutzen und nachholen, was ihnen vorher verwehrt war, für andere wird es zu spät sein.[2]

Maron continues by underscoring the crisis of identity experienced by many: 'Und es gibt Verlierer eines solchen Umbruchs [...] Für sie ist der Gewinn der Freiheit verbunden mit dem Verlust ihres Selbstbildes.' It is precisely this loss of identity following the collapse of the GDR which forms the point of departure for *Endmoränen*. The characters struggle with feelings of insecurity, insignificance and loss. Its sequel *Ach Glück* follows the same characters as they seek orientation and restore meaning to their lives.

In this chapter I will explore the theme of ruptured biographies in *Endmoränen* and *Ach Glück*. The protagonist Johanna Märtin is a historical biographer who struggles to make sense of her own biography in a post-Wende age. Her husband Achim also has difficulty in adjusting to life after socialism. Significantly, both texts offer counter-biographies to the lethargy and stagnation experienced by Johanna and her friends. This chapter will examine the symbolism of the historical figure Wilhelmine Enke, whose biography is gradually revealed to the reader of *Endmoränen* and who represents a vitality to which her biographer Johanna can merely aspire. Similarly, in *Ach Glück*, the Russian aristocrat Natalia Timofejewna and the artist and writer Leonora Carrington provide examples of energetic, idiosyncratic and adventurous biographies. Taken together, the melancholic *Endmoränen* and its more hopeful sequel *Ach Glück* trace the rupture and the subsequent reshaping of individual biographies in a post-GDR age, as this chapter will illustrate.

---

[2] Maron's address at the *Historikertag* was published in the *Süddeutsche Zeitung* as 'Lebensentwürfe, Zeitenbrüche. Vom Nutzen und Nachteil dunkler Brillen: Wer es sich zu einfach macht beim Rückblick auf seine Geschichte, beraubt sich seiner Biografie', 13 September 2002, p. 18.

Endmoränen

As in previous Maron novels, the protagonist of *Endmoränen* is a writer. Until the collapse of the GDR, Johanna Märtin's professional life had involved the composition of historical biographies. She prided herself on the 'geheime Botschaften'[3] inserted therein, oppositional subtexts critical of the political order. Having retreated to the family summer home in Basekow, a remote village some one hour north-east of Berlin, Johanna grapples with the apparent insignificance of her professional life in a post-Wende age. Although her emotionally distant husband Achim, an academic engrossed in a project on Kleist, has returned to work in Berlin, she remains in the countryside, struggling to progress with a biography of Wilhelmine Enke, mistress of the Prussian king Friedrich Wilhelm II.

The retreat to the countryside was a topos in GDR literature. Christa Wolf's *Sommerstück*, a seminal text that anticipated the end of the GDR, provides a particularly interesting point of reference in this regard. It is a story of disillusioned East German intellectuals who have withdrawn to their summer house. The atmosphere is one of 'Langeweile und Leere';[4] the house itself is described as an 'Arche' (SSt, p. 118), whose inhabitants are 'gestrandet' (SSt, p. 95), cut off from the rest of the world. The parallels with *Endmoränen* extend even to the nautical imagery that Johanna employs to describe her retreat: 'wie auf einem Schiff mitten im dunklen Meer, abgeschnitten von den anderen Menschen und allem, was hätte Halt bieten können' (EM, p. 49). However, there is one very significant difference: Wolf's shipwrecked intellectuals have withdrawn from a claustrophobic GDR society; ironically, Maron's first-person narrator is describing the isolation and disillusionment of her post-Wende situation.

---

[3] Monika Maron, *Endmoränen: Roman* (Frankfurt am Main: S. Fischer, 2002), p. 45. Quotations from the novel will be followed in parentheses by the abbreviation EM and the relevant page number.

[4] Christa Wolf, *Sommerstück* (Berlin: Luchterhand, 2002), p. 79. *Sommerstück* was first published in 1989. Quotations from the text will be followed in parentheses by the abbreviation SSt and the relevant page number.

In her self-imposed isolation Johanna begins writing letters to Christian P., an old friend whom she has not seen in years. Maron herself comments on the advantages of the novel's epistolary structure: 'Die Briefe erwiesen sich als glückliche Möglichkeit, Vergangenes zu vergegenwärtigen und zu reflektieren, auch als ein Vehikel, das Johannas Sehnsucht phantomhaft aufscheinen läßt.'[5] She continues by underscoring the importance of the letters in providing another perspective: 'Vor allem aber bescherten sie dem Buch ein zweites Ich, das ebenso legitim spricht und widerspricht wie Johanna' (WIE, p. 22). This 'Flaschenpost [...] in die Nacht geworfen' (EM, p. 97), as Johanna herself describes the renewed contact, quickly assumes an important function. In the course of the correspondence, the reader learns that she once kissed Christian P. Johanna shares an emotional intimacy with him and reveals in the letters what she seems unable or unwilling to discuss with her husband. Their correspondence includes reflections on love, music, faith, familial bonds, the nature of happiness, growing old and missed opportunities.

A '*Herbstbuch*'

Endmoränen is an autumnal text – a 'Herbstbuch', as Uta Beiküfner describes it.[6] In the very opening sentence Johanna reveals her feelings of relief at the arrival of autumn. The rural setting of Basekow is her 'Refugium' (EM, p. 20). Bathed in the enchanting 'Herbstlicht' (EM, p. 20), the landscape provides a suitably evocative setting for her melancholic reflections: 'Und auf allem lag dieses ungeheure Licht, von dem wir später, als unser ganzes Leben sich geändert hatte und auch wir in die Toskana fahren durften, sagten, in Basekow gäbe es ein Licht wie in der Toskana' (EM, p. 21). The place has a mythical quality, reminiscent of another age: 'wie gar nicht zugehörig der realen Welt, sondern übriggeblieben, zurückgelassen von der Zeit wie die als sanfte Hügel

---

[5] Monika Maron, *Wie ich ein Buch nicht schreiben kann und es trotzdem versuche* (Frankfurt am Main: S. Fischer, 2005), p. 22. Quotations from the text will be followed in parentheses by the abbreviation WIE and the relevant page number.
[6] Uta Beiküfner, 'Herbststück', *Berliner Zeitung*, 26 August 2002, *Literatur*, p. 13.

sich breitenden Endmoränen, die ihn umschlossen' (EM, p. 21). Moraine is debris carried by glaciers and forming mounds when deposited, leaving an imprint on the landscape as physical remnants of the Ice Age. This geological image of the title functions as a leitmotif throughout the text and reinforces the extent to which Johanna and her generation feel left behind, remnants of another epoch. In an essay that explores the relationship between buildings and biography, Monika Shafi notes that the moraines 'point toward both a distant history and unfulfilled longing.'[7] Wolfgang Wehdeking locates the moraine image within communist discourse, noting, in particular, the prevalence of *Tauwetter* as a metaphor during the existence of the GDR. He draws interesting parallels between the palaeontological metaphor of Maron's earlier novel *Animal triste* and the geological metaphor of *Endmoränen* – both capture 'das Bild vom eigenen, mit dem ersehnten Mauerfall verblichenen Staatsgebilde und seiner einstigen, eindrucksvollen Utopie.'[8]

In her country retreat Johanna ponders life several years after unification. Writing to Christian P., she recalls the chance of a fresh start and the promise of a new beginning that the fall of the Wall seemed to herald. However, this sense of limitless opportunities has given way to stagnation:

> Und jetzt, ein paar Jahre später, hat mich die Ahnung, eher die Furcht befallen, es könnte schon wieder vorbei sein mit dem eigentlichen Leben, weil es zu spät angefangen hat, weil wir gar nicht mehr dran sind mit dem richtigen Leben, sondern daß für uns bald diese öde lange Restzeit beginnt, zwanzig oder dreißig Jahre Restzeit [...]. (EM, p. 55)

Although only in her early fifties, Johanna already feels superfluous and is at once fearful and fatalistic as she contemplates a future stretching ahead, with no apparent release from the pervasive lethargy and the monotony of her existence.

---

[7] Monika Shafi, 'German and American Dream Houses: Buildings and Biographies in Gregor Hens's *Himmelssturz* and Monika Maron's *Endmoränen*', *The German Quarterly*, 79.3 (2006), pp. 505–24 (p. 514).

[8] Volker Wehdeking, 'Monika Marons rückläufige Erwartungen von *Animal triste* zu *Endmoränen*: das Unbedingte in der Liebe und die Bedingtheiten des Älterwerdens', in *Monika Maron: Begleitheft zur Ausstellung – Wie ich ein Buch nicht schreiben kann und es trotzdem versuche*, ed. by Winfried Giesen (Frankfurt am Main: Universitätsbibliothek Johann Christian Senckenberg, 2005), pp. 60–74 (p. 66).

Endmoränen has been described as an 'Alterselegie',[9] 'ein Buch über das Altern, doch kein Alterswerk',[10] indicating the extent to which reviewers have focused on Maron's portrayal of the ageing process. Through its depiction of this process, the novel represents a natural progression in her oeuvre. In *Stille Zeile Sechs* Beerenbaum's physical frailty had served as potent symptom of a stagnant political state on the eve of its collapse. Contemplating the inevitability of physical decline, the first-person narrator of *Animal triste* had been brutally honest in her unsparing description of gradual, ineluctable decay. Maron returns to this discourse of the ageing body in *Endmoränen*. In the very opening sequence Johanna recalls her first summer in Basekow some thirteen years previously; this was also the summer when her childhood friend Irene died of cancer. She remembers the latter's disfigured body and recalls asking her: 'wie lebst du so in deinem Körper?' (EM, p. 8) When news of her death reaches Johanna, she notes that the many images of dying have coalesced to form a prophetic metaphor for her own mortality: 'von unserer, meiner, gesichtslosen Sterblichkeit' (EM, p. 15).

Johanna describes ageing as a humiliating, helpless state (EM, p. 37) and resents having to engage in what she terms 'diesen aussichtslosen Kampf [...] gegen die Haare, die Haut und das Fleisch' (EM, p. 27). In a letter to Christian P. she writes of society's obsession with physical perfection: 'Eine Generation im Fitneßstudio' (EM, p. 112) is her dismissive description of a narcissistic generation. Registering 'die in grellem Sonnenlicht schon sichtbare Gravur der Greisenhaftigkeit auf meiner Haut' (EM, p. 26), she is very much aware that her body is no longer the object of admiring male glances: 'Ich kannte längst das Gefühl, wenn die Blicke der Männer mich neutralisierten' (EM, p. 27), she comments.

Endmoränen is indeed a 'Herbstbuch'. Just like the moraines of the title, Johanna feels left over; what remains, it seems, is a melancholic contemplation of the 'Restzeit' (EM, p. 55) stretching ahead. The autumnal landscape of Basekow provides an appropriate setting for the protagonist's musings on death and dying and on the inexorability of physical decline.

---

9   Iris Radisch, 'Barfuß in Basekow', *Die Zeit*, 5 September 2002, p. 50.
10 Richard Kämmerlings, 'Hundejahr. Nach Mexico: Monika Marons Frankfurter Poetikvorlesungen', *Frankfurter Allgemeine Zeitung*, 3 February 2005, p. 41.

'Biografien ohne Botschaften': Johanna's Meaningless Biography?

Johanna Märtin is a biographer who struggles to make sense of her own biography in a post-Wende age. Her professional life in the GDR had involved the composition of commentaries to literary editions, of forewords and epilogues, and the production of biographies. For Johanna, the real significance of this work had derived from the insertion of hidden meanings. Her dexterity in applying those writing strategies which had circumvented the censor, thereby ensuring publication, recalls the compromise manoeuvres that had defined both Maron's articles for the *Wochenpost* in the early 1970s and her alter ego's professional practice in her debut novel *Flugasche*. As I demonstrated in Chapter One, Josefa Nadler and her fellow-journalists had been conditioned to conceal the truth 'hinter schönen Sätzen' (FA, p. 34).

Johanna welcomed the thematic freedom heralded by the end of censorship: 'Wörter, die bis dahin dem privaten Gebrauch vorbehalten waren, durfte ich jetzt in meinen Aufsätzen benutzen' (EM, p. 44). She began writing about Ezra Pound, Gottfried Benn, Uwe Johnson, all of them classic taboo figures in the GDR. However, the collapse of the political state suddenly rendered superfluous Johanna's transmission of hidden messages: 'Ich konnte Botschaften in Biografien verstecken', she writes to Christian P., 'und das ist über Nacht eine ganz überflüssige Fähigkeit geworden' (EM, p. 56). Biographies no longer contained secret meanings: 'Biografien [enthielten] keine heimlichen Botschaften mehr, um derentwillen sie überhaupt geschrieben wurden [...] [sie waren] nichts anderes [...] als Biografien, sorgsame Erinnerungen, Wissenspartikel für Liebhaber' (EM, p. 38). During the existence of the state Johanna never had to question the relevance of her work. Its significance had derived from her camouflaged oppositional stance: 'Es war schon wichtig, einfach nur gegen den Staat zu sein', she recalls in her first letter to Christian P., 'mehr mußte man gar nicht tun, um wichtig zu sein' (EM, p. 57). She had viewed her furtive transmission of political subtexts as a rather heroic endeavour to oppose the state. 'Natürlich war das eine ganz idiotische Wichtigkeit', she concedes retrospectively, 'trotzdem fehlt sie mir' (EM, p. 57).

Johanna recognises that she should have stopped writing biographies and embraced the possibilities for change heralded by the Wende. However, she knew no other way of life and lacked the confidence to start afresh: 'Ich konnte nichts anderes [...] In mir rumorte keine unterdrückte Begabung, die nur auf ihre Befreiung wartete' (EM, p. 44). The irony of her position does not escape her. She is a professional biographer who seems unable to refashion her own biography:

> Es ist seltsam, daß ausgerechnet ich, die genug wußte über die zufälligen und schicksalhaften Fügungen in fremden Biografien, nicht auf die Idee kam, meine eigene neu zu erfinden oder wenigstens auf ein anderes Gleis zu lenken. Statt dessen suchte ich neue Auftraggeber für Nachworte und Biografien. (EM, pp. 43–44)

An Exemplary Biography: Wilhelmine Enke

Having withdrawn to the countryside, Johanna contemplates the apparent insignificance of her life. Even the biography of Wilhelmine Enke, mistress of Friedrich Wilhelm II, now seems 'vollkommen bedeutungslos, außer für meinen Kontostand' (EM, p. 37). In her rural retreat she hopes to recover that impetus which, some two years previously, had propelled her to select Enke as suitable figure for a biography, citing her subject's fascinating and original contribution to Prussian history (EM, p. 36) as the reason for her choice. Interwoven with her letters to Christian P. and depiction of life in Basekow, Johanna's notes on Wilhelmine Enke reveal an unorthodox biography.

Enke was born in Potsdam in 1753, the daughter of a court musician. When the crown prince Friedrich Wilhelm first encountered the young Enke, he was instantly smitten. He provided for her education: this included a French governess and trips to Paris. In 1769 she was given a house in Charlottenburg and became Friedrich Wilhelm's official mistress. They had five children, but only two survived: a daughter, Marianna Gräfin von der Mark, and a beloved son, Alexander von der Mark, 'das unlösbare Bindeglied zwischen W.E. und Friedrich Wilhelm' (EM, p. 195), who died in mysterious circumstances at the age of nine. Enke's ingenuity enabled her to thwart the efforts of an opportunistic Rosicrucian group at court who deliberately played upon Friedrich Wilhelm's interest in mysticism and the occult. Following their advice, he sought to dissociate himself from Enke; she, in turn, deliberately invented stories of their dead son Alexander's apparition and thus continued to exert her influence.

In 1796 Friedrich Wilhelm bestowed the title Countess of Lichtenau upon his former mistress. According to her contemporary, the German-Jewish writer Rahel Varnhagen, Enke possessed a special talent: 'daß sie von jedem Mann, der sie liebt, als Ideal angeboten wird, wie sein Spiegelbild' (EM, p. 149). Johanna notes the similarities between Varnhagen's and Enke's biographies. Both were social climbers: the former advanced to host one of the most important salons in Europe, while the latter was elevated to the status of Duchess. Johanna admires her subject's survival instinct, her 'Kampf ums Überleben an der Seite des Königs' (EM, p. 149).

In 1802 she embarked upon a short-lived marriage to a man some twenty-six years her junior – Franz von Holbein, who would later become director of the Burgtheater in Vienna in the 1840s. Enke died in 1820 and was buried in Berlin. Her gravestone in the St Hedwig graveyard, Liesenstraße was levelled in 1961 to make way for the building of the Wall. It was located in what was to become the no-man's land between East and West Berlin. Johanna realises that, pre-1989, this single historical fact would have sufficed to transform a mere historical biography into a politically subversive text:

> Vor fünfzehn Jahren hätte der Leser meiner Biografie über die Gräfin Lichtenau seinen Freunden sofort von der Offenbarung der ungeheuerlichen Grabschändung berichtet, und die hätten es ihren Freunden erzählt, und alle wären mir dankbar gewesen und hätten mich bewundert, weil ich es gewagt hatte, darüber zu schreiben, und zudem so geschickt, dass der Zensor den entscheidenden Satz überlesen hatte. (EM, p. 40)

Johanna writes longingly of such 'Klopfzeichen aus dem Untergrund' (EM, p. 39), which gave meaning to her professional life: 'Wer sie schrieb, hätte sich der Wichtigkeit seines Tuns, ja, seiner ganzen Existenz, gewiß sein dürfen' (EM, p. 39).

Johanna seeks to recapture the exemplary aspect of Enke's life that had initially attracted her to this historical figure: 'Ich hatte damals in dem Schicksal der Wilhelmine Enke und späteren Gräfin Lichtenau ein Gleichnis gefunden, das nicht nur eine Antwort auf die Verwirrungen meines eigenen Lebens zu enthalten schien, sondern etwas Exemplarisches' (EM, p. 36). She describes her subject as 'die einzige preußische Mätresse von Rang' (EM, p. 81), yet she had been discredited by previous biographers and considered a 'Schandfleck auf der Uniform der Hohenzollern' (EM, p. 82). Upon the death of Friedrich Wilhelm II in 1797, his successor had her property confiscated.

She was arrested, falsely accused of treason and of improperly amassing wealth, and banished to the fortress of Glogau for three years. Vilified in defamatory pamphlets, she retaliated with an apologia 'gegen die Beschuldigungen mehrerer Schriftsteller' (EM, p. 104), providing further evidence of her independent spirit.

During a conversation with the Russian gallery-owner Igor towards the end of the text, Johanna dismisses her biographical endeavour as being of interest to nobody. However, that same evening she reads a passage from Enke's memoirs, beginning with the same sentence which formed the dramatic opening of her apologia: 'Meine Geduld ist erschöpft; ich kann nicht länger schweigen' (EM, p. 243). She recognises the importance of Enke in and for her own life. Unlike her current biographer, who struggles with feelings of failure and bemoans missed opportunities, the young Enke enthusiastically embraced her second chance, the opportunity of a new life and elevated social status that Friedrich Wilhelm II offered her. Indebted to the Prussian king for providing her with an education, she sought to advance herself through the acquisition of languages and an appreciation of art, music and philosophy. Johanna writes of her subject's intelligence, her beauty and her thirst for knowledge:

> Die Enke hat die Chance eines zweiten, unverhofften, ihr durch Geburt nicht zugedachten Lebens, die Friedrich Wilhelm ihr gab, als er in dem dreizehnjährigen Kind die Frau erkannte, die er sich zur Geliebten wünschte, mit allem, was ihr gegeben war, mit Intelligenz, Wißbegier, Schönheit, Willenskraft, gepackt und fortan mit Klauen und Zähnen verteidigt. (EM, p. 215)

She lived life to the full: 'Alles, was dieses geschenkte Leben hergab, hat sie aus ihm gesogen' (EM, p. 215). Enke became an essential adviser to the king. We learn that he asked her advice in all things and that she remained his closest friend until his death: 'die WE hat ihre Unersetzlichkeit im Leben Friedrich Wilhelms bis zuletzt behauptet, gegen die Rosenkreuzer, gegen Mätressen und gegen die öffentliche Meinung' (EM, p. 204). This indispensability is in stark contrast to what Johanna views as the apparent superfluity of her own existence in a post-GDR society.

In an essay exploring the manner in which Enke's life has been narrated, Waltraud Maierhofer observes that 'the biography of the Prussian mistress [...] assumes existential meaning for Johanna [...] With her sensuality, courage, and determination, Encke becomes a model of self-assertion'.[11] Johanna's notes reveal a brave, free-spirited and fiercely independent woman. She becomes for her biographer a 'strahlende Kostbarkeit' (EM, p. 82), whose adventurous spirit and love of life represent an exemplary biography.

Resistance as a Form of Biography?: Achim's 'Akt des Widerstands'

Johanna's husband Achim also experiences difficulty in adapting to life after socialism. While his wife was busy inserting secret messages into ostensibly innocuous historical biographies, he had immersed himself in his research on Kleist, to the exclusion of all else: 'Achim [hatte] die Erforschung des Kleistschen Werkes wie eine Barrikade vor sich errichtet' (EM, p. 85), his wife observes. Having barricaded himself behind his research, he was able to pursue 'sein heimliches Gelehrtenleben' (EM, p. 85). For Achim, this research quickly assumed an oppositional aspect, 'ein Akt des Widerstands' (EM, p. 86), which bestowed a feeling of intellectual freedom, 'ein Gefühl geistiger Unabhängigkeit' (EM, p. 86). He had quite literally turned his back on the world, as is clear from Johanna's recurring description of him sitting at his desk, 'den Rücken mir zugekehrt' (EM, p. 46). Before the Wende she could tolerate this stance, interpreting it as an assertion of her husband's independence: 'Achim [kämpfte] hinter der Kleist-Barrikade nicht nur für seinen Ehrgeiz [...], sondern um seine Unabhängigkeit' (EM, p. 86)

The collapse of the GDR brought drastic changes to Achim's professional life. The institute in which he had worked was shut down and his research taken over as a project by a different institute. Surrounded by other Kleist researchers, he suddenly found himself having to prove his indispensability. His previously silent resistance no longer appeared to have any significance; instead he began to exhibit ambition, a trait that he had previously dismissed as 'institutionellen Ehrgeiz' (EM, p. 87). Despite this survival strategy, he was promptly passed over for promotion when a professor from Hamburg was assigned the position of project leader. The Kleist barricade had become a

---

11 Waltraud Maierhofer, 'Wilhelmine Encke-Ritz-Lichtenau: Writing and Reading the Life of a Prussian Royal Mistress', *Biography: An Interdisciplinary Quarterly*, 27.3 (2004), pp. 575–96 (p. 590).

springboard: 'ein Sprungbrett, auf dem Achim unsicher wippte und mit den Armen schlug, wie ein Vogel, der vergessen hat, wie er fliegen kann' (EM, p. 86). This change of metaphor perfectly captures the move from retreat to albeit tentative, but necessary engagement with society. The image of the springboard also represents the opportunities for biographical change heralded by the end of the GDR.

Despite such possibilities for change, Achim continues to turn his back on the world and on his wife. In a letter that Johanna writes from Basekow, but that she does not send, she wonders about his continued refusal to turn towards her and, figuratively, towards the future: 'Kehrst du der Welt und mir den Rücken, weil Dich mehr als der ganze lebendige Rest das bedruckte Papier vor Dir interessiert, oder krallst Du Dich am Papier fest, um Deine Unlust an der Welt zu tarnen?' (EM, p. 58). She reflects on the growing emotional distance between them as they struggle in an environment of disorientation and insecurity: 'Solange Achim hinter seiner Kleist-Barrikade gekämpft hatte, war Kleist für mich das Sinnbild unserer Verschworenheit gewesen [...] Aber jetzt war Kleist ein Projekt, und ein Projekt taugt nicht zum Sinnbild, jedenfalls nicht für mich' (EM, pp. 91–92). She registers their increasing emotional estrangement: 'Ich war entlassen aus dem Kleist-Projekt' (EM, p. 92) is her laconic comment.

In a *Spiegel* interview Maron is quite dismissive of Achim's behaviour and his apparent unwillingness to change. She interprets the motif of turning his back on the world: 'Das konnte in der DDR als Verweigerungshaltung gelten. Aber nach der Wende hat das keinen höheren Sinn mehr.'[12] Johanna's disappointment comes from the realisation that his withdrawal was not, in fact, oppositional at all: 'Es war überhaupt kein Widerstand, es war einfach nur seine Art zu leben.'[13] His silent resistance is revealed to be nothing more than an illusion.

---

12   Romain Leick and Volker Hage, '"Das Glück bleibt unerreicht": Die Schriftstellerin Monika Maron über ihren neuen Roman, die Sehnsucht nach einem gelungenen Leben und das Verlustgefühl im Osten', *Der Spiegel*, 23 July 2007, pp. 140–42 (p. 141).
13   Ibid, p. 141.

Struggling to Adapt: The Other Characters

Other characters also experience feelings of insignificance. Like Achim, Johanna's friend Elli must adapt to drastic changes in her professional life. Her biography reveals a strong-willed, determined character; indeed Johanna describes her own inadequacy when compared with her friend's intelligence and independence. Elli applied for an exit visa; not content to stagnate, she wrote a book during the four-year waiting period. Having been finally granted the permit, she settled in Kreuzberg and went on to become a successful newspaper editor. After the Wende she had to undergo the humiliation of a new, supremely confident and, worst of all, much younger boss: a twenty-eight-year old Harvard graduate, a mere one year older than Johanna's daughter Laura.

Karoline Winter is a successful artist from Berlin and a neighbour of Johanna's in Basekow. The melancholic mood of Maron's text extends even to the minutiae of Karoline's paintings, which exude a 'kühle Melancholie' (EM, p. 70). Johanna is jealous of her much grander country retreat and, more significantly, of her professional success. She is again assailed by feelings of inadequacy: 'Ich fühlte mich selbst armselig und provisorisch, ein mißlungener Prototyp vom Menschen, dem Karolines Eleganz versagt war wie ihr Erfolg, der wirklich ein Erfolg in der Welt war' (EM, p. 71). Johanna's daughter sees Karoline as belonging to a world of adventure and risk: 'Für Laura gehörte Karoline zur Welt des Risikos und des Spiels, der Siege und Niederlagen, in der wir, Achim und ich, wenn überhaupt, nur unfreiwillig spielten und auch nur um die letzten Plätze' (EM, p. 186). It is all the more surprising, then, to learn that this adventurous character suffers from a fear of flying, which renders her hysterical and irrational on the evening before a trip to Moscow. When Johanna arrives to appease her, she finds her friend frantically composing her last will and testament. Karoline is overcome by feelings of insignificance. She dismisses her paintings and the material trappings of her life and is distressed by the fact that she does not have children of her own. Johanna is uncomfortable when confronted with her friend's sense of inadequacy and she attempts to offer a contrary perspective: 'Von dir bleiben immerhin deine Bilder, von mir bleibt nichts. Außer Laura' (EM, p. 182). Even a figure as confident as Karoline is not immune to feelings of 'Bedeutungslosigkeit' (EM p. 182).

Johanna's newly-acquired correspondent, Christian P., is forced to reevaluate his biography when his wife Katrin leaves him for a young Finnish composer, fifteen years her junior. Although he is stunned at the speed with which his life unravels – 'Sie [...] setzte mich ab. Es ging alles sehr schnell, und ich verstand nichts. Sie hatte es so eilig, mich loszuwerden' (EM, p. 159) – he also concedes that, in the years prior to their separation, he had already been plagued by thoughts of a stifling routine: 'die Furcht, ich könnte in den festgefügten Ritualen unseres Zusammenlebens allmählich verkümmern' (EM, p. 160). Although the changes in Christian P's life did not involve anything as dramatic as the collapse of an entire political system, they were equally unexpected: 'Du siehst, liebe Johanna', he writes, 'es müssen nicht ganze Imperien zerbrechen, um in unserem Leben ungeahnte Dinge geschehen zu lassen' (EM, p. 160). In his professional life, too, he has been passed over. The publishing house in which he had worked for twenty years was sold and restructured. The humanities, once its core offering and his area of expertise, have been relegated, 'zum Appendix geschrumpft' (EM, p. 96). New, much younger colleagues now hold power; he has been banished to the attic (EM, p. 96). He empathises with Johanna's sense of disorientation: 'Und jetzt kennst Du auch schon das Gefühl, zu früh aus der Welt gefallen zu sein' (EM, p. 94), he writes in one of his letters. He feels out of step with his contemporary society: 'manchmal denke ich wirklich: laß sie doch ziehen, die Welt' (EM, p. 95). Just as thoughts of an 'öde lange Restzeit' (EM, p. 55) fill Johanna with fear, Christian P. is equally unnerved by the prospect of stagnation: 'Und dann erschrecke ich, weil mir klar wird, daß ich, statistisch gesehen, in solcher Lethargie, noch zwanzig, vielleicht sogar dreißig Jahre verbringen kann' (EM, p. 95).

1989 and the Rupture of Biographies

Johanna recalls her initial delight at what she repeatedly terms the 'Wunder' of 1989. She witnessed the collapse of the old order in the dismantling of economic, administrative and educational institutions. Maron's text also alludes to the physical rebuilding of the former GDR. The castle in Basekow is restored. In one of his final letters, Christian P. describes the transformation of Berlin, urging Johanna to return to the capital and complete her biography of Wilhelmine Enke.

Rather than presenting a romanticised version of a unified Germany, the novel depicts fraught East-West relationships. Achim must endure the ignominy of watching a professor from Hamburg assume the sought-after position of project leader. Johanna, her husband and her friends find it difficult to adapt to an increasingly competitive professional milieu. Instead of heralding limitless opportunities for advancement, the Wende marks a caesura in their career trajectories. They are cast aside, passed over for promotion and, in the case of Christian P., literally removed from view.

Johanna celebrated the end of the old order, but failed to embrace the possibilities of a new beginning that the demise of the GDR afforded: 'Ich habe damals vor allem das Ende dessen, was wir für ewig gehalten hatten, gefeiert und darüber wohl den Anfang vergessen', she realises in retrospect, 'So scheint es mir jedenfalls heute' (EM, p. 214). In her rural retreat she grapples with her apparently insignificant existence. Her husband has quite literally turned his back on her, while her daughter is busy travelling the world and forging a successful career. Laura's fearless disposition and adventurous spirit merely reinforce her mother's sense of inadequacy: 'In Laura wuchs das Mädchen heran, das ich hätte sein wollen' (EM, p. 168). Her very emotions have become superfluous, 'weil alles und jedes, worauf ich sie richtete, sich ihnen entzog' (EM, p. 212). Even the writing of biographies, once a source of pride, now lacks emotional investment: 'selbst das Biografienschreiben, früher ein Geysir meiner Aufregung, ist eine fast gefühllose Angelegenheit geworden' (EM, p. 212). Towards the end of the text, a sexual encounter with Igor, on the eve of her return to Berlin, releases Johanna from her lethargy. The Russian impresses upon her the importance of new beginnings: 'man müsse vor allem im eigenen Leben dafür sorgen, daß es zu jeder Zeit genügend Anfänge gibt, glückliche Anfänge' (EM, p. 240). Rejuvenated, she resolves to complete the biography on Enke in the capital. En route she happens upon an abandoned dog and decides to take it home. The final line of the novel – 'Ein wunderlicher Anfang, dachte ich' (EM, p. 253) – appears to herald a new beginning and a move away from the pervasive 'Schläfrigkeit' (EM, p. 213) of her life since 1989.

In 'Lebensentwürfe, Zeitenbrüche' Maron addresses the crisis of identity experienced by many former GDR citizens in a drastically-altered society – a seminal concern for her characters in *Endmoränen* also: 'Ostdeutsche Lebensläufe offenbarten oft erst im Licht ihrer gesamtdeutschen Fortsetzung, was sie wirklich gewesen waren [...] für die einen mag das den Verlust ihres

Selbstbildes bedeutet haben; andere haben es wiedergefunden.' The characters who populate Maron's melancholic 'Herbstbuch' experience the Wende as a radical rupture, after which they seem doomed to stagnate. Its sequel *Ach Glück* follows these same characters as they seek to refashion their biographies and begin again.

Ach Glück

In the winter semester of 2004–05 Maron was a guest lecturer at the Goethe-Universität Frankfurt. She delivered a series of lectures entitled 'Vom Scheitern I–III', 'Von Schriftstellern, Hunden und Mythenbewahrern', 'Von der Fähigkeit zum Glücklichsein' and 'Versuch'. Subsequently published as *Wie ich ein Buch nicht schreiben kann und es trotzdem versuche*, these four lectures recount the difficulties she experienced in her attempts to write the sequel to *Endmoränen*. Interwoven into each of the lectures were extracts from the work-in-progress, which was later to become *Ach Glück*. As well as reflecting on the process of composition, Maron provides in these texts valuable insights into her characters. She describes her motivation for writing a sequel: 'weil ich herausfinden wollte, wie die Geschichte, die ich in die Welt gesetzt hatte, weitergeht' (WIE, p. 9). She recalls a previous instance when she was unable to separate herself from a character constellation – the main protagonist Rosalind Polkowski and many of the other figures in *Die Überläuferin* reappear in her subsequent novel *Stille Zeile Sechs*. Significantly, Maron establishes a parallel between the ending of *Die Überläuferin* and the final passages of *Endmoränen*: 'beide Bücher enden mit dem entschiedenen Wunsch ihrer Protagonistinnen nach Veränderung der eigenen Lage' (WIE, p. 14). Rosalind Polkowski and Johanna Märtin contemplate society from positions of retreat; however, the desire for change, which is already evident in the closing sequences of both novels, translates into a willingness to re-engage with the world in the sequels *Stille Zeile Sechs* and *Ach Glück* respectively.

Wie ich ein Buch nicht schreiben kann und es trotzdem versuche functions as an intermediary text, referencing *Endmoränen* as its point of departure and prefiguring *Ach Glück*, the sequel that emerges when Maron has overcome her writer's block. In the final lecture, which she entitles 'Versuch', she raises the issue of narrative perspective and ponders the possible use of first-person narrative in relation to Achim. *Ach Glück* is the first text in which Maron narrates from a male perspective. Composed of fifteen chapters and charting a single day in the lives of Johanna and Achim, the alternating of perspectives throughout proves to be a most effective structural device, revealing the characters' thoughts as they respond to a potentially life-changing event for both of them: Johanna's trip to Mexico City. The novel opens with Johanna already in the air; in the concluding scene she is making her way through passport control, having reached her 'Sehnsuchtsort' (WIE, p. 110). In the course of this long-haul flight, she recalls the events that precipitated her decision to reshape her biography in such a dramatic manner. Alternating chapters follow Achim as he spends the day wandering around Berlin, trying to come to terms with the reasons for and significance of his wife's departure.

Endmoränen provided a melancholic meditation on the passage of time and missed opportunities; its sequel develops these themes and follows the progress of the same characters. The title also has its genesis in a scene from the earlier novel during which Elli and Johanna discussed the nature of happiness. Elli recounted an interview she had conducted with a research scientist; Johanna's response to his claim that apes are also capable of experiencing happiness was the laconic, possibly fatalistic, ultimately ambiguous comment 'Ach, Glück' (EM, p. 122). The reviewer Jörg Magenau notes that the title of Maron's most recent novel can be read as a resigned sigh or as an expression of surprised discovery; both interpretations are bound together in what he terms a 'klassische Aufbruchsgeschichte.'[14] In the pursuit of happiness and propelled by a desire to restore meaning to her ruptured biography, the Johanna of *Ach Glück* is ready to embark upon a new chapter in her life.

---

14   Jörg Magenau, 'Mein Hund ist meine wahre Liebe', *Der Tagesspiegel*, 27 July 2007, <http://www.tagesspiegel.de/kultur/literatur-alt/mein-hund-ist-meine-wahre-liebe/997078.html>.

Refashioning her Biography: Johanna's 'wunderlicher Anfang'

In the first of her guest lectures in Frankfurt, Maron recalls her feelings following the completion of *Endmoränen* and the realisation that she needed to continue writing about these characters. It quickly became apparent to her that her protagonist needed to be released from the pervasive lethargy depicted throughout the text: 'Johanna musste aus ihrer Lethargie befreit und Situationen ausgesetzt werden, die zur anderen, mystischen, gefährlichen Seite des Lebens gehören' (WIE, p. 10). Having spent months in Basekow contemplating the prospect of the 'öde lange Restzeit' (EM, p. 55) stretching ahead of her, she returns to Berlin in the final sequence of *Endmoränen*. En route she finds an abandoned dog in a parking lot and takes him home. The animal heralds a new beginning. Johanna's enthusiastic response to Bredow's unexpected arrival into her life indicates an openness to change: 'eigentlich hat alles mit dem Hund angefangen', her husband reflects in retrospect.[15]

Maron describes the illusory nature of the importance Johanna had attached to her professional role as a historical biographer pre-1989: 'Johannas Gleichgewicht beruhte auf einer Täuschung. Abhanden gekommen ist ihr das Gewicht der eigenen Wichtigkeit, einer Wichtigkeit, die keine war' (WIE, p. 90). Painfully aware of the sudden insignificance of her professional life, Johanna has resolved to stop writing biographies. 'Ich beneide Leute mit einem richtigen Schicksal', she reveals in conversation with Hannes Stahl, the man to whom she entrusts Bredow during her trip to Mexico; 'Dabei habe ich lange Zeit gedacht, ich hätte eins' (AG, p. 156), she continues wistfully. Johanna can no longer tolerate the monotony of her existence, 'die Endlosschleife, zu der es [ihr Leben] geraten war' (AG, p. 101); nor can she continue to engage in the depressing rituals, 'die albtraumhaften Wiederholungen, in denen alle Tage zu einem schrumpften' (AG, pp. 101–02). *Ach Glück* returns to the theme of the ageing female body, already an issue of concern for Johanna in the earlier text. Suffocated by the sameness of the company she keeps and depressed by what she terms 'dieses kollektive Altern' (AG, p. 41), she is under no illusions about the loss of sexual power experienced by middle-aged women: 'weil sie in

---

15   Monika Maron, *Ach Glück: Roman* (Frankfurt am Main: S. Fischer, 2007), p. 29. Quotations from the novel will be followed in parentheses by the abbreviation AG and the relevant page number.

den Augen gleichaltriger Männer auf den erotischen Abfallhaufen gehörten' (AG, p. 38), she comments acerbically.

Exploring a further theme of *Endmoränen*, its sequel continues to chart the relationship between Johanna and Achim. From Johanna's perspective their marriage is disintegrating, yet another instance of the stultifying routine from which she must escape: 'die anhaltende Freudlosigkeit, die sich über ihren ehelichen Alltag seit einigen Jahren wie Mehltau gelegt hatte' (AG, p. 104). She has become increasingly intolerant of her husband's work on Kleist and is dismissive of his obsessive attention to detail: 'Alles wurde in seine kleinsten Teile zerlegt, in Szenen, Sätze, Wörter, Silben, Buchstaben, [...] bis das Werk enthäutet, ausgeblutet und skelettiert [...] auf seinem Schreibtisch lag, zu Tode verzehrt von Doktor Achim Märtin' (AG, p. 135). The violence of this imagery indicates her deep-seated anger at her husband's dedication to his academic project to the exclusion of all else, even at the expense of their relationship. Her frustration at his apparent unwillingness to change also finds expression in the final image of Achim as 'ein moderner Kentaur, halb Schreibtisch, halb Mann' (AG, p. 216).

During the transatlantic flight Johanna recalls the sequence of events culminating in her dramatic decision to travel to Mexico City. At a New Year's Eve party hosted by her friend Karoline Winter, she once again encountered Igor, the Russian gallery owner who had also featured in *Endmoränen* and who had emphasised the importance of 'glückliche Anfänge' (EM, p. 240). She agreed to work in his gallery and it is in this context that she began corresponding with his friend, the Russian aristocrat Natalia Timofejewna. The ninety-year-old has already travelled to Mexico in search of the artist and writer Leonora Carrington; 'fassen Sie sich ein Herz, meine Liebe, und kommen Sie her' (AG, p. 7), she urges Johanna in a letter. Responding to this 'Lockruf' (AG, p. 152) from the other side of the world, Johanna quite literally leaves her old life behind.

The flight also affords Johanna the opportunity to reflect on the nature of happiness. The birth of her daughter was the happiest event of her life and the all-consuming feelings of that period had not been replicated, with one notable exception – the fall of the Wall: 'abgesehen also von diesem geschichtlichen Beben war ihr in den letzten siebenundzwanzig Jahren nichts zugestoßen, das ihr als überwältigendes und darum gefährliches Glück erschienen wäre' (AG, p. 103). The abandoned dog discovered en route to Berlin in the final passage of *Endmoränen* is a harbinger of happiness. In Bredow's company

Johanna begins to laugh again. She enjoys nocturnal walks with her newfound companion, thus resuming an activity that had brought her such pleasure in her youth. She is indebted to Bredow for unleashing her independent spirit: 'diese wiedergewonnene Freiheit, sagte Johanna, verdanke sie nur dem Hund' (AG, p. 34). Reflecting on the animal's unconditional love, she realises: 'So einfach ist es also, Glück auszulösen und glücklich zu sein' (AG, p. 62). In the appropriately-entitled lecture 'Von Schriftstellern, Hunden und Mythenbewahrern', Maron sees in the dog's presence the stimulus prompting Johanna to reflect on the meaning of her own life and her understanding of happiness: 'Der Hund als Fragezeichen hinter der eigenen Sinn- und Glücksvorstellung' (WIE, p. 40). She underscores the serendipitous nature of the animal's arrival into her protagonist's world: 'In Gestalt des Hundes begegnet ihr der Zufall, dessen Folgen sie zulassen kann oder zurückweisen' (WIE, p. 32). The 'wunderlicher Anfang' (EM, p. 253) of her chance encounter with Bredow heralds the longed-for change in Johanna's life.

Adventurous Biographies: Natalia Timofejewna and Leonora Carrington

In *Endmoränen* Wilhelmine Enke's life story served as a counter-biography to the monotony of her biographer's existence. In *Ach Glück* the biographies of the fictional character Natalia Timofejewna and of the surrealist artist Leonora Carrington capture a sense of adventure that Johanna seeks to emulate by responding to Natalia's call. The reader of *Endmoränen* was already familiar with much of the Russian aristocrat's life story. According to Igor, she claimed to have been born into a wealthy Muscovite family that had emigrated to Germany during the October Revolution. She studied art in Berlin, where she first became acquainted with Max Ernst and Leonora Carrington. During the Nazi period she fled to Mexico and later married Walter, a German communist, with whom she returned to the GDR. 'Mein Leben war in die Ereignisse meines Jahrhunderts verwoben', she writes in a letter from Mexico, 'und ich habe es so angenommen' (AG, p. 130), thus situating her individual biography in the context of twentieth-century German history.[16]

---

16   Maron's family story *Pawels Briefe* explored the relationship between individual biography and overarching historical structure, as I demonstrated in Chapter Five.

Natalia also seeks to refashion her biography following the death of the man to whom she was married for fifty years. Propelled into action after inadvertently discovering that Leonora Carrington is still alive, she journeys to Mexico in the hope of reuniting with her and thus recapturing the vitality of her youth. Just as Johanna sees her chance encounter with Bredow as part of her destiny, Natalia also interprets the radio programme about Leonora Carrington as being destined for her alone: 'Mein Herz sagte mir, dass diese Botschaft für mich bestimmt war, nur für mich' (AG, p. 57). Johanna is full of admiration for her correspondent's apparent fearlessness in embarking alone upon this 'Reise ins Ungewisse' (AG, p. 66). Natalia, for her part, admires Leonora enormously and reveals that she often wished that she had had the courage to change her life many years previously: '[ich habe] oft gewünscht [...], ich hätte damals mehr von Leonoras Kraft und Talent oder einfach mehr Glück gehabt und mir ein anderes Leben erobert als das, in das Walter mich dann nach Deutschland geführt hat' (AG, p. 129). Determined to transform her biography despite her advanced years, Natalia revisits the city of her youth and captures in her letters the vibrancy, chaos and exotic nature of the South American capital. Johanna's comment about her correspondent's life story – 'fünfzig Jahre in der eigenen Haut als eine Andere, fünfzig Jahre ein fremdes Leben' (AG, p. 134) – has a resonance for her own biography also.

It is Natalia who urges Johanna to read Leonora Carrington's novel *Das Hörrohr*; interestingly, this fantastic tale is also about 'die Malaisen des Alters' (AG, p. 107) and follows the progress of two very old ladies, Marian Leatherby and her friend Carmella Velasquez, both determined to embrace life.[17] Born in Lancashire in 1917, Carrington became famous as a surrealist painter and later as a novelist. Hers is a turbulent biography that includes a relationship with Max Ernst, a mental breakdown and escape to Mexico, where she still lives. In her essay 'Wo war Leonora Carrington?', Maron bemoans the lack of public interest in and information about this important figure. She admires Carrington's 'mutwillige Täterschaft'.[18] This desire to take action is a motif

---

[17] In her text '"Das Hörrohr" von Leonora Carrington', Maron emphasises the fantastical elements of Carrington's novel. *'Doch das Paradies ist verriegelt...': Zum Werk von Monika Maron*, ed. by Elke Gilson (Frankfurt am Main: Fischer Taschenbuch Verlag, 2006), pp. 293–95.

[18] Monika Maron, 'Wo war Leonora Carrington?', in *Nach Maßgabe meiner Begreifungskraft*, pp. 63–65 (p. 65).

throughout Maron's oeuvre and finds expression in the refashioning of individual biographies in *Ach Glück*. Although she has resolved to stop writing biographies, 'weil sie es leid war, fremden Lebenswegen wie ein Schatten zu folgen' (AG, p. 111), Johanna continues to process Carrington's story in her mind, searching for the 'Ursprung ihrer Biografie' (AG, p. 111). Just as she hoped to gain insight into her own life by writing Wilhelmine Enke's life story, Johanna seeks similar answers when confronted with Carrington's creative, tumultuous biography: 'In Johanna regte sich die professionelle Neugier, wie immer, wenn ihr schien, in einer fremden Biografie ließe sich etwas finden, das ihr Aufschluss geben könnte über die Wirrnisse ihres eigenen Lebens' (AG, p. 111).

Carrington's paintings exude energy and teem with phantasmagoric images: 'In Leonoras Bildern tummelten sich phantastische Mischlinge' (AG, p. 112). According to Natalia, Leonora understands 'die Sprache der Tiere' (AG, p. 161). Johanna admires the free-spirited, determined figure depicted in her self-portrait: 'So war ich nie, dachte Johanna [...] nie so wild, nie so entschlossen' (AG, p. 110). Despite repeated attempts on Natalia's part to track down her erstwhile friend, Carrington remains a mystery: 'Es passt zu Leonora, dass sie sich einfach unsichtbar macht' (AG, p. 182), Natalia notes in a letter. Maron echoes this comment. In a *Spiegel* interview she reveals that she herself had travelled to Mexico in 2004, but never actually wanted to meet Leonora Carrington: 'Sie musste ein Phantom bleiben', she explains.[19] For Natalia – and perhaps for Johanna also – Leonora Carrington is 'die Verkörperung eines gelungenen Lebens' (AG, p. 153).

'Wer hat das Leben, das er sich wünscht'?: Achim's Biographical Reflections

While his wife, enthralled by the adventurous biographies of Natalia Timofejewna and Leonora Carrington, journeys to the other side of the world, Achim is left to contemplate the motivation for and consequences of her dramatic departure. The reader of *Endmoränen* encountered in Achim an academic who had apparently turned his back on the world; in *Ach Glück*

---

19   Romain Leick and Volker Hage, '"Das Glück bleibt unerreicht"', *Der Spiegel*, 23 July 2007, p. 142.

the use of first-person narrative affords us insight into his thoughts as he, too, reflects on the biographical rupture that has been brought about by the Wende, but also by a changing relationship with Johanna.

Achim is acutely aware of the importance of Bredow in his wife's life as a catalyst for change. He realises that the dog and 'dieser arrogante Russe' (AG, p. 116), as he calls Igor, could enter Johanna's life precisely because she had been waiting for the opportunity to break with the monotony of her existence: 'ihr gewohntes Leben auf den Kopf zu stellen' (AG, p. 49). Their arrival into her life has radical repercussions for his biography also: 'ein Hund und ein Russe haben mein Leben durcheinandergebracht' (AG, p. 69) is his terse summation. The Berlin cityscape is the backdrop to Achim's reflections; the upheaval in his life is reflected in the topography of change, renaming of streets, demolition and rebuilding. Welcoming the transformation of the capital, he dismisses any physical reminders of the political state; 'die abgetakelte Zwingburg der proletarischen Diktatur [...] enthäutet, grindig' (AG, p. 88) is his caustic description of the infamous Palast der Republik. He recalls his earlier life with Johanna: 'unsere ehemalige Jugend in diesem ehemaligen Staat' (AG, p. 95). Their triumph at the collapse of this state, 'als dessen Feind sie sich beide verstanden hatten' (AG, p. 95), was, according to his wife, the last passionate feeling that they had shared.

Achim's biography was shaped by an innate unwillingness to engage in confrontation of any kind: 'Die Kampffelder hatte er in seinem Leben lieber gemieden' (AG, p. 94), he concedes. Having retreated to his study, he relished the security that his work as a lone researcher brought. He felt 'sicher und am richtigen, an dem für ihn im Leben vorgesehenen Platz' (AG, p. 94). However, he realises that this retreat was simultaneously a self-protective act, sheltering him from any real imperative to engage with the world around him: 'Er hingegen hatte vielleicht wirklich zwischen den Büchern vor allem einen Platz gesucht, der ihn vor dem Leben bewahren sollte' (AG, p. 171). He considers visiting Kleist's grave in Wannsee. His comment 'Da lag auch sein Leben begraben' (AG, p. 68) is tinged with regret; he is forced to recognise the veracity of his wife's observation: 'ein Leben im Dienste des Heinrich von Kleist, wie Johanna kürzlich nicht ohne Bosheit bemerkt hatte' (AG, p. 68). The growing emotional distance between them derives in no small part from Achim's obsession with his academic project. His affair with a younger woman some six years previously is also revealed during the course of his reflections. It is Laura who expresses most cogently the extent to which her parents have grown apart: 'in letzter Zeit seien sie beide ihr wie ein entkoppelter Zug vorgekommen, die eine Hälfte bleibt stehen, die andere fährt weiter' (AG, p. 173).

Alternating chapters chart one fateful day in Achim's life, a day during which he contemplates his relationship with his wife, from their very first encounter at university thirty years earlier to a conversation the previous evening about the search for happiness. He suggests that she may find happiness in Mexico. There is sadness in his interpretation of her response and awareness that his wife has not been happy for a long time:

> Ach Glück, hatte sie nur gesagt, eigentlich nicht gesagt, eher geseufzt, versetzt mit einem kleinen harten Lachen, ach Glück, als sei ihr dieses Wort schon vor langer Zeit entfallen und als erinnere sie sich gerade in diesem Augenblick an seinen Klang, ach Glück, und als sei er schuld, dass ihr ein so kostbares Wort bedeutungslos geworden war. (AG, pp. 198–99)

While a confused Achim may be left alone to contemplate the memories of their life together, the novel's ending is an optimistic one. During a dinner party at the house of a particularly obnoxious colleague – one of several scenes during which Maron takes a satirical swipe at Berlin academic circles – he envisages knowing glances exchanged with Johanna and her clever interventions. He misses his wife. The day reminds him of the day his mother died suddenly in a car accident. He needed to tell her that he loved her, but it was too late: 'Den ganzen Tag war er gegen die Endgültigkeit angelaufen, an diesem Dienstag vor dreißig Jahren. Wie heute' (AG, p. 206). The final line of the chapter 'Nur dass Johanna noch lebte' (AG, p. 206) seems to negate the apparent irrevocability of her departure. Johanna is determined to embrace the opportunities that are presented to her; Achim, too, seems finally ready to reshape his biography by confronting the problems in their relationship. The ending of *Ach Glück* is ultimately a hopeful one.

Conclusion

The autumnal *Endmoränen* and its more hopeful sequel *Ach Glück* explore the search for meaning in a post-GDR age. In her rural retreat of Basekow the biographer Johanna Märtin is left to contemplate 'die ruinösen Reste ihrer früher als sinnvoll empfundenen Lebenskonstruktion' (WIE, pp. 8–9). Her sense of accomplishment in the transmission of 'heimliche Botschaften' (EM, p. 38) has yielded to the disappointment of 'Biografien ohne Botschaften' (EM, p. 138) and to the sudden insignificance of her professional life in a post-GDR society. Privately, too, she is growing increasingly estranged from her husband Achim, who is also struggling to adapt to life after the GDR. The prospect 'in endloser Wiederholung fortzuleben' (EM, p. 138) fills her with dread. The characters of *Endmoränen* experience the Wende as a biographical caesura, after which they seem destined to stagnate and atrophy. The passionate excesses recalled by the narrator of *Animal triste* have ceded to a prevailing sense of lethargy, from which Johanna is rescued only in the closing sequence of the text.

Ach Glück follows the progress of these same characters as they seek to restore meaning and thus overcome the historical and biographical rupture caused by the implosion of the GDR. Johanna is ready to begin again; the 'wunderlicher Anfang' (EM, p. 253) of Bredow's arrival sets in motion a sequence of events that facilitate the reshaping of her biography. While Achim's response is far less radical than departure for Mexico, he, too, realises the need for change. Taken together, *Endmoränen* and *Ach Glück* trace the movement from retreat to re-engagement with society, a movement precipitated by the adventurous, alternative biographies interwoven into the texts. The lives of Wilhelmine Enke, Natalia Timofejewna and Leonora Carrington symbolise a vitality to which Johanna aspires.

Significantly, in her most recent novels, published so many years after the Wende, Maron is still reflecting on the demise of the socialist state, even if the scathing criticism of the GDR, present throughout her writing, has been replaced by a sobering portrayal of post-unification reality. In her address 'Lebensentwürfe, Zeitenbrüche' she foregrounds the sudden loss of identity experienced by many of her contemporaries following the collapse of the GDR; it is precisely this 'Verlust ihres Selbstbildes' with which Johanna and Achim struggle. Suddenly deprived of the 'Illusion über sich selbst' ('Lebensentwürfe, Zeitenbrüche'), they are forced to reflect on the meaning of their lives. *Endmoränen* and *Ach Glück* chart the rupture and the ultimate refashioning of individual biographies in a post-GDR age.

Conclusion

The implosion in late 1989 of an entire political and literary system necessitated a radical review of critical practice. Amidst the rubble of the GDR and its institutions, the literary historian Wolfgang Emmerich called for a rereading of traditional approaches to those texts emerging from a defunct state. His proposal has assumed paradigmatic significance for my study of Maron's oeuvre. Emmerich advocated a movement away from those critical approaches that had privileged the sociopolitical dimension of the texts, proposing instead an analysis that would consider their imaginative elements. Embracing the challenge to reread, I have explored in the present study 'die Mobilisierung von Phantasie' ('Für eine andere Wahrnehmung', p. 17), those imaginative impulses which manifest themselves in various ways throughout Maron's oeuvre.

As I demonstrated in Chapters One and Two, the search for an authentic form of expression defined Maron's writing in the 1970s and 1980s. The transition from journalism to fiction, from her contributions to the *Wochenpost* to her debut novel, the quasi-fictitious *Flugasche*, became, in effect, a process of writing herself out of the prevailing discourse system. This process was accelerated throughout the final decade of the GDR, manifesting itself in the radical stylistic experimentation of the collection *Das Mißverständnis* and of her second novel *Die Überläuferin*. It is literature's role as '"Gegentext", als Subversion des Leitdiskurses' ('Für eine andere Wahrnehmung', p. 17) that Emmerich foregrounded as he urged us to reread; in *Flugasche* and particularly in *Die Überläuferin*, the imaginative realm serves as a potentially subversive counter-text, even if complete escape from the physical and the ideological confines of the political state remains an illusion.

The protagonist of Maron's third novel also creates a powerful counter-text when she writes into her story those marginalised figures who find no place in official GDR historiography. In the claustrophobic setting of Herbert Beerenbaum's study, a bitter struggle to write and rewrite GDR history unfolds. Conflicting versions of a shared GDR past collide as Beerenbaum clings to the teleological narrative of a triumphant socialism, while his amanuensis exposes and demolishes the myth of the antifascist state upon which he has constructed his life story. Rosalind Polkowsi's brutal determination to rewrite his version of the past culminates in an explosive final confrontation, from which Beerenbaum never recovers. By recollecting in the novel's present increasingly fraught transcription sessions, Rosalind writes the story of Beerenbaum's life into her text. In the closing sequence she accepts a parcel containing the memoirs that she has transcribed and amended. Ultimately, then, she remains trapped within the very metanarrative against which she has railed throughout the text. As I illustrated in Chapter Three, the problem of history remains.

Maron's post-Wende writing reflects on the caesura caused by the collapse of the GDR. Like her protagonist Johanna Märtin, she welcomed the thematic freedom heralded by the Wende; the demise of the political system led to an exploration in her writing of more intimate themes. Chapter Four foregrounds this inward turn. Having retreated from her contemporary society, the first-person narrator of *Animal triste* is sustained only by memories of an all-consuming love affair. Even in this tale of sexual obsession, the sociopolitical dimension never disappears completely: a chaotic Berlin in the months immediately following the fall of the Wall serves as fitting backdrop to the lovers' erotic encounters.

It is Maron's family story *Pawels Briefe* that best captures the fragmented experience of twentieth-century German history. Significantly, the GDR experience continues to shape Maron's writing in this powerful memory narrative published a decade after the Wende. As I demonstrated in Chapter Five, the author's attempts to reconstruct her family biography are themselves refracted through contrary versions of a shared GDR past. Chapter Six foregrounds the rupture and the ultimate refashioning of biographies in a post-GDR age as central themes in Maron's most recent novels, the melancholic *Endmoränen* and its more optimistic sequel *Ach Glück*. The protagonist Johanna Märtin is a biographer struggling with the insignificance of her own professional and personal biography in a post-Wende era. Interwoven into the novels, the spirited, unorthodox life stories of Wilhelmine Enke, Leonora Carrington and the fictitious Natalia Timofejewna provide powerful counter-biographies to the stagnation of a life suddenly devoid of purpose.

Maron's protagonists contemplate their contemporary society from positions of retreat. In an interview the author drew attention to what she termed this particular writing constellation: 'Das Leben wird angehalten', she explained, 'Es wird erst aus der Ruhe reflektiert.'[1] A disillusioned Josefa Nadler withdraws from the offices of the *Illustrierte Woche*. Rosalind Polkowski defects into the imaginative realm in *Die Überläuferin* and resigns from her position as historian at a research institute in the sequel *Stille Zeile Sechs*. Necessarily concerned with the preservation of the past in her professional capacity as palaeontologist, the first-person narrator of *Animal triste* has retreated into memories of her doomed love affair. In *Pawels Briefe* the author exposes generational memory gaps, thus forcing re-engagement with a painful family past. Johanna Märtin, the protagonist of *Endmoränen* and *Ach Glück*, has withdrawn to the countryside to contemplate the apparent superfluity of her existence. However, the desire to take action exists in each protagonist and finds expression in various ways throughout the texts. Maron's most recent novel *Ach Glück* charts the movement from retreat to re-engagement with society, thus offering a fitting resolution to the biographical ruptures explored in earlier texts.

Although she creates potent counter-texts and counter-biographies and she embraces the thematic freedom of the post-Wende era, the GDR remains a constant presence in Maron's work. From her depiction of a restrictive society in *Flugasche* and of the ensuing intellectual and emotional stultification, as presented in *Das Mißverständnis* and *Die Überläuferin*, to her portrayal of a stagnant political state on the eve of its collapse in *Stille Zeile Sechs*; from the backdrop to the lovers' encounter in *Animal triste* to the complexities of memory transmission and of a mother–daughter relationship in *Pawels Briefe* – the GDR remains a continuity that she explores and recalls in her writing. Even in the autumnal *Endmoränen*, published some thirteen years after the Wende, she is still reflecting on life in the GDR, on the collapse of the socialist state and on the attendant rupture of individual biographies.

Maron's oeuvre articulates salient aspects of her generation's social and historical experience. Her protagonists are concerned with recording the events and moods of their society, whether as journalists, historians or biographers. Their author, too, articulates the personal experience of living through momentous historical change. She describes historical processes, including the rise and devastating consequences of fascism, the communist response

---

[1] Deirdre Byrnes, Interview with Monika Maron, Berlin-Schöneberg, 29 June 1999.

in the post-war years, the failures and the ultimate collapse of the antifascist state, in terms of biographical experience.

'Wie wird das Leben erzählbar?', Maron pondered during her address 'Lebensentwürfe, Zeitenbrüche', delivered at the *Historikertag* of 2002. She emphasised our need to attribute significance, albeit in retrospect, to the events of our lives, even if this distorts the reality of our experience:

> Um an meinem Misstrauen in die Freiheit unserer Selbsterfindung und in biografische Wahrheiten keinen Zweifel zu lassen, will ich auf unseren unwiderstehlichen Drang verweisen, unseren Lebensgeschichten nachträglich, diesem aus unzähligen Quellen zusammengeflossenen Verlauf unserer Lebenszeit einen Sinn zu geben, indem wir ihm eine Kausalität erfinden und damit uns selbst eine erzählbare Biografie.

However, this narratable biography is itself shaped by the roles that fate and coincidence play in our lives. As she had done in *Pawels Briefe*, Maron again quotes the sociologist Niklas Luhmann: 'Die Komponenten eines Lebenslaufs bestehen aus Wendepunkten, an denen etwas geschehen ist, was nicht hätte geschehen müssen. Das beginnt mit der Geburt.' She is cognisant of our very limited freedom in the shaping of our biographies. Attempting to restore causality to her fractured family past in *Pawels Briefe*, Maron appreciates the full import of Luhmann's words. She comes to realise that, despite a deep-seated desire to break with the GDR, her own biography cannot be extricated from her family's GDR experience: 'Eigentlich weiß ich es längst: den verpaßten Ausweg aus Hellas und damit meiner Biographie, nach dem ich mit Hilfe aller denkbaren Vielleichts immer wieder fahnde, gibt es nicht' (PB, p. 178–79).

Maron's texts go far beyond sociopolitical interpretations, even if, as I have shown in this study, it does not seem possible to prize them apart completely from the context in which they were composed. Each chapter has been informed by awareness not only of Emmerich's incitement to reread, but also of the author's repeated exhortations – most recently during her acceptance speech on receipt of the *Deutscher Nationalpreis* in 2009[2] – to consider the

---

2   Together with Erich Loest and Uwe Tellkamp, Maron was awarded the *Deutscher Nationalpreis* in June 2009. The awarding body, the *Deutsche Nationalstiftung*, explained that these authors, belonging to three different generations, were being honoured for their contribution to furthering in their literary work an understanding of German history, more particularly the history of the GDR.

literary quality of texts written in the GDR. In Maron's own case the constant rethinking and reimagining that underlie her work bear fruit in the remarkable qualities of her writing.

Monika Maron displays extraordinary versatility and is equally at ease in the genres of journalism, essay-writing, fiction and autobiography. While the focus of this study has been on her novels, she is also a brilliant essayist. In the collections *Nach Maßgabe meiner Begreifungskraft* and *Quer über die Gleise*, she reflects on an array of issues and provides a characteristically forthright and acerbic commentary on her contemporary society. In *Bitterfelder Bogen*, published in 2009, she revisits the East German town that played such an important role in her early writing career. She returns to her journalistic roots as she documents the decline and subsequent rebirth of the once-notorious Bitterfeld, now a world leader in the production of solar energy. The documentary quality of some Maron texts – the scathing depiction of Bitterfeld in *Flugasche*, the use of documents and letters in *Pawels Briefe* – is the legacy of her journalistic background. However, her writing, particularly her early novels, also demonstrates a willingness to experiment with form and to flout stylistic conventions. The imaginative realm acts a potent counter-text to the scripted existence of life in the GDR; the 'Mobilisierung von Phantasie' manifests itself in multiple narrative perspectives, frequent interruption of the linear narrative and, most obviously, in the phantasmagoric journeys undertaken by the protagonists of *Flugasche* and *Die Überläuferin*. As a novelist, Maron is highly skilled in the creation of dramatic tension. Nowhere is this more obvious than in the escalating conflict between Herbert Beerenbaum and his amanuensis that culminates in a highly-charged final confrontation in *Stille Zeile Sechs*.

Maron's writing is characterised by a keen awareness of linguistic subtleties. This is particularly apparent in her use of humour and irony. We recall the comic exchanges that occur in the pub, itself a potentially transgressive space in *Die Überläuferin* and *Stille Zeile Sechs*. Gentle irony is employed at the expense of the eccentric, endearing Karl-Heinz Baron and of the lovestruck, child-like piano-teacher Thekla Fleischer. Black humour is a feature of her texts – the description of Beerenbaum's funeral service in *Stille Zeile Sechs* and the grotesque circumstances that culminate in Franz's meeting a bloody end in *Animal triste* come to mind. Maron's use of irony is as effortless as it is effective. The frequently ironic tone of her articles and essays reinforces her incisive commentary on society. In *Animal triste* the gaping disparity between the passionate excesses of Kleist's anti-heroine and the banality of the context in which Penthesilea is invoked undermines, in ironic fashion, the narrator's identification with this literary and historical figure.

Maron creates a tangible sense of place, particularly in her nuanced, sustained portrayal of the Berlin cityscape, itself a constant presence in her writing. The oppression and stagnation of East Berlin gives way to the turbulence of the immediate post-Wende period. In the collection *Geburtsort Berlin*, published in 2003, she returns to observing her fellow city-dwellers, as she did three decades previously when writing for the *Wochenpost*. This collection is Maron's 'Liebesbekenntnis zu Berlin', homage to the city that has always been her emotional home.[3]

Monika Maron's biography reflects a deeply complex relationship with the GDR state, from initial ideological identification to disillusionment, from a collaboration of sorts to a sustained, radical rejection. Her oeuvre captures the difficulties for writers from the GDR, emerging from a system whose deeper structures continue to exert an influence. Growing from this past, her post-Wende writing turns towards more intimate themes, such as the female body, the passage of time, and, perhaps most significantly, memory and its repression. It is this merger of her textual reflection on life during and after the GDR with the paradigm shift in recent decades in German critical thinking towards the memory culture which is of particular interest to contemporary readers.

In this book I set out to reread Monika Maron's writing in a post-Wende light. As I explored the work of this incisive and complex literary voice, a number of interrelated themes emerged: the search for an authentic form of expression, history, memory, biographical rupture. From her journalistic beginnings she has evolved as a writer, creating a rich textual tapestry in which such themes find expression. This study offers new perspectives on Maron's writing and illuminates the significance of her contribution to contemporary German literature.

---

[3] Monika Maron, *Geburtsort Berlin* (Frankfurt am Main: S. Fischer, 2003), p. 50. A more detailed exploration of the importance of Berlin in Maron's oeuvre can be found in my article 'Berlin in the Writing of Monika Maron', which was published in *Berlin's Culturescape in the Twentieth Century*, edited by Thomas Bredohl and Michael Zimmermann (Regina: Canadian Plains Research Centre, 2008), pp. 229–43.

Bibliography

Primary Literature: Monika Maron

Articles for the Wochenpost

Articles on Pages Four and Five

'Bauen lernen', *Wochenpost*, 24 September 1976
'Drachentöter', *Wochenpost*, 21 June 1974
'Eva in Bitterfeld', *Wochenpost*, 1 August 1975
'Ist Geld die Hauptsache?', *Wochenpost*, 9 August 1974
'Der Marktplatz in Greifswald', *Wochenpost*, 20 December 1974
'Musketiere in Arnstadt?', *Wochenpost*, 29 March 1974
'Der Prellbock', *Wochenpost*, 15 November 1974
'Das Schiff auf der Insel', *Wochenpost*, 1 February 1974
'Traktoristen', *Wochenpost*, 20 September 1974
'Was macht der Technologe?', *Wochenpost*, 7 May 1976

Articles on Page Eighteen

'Als Wurschtmaxe auf dem Alex', *Wochenpost*, 11 October 1974
'Durch die Hintertür', *Wochenpost*, 17 January 1975
'Erzieh' mich mal', *Wochenpost*, 25 April 1975
'Hinter dem Tresen', *Wochenpost*, 24 January 1975
'Ich werde eingeschult', *Wochenpost*, 29 August 1975
'Im Laden an der Ecke', *Wochenpost*, 24 May 1974
'"Liebes Brautpaar ..."', *Wochenpost*, 26 December 1975
'Ein Mann im Hort', *Wochenpost*, 9 July 1976
'Mit Eis und Brause unterm Turm', *Wochenpost*, 25 October 1974
'Neptunfest', *Wochenpost*, 26 September 1975
'Wir und der Hut', *Wochenpost*, 2 April 1976

Book Publications

Ach Glück: Roman (Frankfurt am Main: S. Fischer, 2007)
Animal triste: Roman (Frankfurt am Main: S. Fischer, 1996)
Bitterfelder Bogen: Ein Bericht (Frankfurt am Main: S. Fischer, 2009)
Endmoränen: Roman (Frankfurt am Main: S. Fischer, 2002)
Flugasche: Roman (Frankfurt am Main: S. Fischer, 1981; Frankfurt am Main: Fischer Taschenbuch Verlag, 1995)
Geburtsort Berlin (Frankfurt am Main: S. Fischer, 2003)
Das Mißverständnis: Vier Erzählungen und ein Stück (Frankfurt am Main: S. Fischer, 1982; Frankfurt am Main: Fischer Taschenbuch Verlag, 1993)
Nach Maßgabe meiner Begreifungskraft: Artikel und Essays (Frankfurt am Main: S. Fischer, 1993; Frankfurt am Main: Fischer Taschenbuch Verlag, 1995)
Pawels Briefe: Eine Familiengeschichte (Frankfurt am Main: S. Fischer, 1999)
Quer über die Gleise: Artikel, Essays, Zwischenrufe (Frankfurt am Main: S. Fischer, 2000)
Stille Zeile Sechs: Roman (Frankfurt am Main: S. Fischer, 1991; Frankfurt am Main: Fischer Taschenbuch Verlag, 1996)
Trotzdem herzliche Grüße: Ein deutsch-deutscher Briefwechsel with Joseph von Westphalen (Frankfurt am Main: S. Fischer, 1988)
Die Überläuferin: Roman (Frankfurt am Main: S. Fischer, 1986; Frankfurt am Main: Fischer Taschenbuch Verlag, 1995)
Wie ich ein Buch nicht schreiben kann und es trotzdem versuche (Frankurt am Main: S. Fischer, 2005)

Essays and Articles

'Ernst Toller', in *Nach Maßgabe meiner Begreifungskraft*, pp. 60–62; first published in *Du: Die Zeitschrift der Kultur*, 6 (June 1989), 113
'Heuchelei und Niedertracht', in *Quer über die Gleise*, pp. 34–43; first published in *Frankfurter Allgemeine Zeitung*, 14 October 1995, *Bilder und Zeiten*, p. B1
'"Das Hörrohr" von Leonora Carrington', in *'Doch das Paradies ist verriegelt ...': Zum Werk von Monika Maron* (Frankfurt am Main: Fischer Taschenbuch Verlag, 2006), pp. 295–95
'Ich war ein antifaschistisches Kind', in *Nach Maßgabe meiner Begreifungskraft*, pp. 9–28; first published in *Die Zeit*, 1 December 1989, pp. 70–71
'Lebensentwürfe, Zeitenbrüche. Vom Nutzen und Nachteil dunkler Brillen: Wer es sich zu einfach macht beim Rückblick auf seine Geschichte, beraubt sich seiner Biografie', *Süddeutsche Zeitung*, 13 September 2002, p. 18
'Nach Maßgabe meiner Begreifungskraft', in *Nach Maßgabe meiner Begreifungskraft*, pp. 103–11; first published in *Frankfurter Allgemeine Zeitung*, 30 June 1992

'Das neue Elend der Intellektuellen', in *Nach Maßgabe meiner Begreifungskraft*, pp. 80–90; first published in *die tageszeitung*, 6 February 1990, p. 7

'Rollenwechsel: Über einen Text und seine Kritiker', in *Quer über die Gleise*, pp. 95–116; first published in *Neue Rundschau* 111.2 (2000), 135–50

'Ein Schicksalsbuch', in *Quer über die Gleise*, pp. 7–23; first published in *Die Zeit*, 28 November 1997, p. 63

'Wo war Leonora Carrington?', in *Nach Maßgabe meiner Begreifungskraft*, pp. 63–65; first published in *Du: Die Zeitschrift der Kultur*, 10 (October 1988), 109

'Zonophobie', in *Nach Maßgabe meiner Begreifungskraft*, pp. 112–20; first published as 'Peinlich, blamabel, lächerlich: Monika Maron über das neue Opfergefühl ihrer ostdeutschen Mitmenschen', *Der Spiegel*, 24 August 1992, pp. 136–41

'Zwei Berichte an die Stasi, 1976', in *Quer über die Gleise*, pp. 24–33

Primary Literature: Other Writers

Benjamin, Walter, 'Über den Begriff der Geschichte', in *Illuminationen: Ausgewählte Schriften 1* (Frankfurt am Main: Suhrkamp Taschenbuch, 1977), pp. 251–61; first published 1942

Freud, Sigmund, 'Traumreize und Traumquellen', in *Gesammelte Werke: Chronologisch geordnet*, ii und iii: *Traumdeutung und Über den Traum* (London: Imago Publishing, 1942), pp. 22–45

—— 'Über Deckerinnerungen', in *Gesammelte Werke: Chronologisch geordnet*, i: *Werke aus den Jahren 1892–1899* (London: Imago Publishing, 1952), pp. 531–54

—— 'Über Psychoanalyse, Zweite Vorlesung', in *Gesammelte Werke: Chronologisch geordnet*, viii: *Werke aus den Jahren 1909–1913* (London: Imago Publishing, 1943), pp. 17–26

Kleist, Heinrich von, *Penthesilea: Ein Trauerspiel* (Cotta, 1808; Stuttgart: Reclam, 1999)

Kraus, Karl, 'Franz Ferdinand und die Talente', *Die Fackel*, 400–03 (10 July 1914), 1–4

Raabe, Wilhelm, *Sämtliche Werke: Braunschweiger Ausgabe*, ed. by Karl Hoppe, xviii: *Stopfkuchen* und *Gutmanns Reisen*, 2nd edn (Göttingen: Vandenhoeck & Ruprecht, 1969)

Wolf, Christa, *Der geteilte Himmel: Erzählung* (Halle/Saale, 1963; Munich: Deutscher Taschenbuch Verlag, 1997)

——*Kein Ort. Nirgends* (Ost-Berlin: Aufbau Verlag, 1979)

——*Kindheitsmuster: Roman* (Ost-Berlin, 1976; Frankfurt am Main: Luchterhand, 1988)

——*Nachdenken über Christa T.* (Halle/Saale, 1968; Munich: Deutscher Taschenbuch Verlag, 1993)

——*Sommerstück* (Darmstadt, 1989; Munich: Luchterhand, 2002)

Interviews

Byrnes, Deirdre, Interview with Monika Maron, Zürich, 22 April 1996
—— Interview with Monika Maron, Berlin-Schöneberg, 29 June 1999
Doerry, Martin, and Volker Hage, 'Ich hab' ein freies Herz: Monika Maron über Autoren in der Politik und die Zukunft des VS', *Der Spiegel*, 25 April 1994, pp. 185–92
Hametner, Michael, 'Von Opfern, die Täter wurden', *Börsenblatt für den Deutschen Buchhandel*, 26 June 1992, pp. 40–44
Krause, Tilman, 'Wir waren ja immer ganz eng: Ein Gespräch mit Monika Maron über ihre Familie, das Erinnern und das Verschwinden der DDR', *Die Welt*, 27 February 1999, <http://www.welt.de/print-welt/article567167/Wir_waren_ja_immer_ganz_eng.html>
Krause, Walter, 'Zwischentöne', Gespräch mit Monika Maron, Deutschlandfunk, 7 February 1999
Leick, Romain, and Volker Hage, '"Das Glück bleibt unerreicht": Die Schriftstellerin Monika Maron über ihren neuen Roman, die Sehnsucht nach einem gelungenen Leben und das Verlustgefühl im Osten', *Der Spiegel*, 23 July 2007, pp. 140–42
Richter, Gerhard, 'Verschüttete Kultur – Ein Gespräch mit Monika Maron', *GDR Bulletin*, 18 (1992), 2–7
Schoeller, Wilfried F., 'Literatur, das nicht gelebte Leben: Gespräch mit der Ostberliner Schriftstellerin Monika Maron', *Süddeutsche Zeitung*, 6 March 1987, p. 47
Sütterlin, Sabine, '"Soll ich Not beschwören, damit Leute nett sind?": Die im Westen lebende DDR-Autorin Monika Maron über deutsche Einheit und Irrtümer ihrer Schriftsteller-Kollegen', *Die Weltwoche*, 8 February 1990, p. 59

Readings

Reading from *Pawels Briefe*, Schaubühne, Berlin, 21 February 1999
Reading from *Pawels Briefe*, Literaturforum im Brecht-Haus, Berlin, 22 April 1999

Secondary Literature

Anderson, Susan C., 'Creativity and Nonconformity in Monika Maron's *Die Überläuferin*', *Women in German Yearbook: Feminist Studies in German Literature & Culture*, 10 (1995), 143–60

Assmann, Aleida, *Erinnerungsräume: Formen und Wandlungen des kulturellen Gedächtnisses* (Munich: Beck, 1999)

Assmann, Jan, 'Collective Memory and Cultural Identity', in *New German Critique*, 65 (1995), 125–33

Bakhtin, Mikhail, 'Forms of Time and of the Chronotope in the Novel: Notes Towards a Historical Poetics', in *The Dialogic Imagination: Four Essays*, ed. by Michael Holquist (Austin: Texas University Press, 1981), pp. 84–258

—— *Rabelais and his World*, trans. by Hélène Iswolsky (Cambridge, MA: Massachusetts Institute of Technology Press, 1968)

Barthes, Roland, *La chambre claire: Note sur la photographie* (Poitiers: Gallimard Seuil, 1980)

Beckermann, Thomas, '"Die Diktatur repräsentiert das Abwesende nicht": Essay on Monika Maron, Wolfgang Hilbig and Gert Neumann', in *German Literature at a Time of Change 1989–1990: German Unity and German Identity in Literary Perspective*, ed. by Arthur Williams, Stuart Parkes and Roland Smith (Bern, Frankfurt am Main, Paris, New York: Peter Lang, 1991), pp. 97–116

Beiküfner, Uta, 'Herbststück', *Berliner Zeitung*, 26 August 2002, *Literatur*, p. 13

Bilke, Jörg, 'Wo die Bronchien schmerzen', *Die Welt*, 24 March 1981, p. 23

Bluhm, Lothar, '"Irgendwann, denken wir, muß ich das genau wissen": Der Erinnerungsdiskurs bei Monika Maron', in *Mentalitätswandel in der deutschen Literatur zur Einheit (1999–2000)*, ed. by Volker Wehdeking (Berlin: Erich Schmidt, 2000), pp. 141–51

Boa, Elizabeth, 'Schwierigkeiten mit der ersten Person: Ingeborg Bachmanns *Malina* und Monika Marons *Flugasche*, *Die Überläuferin* und *Stille Zeile Sechs*', in *Kritische Wege der Landnahme: Ingeborg Bachmann im Blickfeld der neunziger Jahre*, ed. by Robert Pichl and Alexander Stillmark (Vienna: Hora Verlag, 1994), pp. 125–45

Bolterauer, Alice, '"Brombeergeruch" und "Vogelfedern": Die Erfahrung von Gegenwart in Monika Marons Prosatext *Das Mißverständnis*', in *Monika Maron in Perspective: 'Dialogische' Einblicke in zeitgeschichtliche, intertextuelle und rezeptionsbezogene Aspekte ihres Werkes*, ed. by Elke Gilson, German Monitor, 55 (Amsterdam and New York: Rodopi, 2002), pp. 21–33

Brändle, Rea, 'Erkundungsfahrten zu neuen Fragen', *Tages-Anzeiger Zürich*, 2 June 1986

Byrnes, Deirdre, 'Berlin in the Writing of Monika Maron', in *Berlin's Culturescape in the Twentieth Century*, ed. by Thomas Bredohl and Michael Zimmermann (Regina: Canadian Plains Research Centre, 2008), pp. 229–43

—— 'Exposing the Gaps in Memory: Forgetting and Remembering in Monika Maron's *Pawels Briefe*', in *Cultural Memory: Essays in European Literature and History*, ed. by Edric Caldicott and Anne Fuchs (Oxford: Peter Lang, 2003), pp. 147–59

—— 'Der Körper als Symptom, die Gefühle als Metaphern: Monika Marons Roman *Stille Zeile Sechs*', in *Sentimente, Gefühle, Empfindungen: Zur Geschichte und Literatur des Affektiven von 1770 bis heute*, ed. by Anne Fuchs and Sabine Strümper-Krobb (Würzburg: Königshausen & Neumann, 2003), pp. 221–26

—— 'Monika Marons Beiträge zur *Wochenpost*: Eine Analyse', in *Denkbilder: Festschrift für Eoin Bourke*, ed. by Hermann Rasche and Christiane Schönfeld (Würzburg: Königshausen & Neumann, 2004), pp. 248–56

Cramer, Sibylle, 'Der Sprung durch die Zeit und die gerettete Geschichte', *Süddeutsche Zeitung*, 20/21 February 1999, *Literatur*, p. IV

Eckart, Gabriele, 'Ost-Frau liebt West-Mann: Zwei neue Romane von Irina Liebmann und Monika Maron', *Colloquia Germanica*, 30.4 (1997), 315–21

Eigler, Friederike, 'Engendering Cultural Memory in Selected Post-*Wende* Literary Texts of the 1990s', *The German Quarterly*, 74.4 (2001), 392–406

—— 'Nostalgisches und kritisches Erinnern am Beispiel von Martin Walsers *Ein springender Brunnen* und Monika Marons *Pawels Briefe*, in *Monika Maron in Perspective: 'Dialogische' Einblicke in zeitgeschichtliche, intertextuelle und rezeptionsbezogene Aspekte ihres Werkes*, ed. by Elke Gilson, German Monitor, 55 (Amsterdam and New York: Rodopi, 2002), pp. 157–80

Emmerich, Wolfgang, 'Für eine andere Wahrnehmung der DDR-Literatur: Neue Kontexte, neue Paradigmen, ein neuer Kanon', in *Geist und Macht: Writers and the State in the GDR*, ed. by Axel Goodbody and Dennis Tate, German Monitor, 29 (Amsterdam and Atlanta, GA: Rodopi, 1992), pp. 7–22

—— *Kleine Literaturgeschichte der DDR*, 3rd edn (Leipzig:Kiepenheuer, 1996)

Fox, Thomas, *Border Crossings: An Introduction to East German Prose* (Ann Arbor: University of Michigan Press, 1993)

Franke, Eckhard, and Roman Luckscheiter, 'Monika Maron', in *Kritisches Lexikon zur deutschsprachigen Gegenwartsliteratur*, March 2005

Fuchs, Anne, *Phantoms of War in Contemporary German Literature, Films and Discourse: The Politics of Memory* (Basingstoke: Palgrave Macmillan, 2008)

Geier, Andrea, 'Paradoxien des Erinnerns: Biografisches Erzählen in *Animal triste*', in *Monika Maron in Perspective: 'Dialogische' Einblicke in zeitgeschichtliche, intertextuelle und rezeptionsbezogene Aspekte ihres Werkes*, ed. by Elke Gilson, German Monitor, 55 (Amsterdam and New York: Rodopi, 2002), pp. 93–122

Gilson, Elke, ed., *'Doch das Paradies ist verriegelt ...': Zum Werk von Monika Maron* (Frankfurt am Main: Fischer Taschenbuch Verlag, 2006)

—— ed., *Monika Maron in Perspective: 'Dialogische' Einblicke in zeitgeschichtliche, intertextuelle und rezeptionsbezogene Aspekte ihres Werkes*, German Monitor, 55 (Amsterdam and New York: Rodopi, 2002)

——*Wie Literatur hilft, 'übers Leben nachzudenken': Das Oeuvre Monika Marons*, Studia Germanica Gandensia, 47 (Gent, 1999)

Grunenberg, Antonia, 'Der Traum als Heilmittel gegen die verordnete Infantilität – "Flugasche" von Monika Maron', in *Aufbruch der inneren Mauer: Politik und Kultur in der DDR 1971–1990* (Bremen: Edition Temmen, 1990), pp. 209–15

Hage, Volker, 'Alles zu wenig, alles zu spät: Steht die Kulturpolitik der DDR vor einer Wende?', *Die Zeit*, 17 June 1988, p. 38

——'Deutschland im Herbst', *Der Spiegel*, 21 September 2002, pp. 180–83

Halbwachs, Maurice, *On Collective Memory*, ed., trans., and with an Introduction by Lewis A. Coser (Chicago and London: University of Chicago Press, 1992)

Harbers, Henk, 'Gefährliche Freiheit: Zu einem Motivkomplex im Werk von Monika Maron', in *Monika Maron in Perspective: 'Dialogische' Einblicke in zeitgeschichtliche, intertextuelle und rezeptionsbezogene Aspekte ihres Werkes*, ed. by Elke Gilson, German Monitor, 55 (Amsterdam and New York: Rodopi, 2002), pp. 123–37

Hielscher, Martin, 'Die Täter werden die Opfer sein', *Deutsches Allgemeines Sonntagsblatt*, 15 November 1991, p. 29

Hirsch, Marianne, *Family Frames: Photography, Narrative and Postmemory* (Cambridge, MA and London: Harvard University Press, 1997)

Jäger, Manfred, *Kultur und Politik in der DDR: Ein historischer Abriß*, Edition Deutschland Archiv (Cologne: Verlag Wissenschaft und Politik, 1982)

Kämmerlings, Richard, 'Hundejahr. Nach Mexico: Monika Marons Frankfurter Poetikvorlesungen', *Frankfurter Allgemeine Zeitung*, 3 February 2005, p. 41

Kane, Martin, 'Culpabilities of the Imagination: The Novels of Monika Maron', in *Literature on the Threshold: The German Novel in the 1980s*, ed. by Arthur Williams, Stuart Parkes and Roland Smith (New York: Berg, 1990), pp. 221–34

Kittler, Friedrich A., *Grammophon Film Typewriter* (Berlin: Brinkmann und Bose, 1987)

Köhler, Andrea. 'Der Mensch, das traurige Tier', *Neue Zürcher Zeitung*, 22 February 1994, p. 41

Koselleck, Reinhart, 'Darstellung, Ereignis und Struktur', in *Vergangene Zukunft: Zur Semantik geschichtlicher Zeiten*, 3rd edn (Frankfurt am Main: Suhrkamp, 1995), pp. 144–57; first published 1988

Kraft, Renate, 'Was der Schlaf der Vernunft gebiert ...: Über die Funktion der Träume in Monika Marons Roman "Flugasche"', *Frauen in der Literaturwissenschaft*, 25/26 (1990), 34–36

Lee, Hyunseon, 'Die Dialektik des Geständnisses: Monika Marons *Stille Zeile Sechs* und die autobiografischen Diskurse nach 1989', in *Monika Maron in Perspective: 'Dialogische' Einblicke in zeitgeschichtliche, intertextuelle und rezeptionsbezogene Aspekte ihres Werkes*, ed. by Elke Gilson, German Monitor, 55 (Amsterdam and New York: Rodopi, 2002), pp. 57–73

Leisten, Georg, '"Leib wart ihr euch selbst genug ...": Schrift und Körper in Monika Marons Roman *Stille Zeile Sechs*', in *Monika Maron in Perspective: 'Dialogische' Einblicke in zeitgeschichtliche, intertextuelle und rezeptionsbezogene Aspekte ihres Werkes*, ed. by Elke Gilson, German Monitor, 55 (Amsterdam and New York: Rodopi, 2002), pp. 139–56

Lenckos, Frauke E., 'Monika Maron: *Stille Zeile Sechs*', *New German Review: A Journal of Germanic Studies*, 8 (1992), 106–16

Lewis, Alison, 'Re-Membering the Barbarian: Memory and Repression in Monika Maron's *Animal triste*', *The German Quarterly*, 71.1 (1998), 30–46

Löffler, Dietrich, 'Publikumszeitschriften und ihre Leser', in *Zwischen 'Mosaik' und 'Einheit': Zeitschriften in der DDR*, ed. by Simone Barck, Martina Langermann and Siegfried Lokatis (Berlin: Links, 1999), pp. 48–60

Lukács, Georg, 'Reportage oder Gestaltung?', in *Essays über Realismus* (Neuwied and Berlin: Luchterhand, 1971), pp. 35–55

Magenau, Jörg, 'Mein Hund ist meine wahre Liebe', *Der Tagesspiegel*, 26 July 2007, <http://www.tagesspiegel.de/kultur/literatur-alt/mein-hund-ist-meine-wahre-leibe/997078.html>

Maierhofer, Waltraud, 'Wilhelmine Encke-Ritz-Lichtenau: Writing and Reading the Life of a Prussian Royal Mistress', *Biography: An Interdisciplinary Quarterly*, 27.3 (2004), pp. 575–96

Matschke, Günther, *Die Isolation als Mittel der Gesellschaftskritik bei Wilhelm Raabe* (Bonn: Bouvier, 1975)

Menninghaus, Winfried, *Ekel: Theorie und Geschichte einer starken Empfindung* (Frankfurt am Main: Suhrkamp, 1999)

Nora, Pierre, 'Entre Mémoire et Histoire: La problématique des lieux', in *Les Lieux de Mémoire*, sous la direction de Pierre Nora (Paris: Éditions Gallimard, 1997), pp. 23–43; first published 1984–92

—— *Realms of Memory: The Construction of the French Past*, trans. by Arthur Goldhammer (New York: Columbia University Press, 1996)

Plowman, Andrew, 'Escaping the Autobiographical Trap?: Monika Maron, the Stasi and *Pawels Briefe*', in *German Writers and the Politics of Culture: Dealing with the Stasi*, ed. by Paul Cooke and Andrew Plowman (Hampshire and New York: Palgrave Macmillan, 2003), pp. 227–42

Polkehn, Klaus, *Das war die Wochenpost: Geschichte und Geschichten einer Zeitung* (Berlin: Links, 1997)

—— 'Ein Nischenblatt?: Die *Wochenpost* als "sozialistische Familienzeitschrift"', in *Zwischen 'Mosaik' und 'Einheit': Zeitschriften in der DDR*, ed. by Simone Barck, Martina Langermann and Siegfried Lokatis (Berlin: Links, 1999), pp. 61–68

Radisch, Iris, 'Barfuß in Basekow', *Die Zeit*, 5 September 2002, p. 50

Reich-Ranicki, Marcel, 'Keine Frucht ohne Schale: Rede bei der Verleihung des Kleist-Preises 1992 an Monika Maron', in *Kleist Jahrbuch 1993*, ed. by Hans Joachim Kreutzer (Stuttgart: Metzler, 1993), pp. 8–20

—— 'Der Liebe Fluch', *Der Spiegel*, 12 February 1996, pp. 185–89
Ring, Annie, '"Eine Bindung durch Hass": Double-Agency, Mimesis and the Role of Hands in Monika Maron's *Stille Zeile Sechs*', *German Life and Letters*, 63.3 (July 2010), 250–64
Rossbacher, Brigitte, '(Re)visions of the Past: Memory and Historiography in Monika Maron's *Stille Zeile Sechs*', *Colloquia Germanica*, 27.1 (1994), 13–24
—— 'The Status of State and Subject: Reading Monika Maron from *Flugasche* to *Animal triste*', in *Wendezeiten, Zeitenwenden: Positionsbestimmungen zur deutschsprachigen Literatur 1945–1995*, ed. by Robert Weninger and Brigitte Rossbacher (Tübingen: Stauffenberg, 1997), pp. 193–214
Schichtel, Alexandra, 'Monika Maron: Flugasche (1981)', in *Zwischen Zwang und Freiwilligkeit: Das Phänomen Anpassung in der Prosaliteratur der DDR* (Opladen: Westdeutscher Verlag, 1998), pp. 143–59
Schirrmacher, Frank, Introduction to Maron's reading, Literaturforum im Brecht-Haus, 22 April 1999
Shafi, Monika, 'German and American Dream Houses: Buildings and Biographies in Gregor Hens's *Himmelssturz* and Monika Maron's *Endmoränen*', *The German Quarterly*, 79.3 (2006), pp. 505–24
Siebenhaar, Klaus, 'Ach Pankow!: Ein Endspiel in einem unwirtlichen System', *Der Tagesspiegel*, 9 October 1991, *Literatur*, p. v
Sontag, Susan, *Illness as Metaphor* (New York: Farrar, Straus & Giroux, 1978)
—— *On Photography* (Harmondsworth: Penguin 1979)
'Stasi-Deckname "Mitsu"', *Der Spiegel*, 7 August 1995, pp. 146–49
Tate, Dennis, *The East German Novel: Identity, Community, Continuity* (New York: St Martin's Press, 1984)
Wehdeking, Volker, 'Monika Marons rückläufige Erwartungen von *Animal triste* zu *Endmoränen*: das Unbedingte in der Liebe und die Bedingtheiten des Älterwerdens', in *Monika Maron: Begleitheft zur Austellung – Wie ich ein Buch nicht schreiben kann und es trotzdem versuche*, ed. by Winfried Giesen (Frankfurt am Main: Universitätsbibliothek Johann Christian Senckenberg, 2005), pp. 60–74; first published in *Deutschsprachige Erzählprosa seit 1990 im europäischen Kontext: Interpretationen, Intertextualität, Rezeption*, ed. by Volker Wehdeking and Anne-Marie Corbin (Trier: Wissenschaftlicher Verlag Trier, 2003), pp. 131–47
Winter, Hans-Gerd, 'Vom gefürchteten und gewünschten Tod und von den Freuden des Überlebens: Darstellungen des Todes bei Monika Maron und Dieter Wellershoff', in *Neue Generationen – Neues Erzählen: Deutsche Prosa-Literatur der achtziger Jahre*, ed. by Walter Delabar, Werner Jung and Ingrid Pergande (Opladen: Westdeutscher Verlag, 1993), pp. 127–38
Wittstock, Uwe, 'Verordnetes Schweigen', *Frankfurter Allgemeine Zeitung*, 14 April 1981, *Literaturbeilage*, p. L2
Young, James E., *The Texture of Memory: Holocaust Memorials and Meaning* (New Haven, Connecticut: Yale University Press, 1993)

Index

Ach Glück 8, 13, 15, 149, 150, 164–73, 176, 177
'Ada und Evald' 45, 46–47, 48, 49, 50
ageing, *see* body
amanuensis 64, 65, 74, 75, 80, 83, 85, 90, 93, 94, 95, 100, 175–76, 179
Animal triste 7, 14, 97–116, 117, 149, 153, 154, 173, 176, 177, 179–80
'Annaeva' 45, 46, 47, 49–50, 50–51
antifascist state 9, 96, 118, 120, 138, 176, 178
Assmann, Aleida 121, 124, 128, 130, 131, 141
Assmann, Jan, *see* communicative memory
'Audienz' 45

Bakhtin, Mikhail 55, 70–73, 91, 101
Barthes, Roland 122, 126
Becher, Johannes R. 9, 89
Belchatow 124, 128, 132, 136
Benjamin, Walter 83, 87–88
Berlin 2, 4, 14, 15, 83, 98, 107, 118, 119, 120, 124, 125, 126, 128, 132, 137, 151, 157, 161, 162, 163, 165, 166, 167, 168, 171, 172, 176, 180
    East Berlin 3, 5, 13, 17, 23, 24, 36, 52, 64, 73, 98, 108, 141, 157, 180
    West Berlin 3, 6, 7, 141, 142, 143, 157
Berlin Wall 10, 16, 85, 107–11, 157, 176
Biermann, Wolf 9–10
biographer 15, 109, 113, 150, 155–59, 166, 168, 172, 176, 177
biography 1–8, 15, 57, 73, 76–79, 82, 83, 93, 94, 110, 116, 118, 135, 136, 143, 144–47, 149–73, 176–80
Bitterfeld 1, 24–29, 42, 179
Bitterfeld Conference 29
Bitterfelder Bogen 8, 26, 179
Bitterfelder Weg 29

body
    ageing body 70, 98, 104–05, 107, 116, 154
    grotesque body, *see* Bakhtin, Mikhail
    hand 64, 70–71, 85, 89, 92
    paralysis 43, 52, 55, 56, 73, 105

Carrington, Leonora 94, 150, 167, 168–70, 173, 176
chronotope, *see* Bakhtin, Mikhail
collective memory 15, 121, 137, 147
communicative memory 121–22, 144
communism 4, 23, 64, 67, 97, 108, 139, 144, 146
counter-text 12, 13–14, 17, 32, 42, 43–44, 45, 48, 49–51, 52, 55, 58, 61, 62, 96, 175, 177, 179
cultural memory 15, 122

decay, images of 38, 50, 60, 64, 67–73
Deutscher Nationalpreis 1, 178
'Drachentöter' 26–30, 35, 42
dreams 36–41, 50, 56

Ekel 72, 104
Emmerich, Wolfgang 8, 10, 12–13, 62, 72, 175, 178
    'Für eine andere Wahrnehmung der DDR-Literatur' 11–12, 41, 43, 44, 79, 103, 175
    Kleine Literaturgeschichte der DDR 8, 10, 12, 138–39
Endmoränen 8, 15, 116, 149–64, 165, 166, 167, 168, 170, 172–73, 176, 177
Enke, Wilhelmine 150, 151, 156–59, 162, 163, 168, 170, 173, 176
'Eva in Bitterfeld' 24–25

father–daughter relationship 3–4,
    65–67, 75, 96, 112–13
Flugasche 1, 5, 10, 13, 17, 28–42, 43,
    44, 50, 52, 54, 61, 64, 99, 100,
    106, 119, 155, 175, 177, 179
Freud, Sigmund 37, 104, 113–14, 134, 147
Friedrich Wilhelm II 151, 156–58
Für Dich 4, 17, 19

Geburtsort Berlin 7, 180
Der geteilte Himmel, see Wolf, Christa

Hadrian's Wall 101, 109, 113
Halbwachs, Maurice, *see* collective memory
hand, symbol of, *see* body
'Herr Aurich' 45, 46, 47–48, 50, 68
Hirsch, Marianne 122–23,
    124, 126, 130, 147
historical materialism 83
historicism 83
historiography 12, 64, 73, 79, 83, 175
Holocaust 123, 130, 131, 133, 136, 140, 149
Honecker, Erich 9, 23, 25, 110
Hotel Lux 84, 86, 87, 94, 96

'Ich war ein antifaschistisches
    Kind' 3, 6, 120, 138, 139
imagination 36–41, 51–52, 54, 55,
    58, 60, 62, 69, 132, 147
intertextuality 36–37, 43, 53, 98,
    99–103, 110–11, 113, 115
irony 21–22, 79, 103, 104, 115, 179–80

journalism in the GDR 1, 4–5, 13,
    17–36, 41–42, 99–100, 175

Kafka, Franz 14, 52
Kein Ort. Nirgends, see Wolf, Christa
Kindheitsmuster, see Wolf, Christa
Klasseninstinkt 82, 84, 145
Kleist, Heinrich von 98, 101,
    159–60, 167, 171
    Penthesilea 98, 100, 101–03, 113, 115, 180

Kleist Prize 1, 63, 101
Koselleck, Reinhart 15
Kulmhof 130, 136
Kurow 124, 129, 132

'Lebensentwürfe, Zeitenbrüche' 2,
    149–50, 163–64, 173, 178
Lenin, Vladimir Ilyich 23, 54, 82, 99
letters 5, 15, 18, 31, 45, 118, 120–21, 127–28,
    130, 132–33, 135, 137, 145, 147,
    149, 152, 156, 162, 169, 179
lieu de mémoire 128–29, 147
Literatur als Ersatzöffentlichkeit 10–11, 12
Luhmann, Niklas 178
Lukács, Georg 76

Maron, Karl 3, 5, 30, 137, 138, 145
Marx, Karl 23, 54, 82, 99
memoirs 14, 64, 65, 67, 74, 76–77,
    82, 85, 89, 92, 93, 95, 96,
    137, 139, 145, 158, 176
memory 14–15, 39, 53, 60, 71, 86,
    95, 99, 149, 176, 177, 180
    remembering 65–67, 98–99,
    112–16, 117–48
    see also collective memory; communicative memory; cultural memory; postmemory; repression
Mexico 165, 166, 167, 168–70, 172, 173
Das Mißverständnis 5, 13–14, 43–51,
    57, 62, 68, 175, 177
'Das Mißverständnis' 40,
    44–46, 47, 49–50
montage 15, 122–31, 145, 147
mother–daughter relationship 118–19,
    121, 125, 144–46, 177

*Nachdenken über Christa T.,
    see* Wolf, Christa
*Nach Maßgabe meiner
    Begreifungskraft* 6, 179
'Nach Maßgabe meiner
    Begreifungskraft' 101–02

Index

'Das neue Elend der Intellektuellen' 11
Neukölln 2, 120, 126–27
Nora, Pierre, *see* lieu de mémoire

Ostrow-Mazowiecka 121, 123, 129, 130, 132

Pankow 4, 5, 64, 68–69, 80
paralysis, *see* body
Pawels Briefe 2–3, 5, 6–7, 14–15, 30, 96, 99, 112, 113, 114, 116, 117–48, 149, 168, 176, 177, 178, 179
Penthesilea, see Kleist, Heinrich von
photographs 15, 118, 120, 121, 122–26, 128, 130, 137, 147, 149
Polkehn, Klaus 18–21, 22, 28, 34
postmemory 122–23, 126, 147
Prenzlauer Berg 10, 80

Quer über die Gleise 7, 143, 179

Raabe, Wilhelm 100, 110–11
Ravensbrück 87–88
Reich-Ranicki, Marcel 4, 97, 101
repression 14, 15, 99, 112–16, 117–19, 131–40, 143, 147, 148, 149, 180
rereading 8, 12–13, 16, 18, 65, 72, 73, 82, 96, 175
see also Emmerich, Wolfgang
'Rollenwechsel' 117–18, 122, 131, 136, 143, 146

SED (Sozialistische Einheitspartei Deutschlands) 5, 8, 9, 19, 28
self-censorship 34, 36
socialist realism 9, 10, 76
Sommerstück, see Wolf, Christa
Sontag, Susan 68, 122, 124
Stasi (Ministerium für Staatssicherheit) 6–7, 8, 10, 80, 118, 141–43

Stille Zeile Sechs 4, 5, 14, 47, 58, 62, 63–96, 100, 101, 104, 105, 112, 116, 117, 137, 145, 154, 164, 177, 179

Toller, Ernst 93–94
transcription 64, 65, 70, 74, 75, 80, 87, 88, 90, 96, 176
Trotzdem herzliche Grüße: Ein deutschdeutscher Briefwechsel 5
typewriter 90, 91

'Über den Begriff der Geschichte', *see* Benjamin, Walter
Die Überläuferin 5, 14, 39, 41, 42, 43–44, 45, 47, 50, 51–62, 66, 73, 98, 104, 105, 112, 164, 175, 177, 179

Vater Staat 65–67, 118, 146

Wende 7, 10, 11, 13, 14, 16, 19, 65, 73, 91, 97–98, 99, 103, 107, 108, 109, 111, 114, 120, 133, 134, 143, 148, 149, 150, 151, 155, 159, 160, 161, 163, 164, 171, 173, 176, 177, 180
Westphalen, Joseph von 5, 31
Wie ich ein Buch nicht schreiben kann und es trotzdem versuche 8, 152, 164, 165, 166, 168, 172–73
Die Wochenpost 1, 4, 13, 17–30, 33, 41–42, 99, 155, 180
Wolf, Christa
  Der geteilte Himmel 108
  Kein Ort. Nirgends 99
  Kindheitsmuster 134, 144
  Nachdenken über Christa T. 68, 135
  Sommerstück 151

Zhdanov, Andrei 9
'Zonophobie' 6
'Zwei Berichte an die Stasi, 1976' 7, 143

Britische und Irische Studien zur deutschen Sprache und Literatur

Nr. 1   Geoffrey Perkins: Contemporary Theory of Expressionism, 1974. 182 S.
Nr. 2   Paul Kussmaul: Bertolt Brecht und das englische Drama der Renaissance, 1974. 175 S.
Nr. 3   Eudo C. Mason: Hölderlin and Goethe, 1975. 145 S.
Nr. 4   W.E. Yates: Tradition in the German Sonnet, 1981. 98 S.
Nr. 5   Rhys W. Williams: Carl Sternheim. A Critical Study, 1982. 282 S.
Nr. 6   Roger H. Stephenson: Goethe's Wisdom Literature, 1983. 274 S.
Nr. 7   John Hennig: Goethe and the English Speaking World, 1983. 288 S.
Nr. 8   John R.P. McKenzie: Social Comedy in Austria and Germany 1890–1933, 1992. 262 S., 2nd Edition 1996.
Nr. 9   David Basker: Chaos, Control and Consistency: The Narrative Vision of Wolfgang Koeppen, 1993. 352 S.
Nr. 10 John Klapper: Stefan Andres. The Christian Humanist as a Critic of his Times, 1995. 188 S.
Nr. 11 Anthony Grenville: Cockpit of Ideologies. The Literature and Political History of the Weimar Republic, 1995. 394 S.
Nr. 12 T.M. Holmes: The Rehearsal of Revolution. Georg Büchner's Politics and his Drama *Dantons Tod,* 1995. 214 S.
Nr. 13 Andrew Plowman: The Radical Subject. Social Change and the Self in Recent German Autobiography, 1998. 168 S.
Nr. 14 David Barnett: Literature versus Theatre. Textual Problems and Theatrical Realization in the Later Plays of Heiner Müller, 1998. 293 S.
Nr. 15 Stephen Parker: Peter Huchel. A Literary Life in 20th-Century Germany, 1998. 617 S.
Nr. 16 Deborah Smail: White-collar Workers, Mass Culture and *Neue Sachlichkeit* in Weimar Berlin. A Reading of Hans Fallada's *Kleiner Mann – Was nun?,* Erich Kästner's *Fabian* and Irmgard Keun's *Das kunstseidene Mädchen,* 1999. 236 S.
Nr. 17 Ian Roe and John Warren (eds): The Biedermeier and Beyond. Selected Papers from the Symposium held at St. Peter's College, Oxford from 19–21 September 1997, 1999. 253 S.
Nr. 18 James Trainer (ed.): Liebe und Trennung. Charlotte von Ahlefelds Briefe an Christian Friedrich Tieck, 1999. 235 S.
Nr. 19 Anthony J. Harper and Margaret C. Ives (eds): Sappho in the Shadows. Essays on the work of German women poets of the age of Goethe (1749–1832), with translations of their poetry into English, 2000. 280 S.
Nr. 20 Peter Hutchinson (ed.): Landmarks in German Poetry, 2000. 218 S.
Nr. 21 Rachel Palfreyman: Edgar Reitz's *Heimat*. Histories, Traditions, Fictions, 2000. 237 S.

Nr. 22 Meg Tait: Taking Sides. Stefan Heym's Historical Fiction. 2001. 208 S.

Nr. 23 Fred Whalley: The Elusive Transcendent. The Role of Religion in the Plays of Frank Wedekind, 2002. 204 S.

Nr. 24 Philip Ward: Hofmannsthal and Greek Myth: Expression and Performance, 2002. 295 S.

Nr. 25 Florian Krobb and Jeff Morrison (eds): Poetry Project. Irish Germanists Interpret German Verse, 2003. 276 S.

Nr. 26 Andreas Kramer, Eric Robertson and Robert Vilain: A Bibliography of Yvan Goll. 2006. 377 S.

Nr. 27 Peter Hutchinson (ed.): Landmarks in German Drama, 2002. 244 S.

Nr. 28 W. E. Yates, Allyson Fiddler and John Warren (eds): From Perinet to Jelinek. Viennese Theatre in its Political and Intellectual Context, 2001. 290 S.

Nr. 29 Hannah Burdekin: The Ambivalent Author. Five German Writers and their Jewish Characters, 1848–1914, 2002. 338 S.

Nr. 30 Elizabeth M. Wilkinson and L. A. Willoughby: Models of Wholeness. Some Attitudes to Language, Art and Life in the Age of Goethe. Edited by Jeremy Adler, Martin Swales and Ann Weaver, 2002. 271 S.

Nr. 31 Martin Kane (ed.): Legacies and Identity. East and West German Literary Responses to Unification, 2002. 209 S.

Nr. 32 Peter Hutchinson and Reinhard K. Zachau (eds): Stefan Heym: Socialist – Dissenter – Jew; Stefan Heym: Sozialist – Dissident – Jude, 2003. 220 S.

Nr. 33 Peter Hutchinson (ed.): Landmarks in German Short Prose, 2003. 208 S.

Nr. 34 Matthew Philpotts: The Margins of Dictatorship: Assent and Dissent in the Work of Günter Eich and Bertolt Brecht, 2003. 377 S.

Nr. 35 Peter Hutchinson (ed.): Landmarks in German Comedy. 2006. 245 S.

Nr. 36 Eleoma Joshua: Friedrich Leopold Graf zu Stolberg and the German Romantics, 2005. 206 S.

Nr. 37 Janet Stewart and Simon Ward: Blueprints for No-Man's Land, 2005. 228 S.

Nr. 38 Paul E. Kerry (ed.): Friedrich Schiller. Playwright, Poet, Philosopher, Historian, 2007. 343 S.

Nr. 39 Hilary Brown (ed.): Landmarks in German Women's Writing, 2007. 213 S.

Nr. 40 Ruth Whittle & Debbie Pinfold: Voices of Rebellion: Political Writing by Malwida von Meysenbug, Fanny Lewald, Johanna Kinkel and Louise Aston, 2005. 208 S.

Nr. 41 John Warren and Ulrike Zitzlsperger (eds): Vienna Meets Berlin: Cultural Interaction 1918–1933, 2005. 298 S.

Nr. 42 Lesley Sharpe: A National Repertoire: Schiller, Iffland and the German Stage, 2007. 306 S.

Nr. 43 Frazer Clark: *Zeitgeist* and *Zerrbild*: Word, Image and Idea in German Satire 1800–1848, 2006. 297 S.

Nr. 44 Barbara Burns: The Prose Fiction of Louise von François (1817–1893), 2006. 151 S.
Nr. 45 Peter Hutchinson (ed.): Landmarks in the German Novel (1), 2007. 237 S.
Nr. 46 Forthcoming.
Nr. 47 Peter Hutchinson and Michael Minden (eds): Landmarks in the German Novel (2), 2010. 170 S.
Nr. 48 Daniel Greineder: From the Past to the Future: The Role of Mythology from Winckelmann to the Early Schelling, 2007. 227 S.
Nr. 49 John Heath: Behind the Legends: The Cult of Personality and Self-Presentation in the Literary Works of Stefan Heym, 2008. 179 S.
Nr. 50 Deirdre Byrnes: Rereading Monika Maron: Text, Counter-Text and Context, 2011. 203 S.
Nr. 51 Lorenzo Bellettini and Peter Hutchinson (eds): Schnitzler's Hidden Manuscripts, 2010. 218 S.
Nr. 52 Geraldine Horan, Nils Langer and Sheila Watts (eds): Landmarks in the History of the German Language, 2009. 320 S.
Nr. 53 John Ward: Jews in Business and their Representation in German Literature 1827–1934, 2010. 260 S.